Every Last Crumb

Paleo Bread and Beyond

Written & Photographed
by **Brittany Angell**

Cover Photo & Styling by
Bill Staley & Hayley Mason

Portraits by Tré

VICTORY BELT PUBLISHING INC.
Las Vegas

This book is dedicated to my other half, Rich Angell.

Thank you for cleaning up my giant kitchen messes. I love you.

Contents

My Story

In the winter of 2009, at the age of twenty-five, I became pregnant. It was a surprise, but we were overjoyed. With that pregnancy came horrible morning sickness. Well, that's what I thought it was. I was having severe sinus issues, and my digestion became a complete mess. Headaches, nausea from postnasal drip, and more headaches. Each day was a struggle. Then, just as I entered the second trimester, I miscarried. From that point on, my health has never been the same.

Months after the pregnancy, my digestion continued to be "off." Six months after the miscarriage, I woke up with a stabbing pain in my right side—as if someone was jabbing a pencil into me, over and over. This began my serious quest to get better.

Doctor after doctor after doctor, no one knew what was wrong. I tested negative for celiac disease, and my health looked perfect on every other front, according to the blood work. I suspected hypothyroidism because it runs in my family, but my doctors refused to treat me for it. Finally, after seeing my second gastroenterologist, I was told that my gallbladder was acting up. Though I did not have gallstones, it was overactive and causing the cramping and stabbing sensation. It took seven months to get that diagnosis. During this time, my digestion literally came to a halt. I became dependent on heavy laxatives, coffee drinking, and fiber, which barely worked.

My gallbladder was removed, with the promise that my health would return to a perfect state thereafter. What they found during surgery was an extremely inflamed organ. I thought my struggles were over. Little did I know, they had just begun!

The stabbing pain went away, but my digestion worsened. Again I went on the "medical circuit" to find a doctor to improve my health. During this time I was in and out of the emergency room with

heartburn so severe I was afraid to eat. I was exhausted and cold all the time, my hair was falling out, my face and eyelids were always puffy, and I had muscle and joint pain so severe it was impossible to get out of bed some days. I was falling apart, and no one could tell me why.

Finally, I struck gold. Doctor number thirteen had the answer: hypothyroidism coupled with Hashimoto's disease. I sobbed tears of joy in the doctor's office that day. She could have given me any diagnosis and I would have rejoiced. I had an answer! With that answer, I knew that if I worked hard enough, I would get better. And that is just what I did.

Due to the fact that I went undiagnosed for so long, my health issues had grown and spiraled into a much more complicated state than I had ever imagined. In addition to Hashimoto's, I had severe adrenal fatigue, a candida infection that had become systemic, a leaky gut, and metabolic syndrome (I was borderline diabetic).

Nothing was going to stop me from turning my health around. I tried multiple diets and finally fell into Paleo, noticing instant relief from the inflammation that had been making my joints throb each day. Bringing my damaged body back to good health took me two years of trial and error. I followed Paleo faithfully each of those days, feeling so thankful for food I could digest and the real progress I was starting to see.

Fast-forward to today: I have been in remission from my Hashimoto's for two years, I'm no longer diabetic, and I've rebuilt my immune system, which now keeps my former candida issues under control. Eating Paleo is my rock! These days I don't have to be as strict, because my gut has healed and my once-giant list of food intolerances has diminished significantly. (To learn about the nondietary treatment regiments I followed to complement my progress on Paleo, you can read my full story on BrittanyAngell.com.)

Being a young woman who once faced an overwhelmingly long list of foods that had become weapons, triggering my immune system to go haywire, I feel sincere compassion for others in this position. Food is and should bring happiness—it's what brings people together! My number-one purpose has become to give people back every single one of their favorite foods. A delicious treat can symbolize hope and give a person suffering from food intolerances and allergies the opportunity to feel normal and forget for a few moments any troubles they may have.

I hope this book gives you happiness and the opportunity to feel healthy and whole again—and to just eat good food. Enjoy the journey you are on, every bite of the way!

Foreword

by Diane Sanfilippo, *New York Times* bestselling author of *Practical Paleo* and *The 21-Day Sugar Detox* and coauthor of *Mediterranean Paleo Cooking*

We all know that Paleo eaters should focus on meat, seafood, eggs, vegetables, fruits, and fat, right? I know this so well, in fact, that I've written what some have dubbed "the Paleo Bible" (their words, not mine) in my first book, a perennial *New York Times* bestseller, *Practical Paleo*.

So why would I be so excited about, and even enthusiastically recommend, a book that seems to go so far against that idea?

For starters (and perhaps most important, since integrity is a quality I absolutely value in others), I know that Brittany Angell wholeheartedly agrees with the basic tenets of Paleo eating for health and follows them herself. Brittany eats Paleo largely to keep her own autoimmune condition in remission—I'm sure many of you can relate. She's also allergic to many of the common ingredients that are included in what might be considered more "standard" Paleo-friendly baking. What's more, she has no intention of attempting to convince anyone that even her own recipes should make up the bulk of your daily diet. Treats are treats—she's not one to convince you otherwise, and will quickly share with anyone who asks about her own diet that what fills her plate most of the time are simple, whole foods.

Next, the last thing I want to create by educating folks on this way of eating is a dogmatic, limiting set of beliefs that creates a construct so rigid that your only option is to break from its chains and perhaps even feel some guilt around wanting to enjoy a treat. Food should be a guilt-free zone, and we all should be allowed to choose what we want to eat without scrutiny from anyone! And without the allergens that might make us sick.

Lastly, I don't know a single human being who never wants a treat—not one. Perhaps our modern food landscape and social settings or celebrations created around food are to blame. I'd argue that the feelings that eating foods we love evoke, perhaps from our childhood or from family gatherings, are an important part of what keeps us sane and calm in an overstressed, nutrient-poor world. When we take pleasure in food, we relieve stress. And we all could use a little of that, right?

Oh, and completely selfishly, my father really needs to reignite his passion for making bagels and bread. Only now he needs to make them from ingredients everyone in the family will be able to eat—without gluten or nuts!

Enter *Every Last Crumb*.

Today, everyone seems to have at least one food allergy, intolerance, or sensitivity, if not more than one. The reasons for these issues are multifaceted and often completely out of our hands, despite possibly doing everything we know to do to maintain a healthy and balanced diet. And, while I certainly recommend that the majority of your diet be made up of whole foods like meat and vegetables, we all know that the day will come when you need to bake an allergen-free treat for your child to bring to school, or you're going to celebrate Thanksgiving and want to keep everyone happy and healthy. You can't simply replace wheat flour with almond flour and expect amazing results. You can't even use almond flour if you're allergic to almonds (which I am). Without the precisely measured and tested recipes that Brittany presents in this book, we'd all be lost.

I thank Brittany for her constant passion and pursuit of an option for everyone. She truly puts her heart and soul into developing recipes that will work for anyone, knowing how much of a struggle it can be when you find out that you can no longer eat so many different foods. It's rare to find someone who puts this much energy into trying to help everyone have a darned cupcake again.

Thanks, Brittany, for caring about that little moment of joy that we all get upon seeing a treat and realizing that we can, in fact, enjoy it—*Every Last Crumb* of it.

INTRODUCTION

Bread? Paleo? Doesn't that sort of go against what Paleo is? Nope.

I have a list of food intolerances that I must follow to keep my Hashimoto's disease in remission. When I want to have a treat, I can't head over to our grocery store and get a loaf of white bread to make into French toast with chocolate and whipped cream on top. So I make my own, much healthier Paleo bread that includes only the ingredients that I allow in my diet. Do I eat bread every day? No. I'm all about eating Paleo 80/20. Meat and veggies fill my plate from day to day, but that 20 percent is for the fun recipes that you'll find in this book. Life is about balance—and enjoying food! To me, that doesn't equate with some extreme diet. Not having treats to look forward to is no way to live.

As you read these pages, I hope you feel profoundly happy with the selection of fun things you can have without regret and without feeling sick. The beauty of Paleo is that you can customize it to make it the perfect lifestyle for you. I recommend not following a rule book, but rather finding what works for you—the Paleo that makes you feel your very best. (Check out Robb Wolf's blog post "Seven Shades of Paleo" at robbwolf.com, which perfectly describes the wide range of differences that can be found from person to person on this diet.)

Thanks to the Paleo-inspired recipes in this book, I can show up to any gathering with a plate of real food to share and watch the crowds go wild. I'll be so bold as to say that my recipes are always the first to vanish, whether the crowd is Paleo or not. Take the PMS Brownies in Chapter 13, for example. You'd better hide those in the back of the freezer, or else you won't get to eat one before they disappear! I promise, no one will know that you are handing them a gluten-free, Paleo treat. Don't feel the need to tell them, either, because the food is just good.

No matter how strict or relaxed you choose to be about your diet, you'll find recipes that work for you in *Every Last Crumb*. Get ready to have fun adventures with food in ways you never thought possible. Best of all, you'll discover that making gluten- and grain-free bread is really fun!

Use the hashtag #EveryLastCrumb on social media to share your journey while baking and cooking the recipes in this book. Let's show the world that we can be healthy, eat allergen-free, and eat every last crumb, too!

INGREDIENTS

& Substitutions

Dairy and Eggs

milk

For the recipes in this book, feel free to use any variety of milk that you choose: dairy milk, almond milk, coconut milk, you name it. Regular or unsweetened is fine—they will all work. The only exceptions are heavy cream and coconut cream (the heavy, thick cream scooped off the top of a can of chilled full-fat coconut milk); these should not be used unless specified in a recipe.

cheese

I prefer raw, grass-fed, and antibiotic-free cheese. Not only does it taste better, but you know that you are eating quality dairy without added hormones.

Though there is no dairy-free cheese labeled "Paleo," if you are looking for a pretty clean gluten-and soy-free substitute for occasional use, I recommend Daiya cheese shreds and slices, which are made from tapioca. Daiya makes mozzarella-style shreds, cheddar-style shreds, and pepper Jack-style shreds. The shreds perform almost like the real thing. If you are using them to make a pizza or other baked good in a hot oven, cover the baking sheet with foil, as the shreds tend to burn before they melt under high heat. I do not recommend Daiya's cream cheese substitute; instead, I suggest using fresh goat cheese (chèvre) as a substitute for cow's milk–based cream cheese.

eggs

Use large eggs whenever eggs are called for in this book.

I do not recommend trying to remove eggs from my grain-free recipes. It's a tricky business, and not worth attempting unless you are prepared to remake a recipe many, many times until you get it right. I have an egg intolerance, and as a result I removed eggs from every recipe I could. You'll find that a large percentage of the recipes in this book are already egg-free!

heavy cream and coconut cream

Heavy cream and coconut cream can be subbed beautifully one for the other.

To source your own coconut cream, buy a can of full-fat coconut milk (make sure that the can is not labeled "light coconut milk"). Place the can in the fridge overnight. Then, when you open the can, you can scoop out the thick, heavy coconut cream that has separated from the water and risen to the top. If you are using this cream to make whipped coconut cream, be sure to avoid pulling any of the coconut water out of the can with the cream.

Avoid purchasing cream of coconut, which is a sweetened product and not what is needed in these recipes!

Fats, Shortening, and Oils

butter (salted)

I use salted organic butter when baking or cooking. If you wish to use unsalted butter in this book's recipes, you may need to add an extra pinch or two of salt to adjust the seasoning, depending on the quantity of butter used. Ghee can be used as a substitute for salted butter in many of my recipes, except for applications when the butter needs to be cut into flours. Because ghee is unsalted, you may wish to add a touch more salt.

When using butter in solid form, as when cutting it into flours to make dough, the ideal texture is softened but still firm—not hard—and the ideal temperature is semi-chilled. To achieve this, I usually take the butter out of the fridge 20 to 30 minutes before making a recipe, depending on how warm my kitchen is that day. During the cold winter months, room-temperature butter works well.

bacon fat

In savory recipes, I sometimes list bacon fat as an optional baking or cooking fat. When using solid bacon fat in baking recipes, such as when cutting it into flours to make dough, it should be used chilled, directly from the refrigerator.

spectrum vegetable shortening

Spectrum is the brand of vegetable shortening that I use in all of my baking. It's made from clean ingredients, is not hydrogenated, and works beautifully in any recipe that calls for shortening. You'll notice that I call for shortening often in this book. It does amazing things to help make grain-free bread airy and fluffy. There is no substitute that will work exactly the same as shortening; I recommend that you use it when it is called for. If you want to use a brand of vegetable shortening other than Spectrum, check the label carefully, as most shortenings are made with low-quality ingredients.

Vegetable shortening can be used at room temperature in all baking recipes because it remains solid.

oils

My favorite oils to work with are coconut oil and palm shortening for frying, mild-flavored grapeseed oil for baking, and olive oil and avocado oil when I'm looking for a bit more flavor. When I call for a mild-flavored oil in my recipes, I suggest that you use coconut oil, grapeseed oil, or macadamia nut oil.

Xanthan Gum and Guar Gum

Gums are essential to making grain-free bread taste like conventional bread and giving it shape and structure. Gluten is the glue in bread. In fact, bread flour is higher in gluten than all-purpose flour. So, to mimic the qualities of conventional bread as closely as possible, I include xanthan gum in many of my recipes. I recommend Bob's Red Mill brand.

Xanthan gum and guar gum work exactly the same. You can use either option in all of these recipes.

Flours

blanched almond flour

I recommend using blanched almond flour in my recipes. It typically has a finer grind and therefore will absorb more moisture when baked. Recipes that use almond flour do not require as much liquid or fat, as almond flour is naturally loaded with those two things. Depending on how this flour is used, it can create a dense, chewy chocolate chip cookie or a fluffy bread with a crispy crust! It may be one of the most versatile flours and without question is my favorite to work with.

Baking tips. When baking with almond flour, be careful not to bake at high temperatures for long periods. Almond flour tends to brown more quickly than other gluten-free flours due to its high fat content, so keep an eye on your baked goods and cover them with aluminum foil as needed.

Substitutions. If you are sensitive or allergic to almonds, I suggest that you try another nut or seed flour in place of almond flour. Choose one with a similarly low-carb/low-fat profile, such as pistachio, hazelnut, sunflower seed, or cashew flour. Sadly, none of these are available for purchase ground as finely as blanched almond flour. Try making your own by processing the raw nuts or seeds of your choice in a high-powered blender until they become powdery like flour. The finer you can get the flour, the better it will work!

Under no condition can coconut flour or chestnut flour be substituted for almond flour in any recipe.

Storage. If you intend to use within a month or so, you can leave your almond flour at room temperature in a sealed bag or container. If you buy the flour in bulk and wish to keep it fresh long-term, you can store it in the freezer for up to two years.

Brands to buy. Nuts.com, Honeyville.com, or Jkgourmet.com

coconut flour

Coconut flour has a strong, sweet flavor. It's one of those love-it-or-hate-it flavors. For this reason, I choose to neutralize the flavor in my recipes by adding starch, which also improves the texture.

Baking tips. When combined with starch and eggs, the fluffy texture of coconut flour works great for pancakes, cakes, cupcakes, and muffins. I use it in applications that require a soft crust. When working with coconut flour, use a little extra fat (shortening or butter) to further improve the texture of your baked goods. My recipes include the extra fat required to give them the perfect texture.

Substitutions. Coconut flour is unlike all other gluten-free flours. It cannot be exchanged with any other flour.

Storage. This flour keeps well and can be stored at room temperature in a sealed bag or container.

Brand to buy. Nuts.com

chestnut flour

This flour tastes like Christmas! Its flavor works incredibly well with warm spices, such as cinnamon, nutmeg, and ginger, which is why I use it in my Carrot Cake (page 332). This grain-free flour is extra-special because it's one of the only flours in this category that does not need eggs to create a light, soft, cakey texture. I especially love using it to make egg-free muffins.

Baking tips. While chestnut flour fluffs up beautifully and creates a tender crumb, it can lead to somewhat crumbly baked goods. For this reason, I like to add a little xanthan gum or guar gum to help it hold together and to give my baked goods a nice structure and shape. The flavor of chestnut flour is distinct; some people love and others don't. To moderate its flavor, you can mix chestnut flour with starch. The more starch you add, the less you'll be able to detect the flavor of the chestnut flour in the baked good. I typically use a 50/50 blend of starch and chestnut flour.

Substitutions. No flour substitutes perfectly for chestnut flour at a 1:1 ratio; rice flour is probably your closest bet.

Storage. Chestnut flour does not have a very high fat content, and as a result it won't go rancid quickly. You can store it at room temperature in a sealed bag or container for several months or in the freezer for two years or longer.

Brand to buy. Nuts.com

superfine white rice flour

This is one of those gray-area Paleo ingredients. Some people are team white rice, and others are not. I happen to love rice flour, and my readers have been excited to see some modified Paleo recipes on my blog that use it. Rice flour is a great option for those who are allergic to nuts and coconut flour, and for that reason I have included a small selection of rice flour recipes throughout this book.

Baking tips. Rice flour is one of the easiest flours to bake with: You can get it to create just about any texture with the right combination of ingredients. In all of my recipes, I use superfine white rice flour. Regular rice flour is gritty, like sand. This coarse texture is part of what gives gluten-free baked goods a bad rap!

Substitutions. A lot of other grain-based, gluten-free flours work well as substitutes for rice flour. For more info, check out my *Essential Gluten-Free Baking Guide, Parts 1 and 2,* available on Amazon. com.

Storage. This flour won't go bad. It can be stored at room temperature in a sealed bag or container.

Brand to buy. Authenticfoods.com. Avoid Bob's Red Mill rice flour, which is coarse and gritty. Your baked goods may end up too moist if you use Bob's. If you want to save some money, look for white rice flour at an Asian grocery store. Despite the fact that the rice flour at these stores is not labeled "superfine," it technically is, and it will work great in my recipes.

potato flour

This flour, commonly confused with potato starch, is made from whole, peeled, dehydrated potatoes rather than just the starch portion.

Baking tips. I use potato flour when I want a chewy crust or flakiness. For example, the addition of potato flour helps give my croissants a flaky exterior. I also like to use it in bagels and soft pretzels to help give them the classic skin. When using this flour, you only need a small amount, never more than a tablespoon or so. It soaks up a lot of liquid and has a bit of a potato flavor. It also works as an all-purpose binder and does a pretty sturdy job of helping gluten-free baked goods hold together. Adding too much potato flour can create a gummy texture.

Substitutions. There is no substitution for potato flour; if it is called for in a recipe, you must use it.

Storage. Store this flour at room temperature in a sealed bag or container. It won't go bad!

Brands to buy. Bob's Red Mill or Nuts.com

Starches

potato starch

Potato starch makes baked goods a little lighter and fluffier than tapioca starch. I use it in breads and pancakes for extra lift. I've also found that potato starch soaks up more liquid than the other starches do. If possible, stick to potato starch when a recipe calls for it. If you are sensitive to nightshades, feel free to use tapioca or arrowroot starch instead, but know that the recipe will turn out less fluffy and chewier than intended.

tapioca starch

Tapioca starch, which is sometimes labeled tapioca flour, tends to make baked goods like cookies both crispy and chewy. Using too much tapioca starch in a recipe can result in a gummy texture.

sweet potato starch / flour

Sweet potato starch is confusing because it's called sweet potato flour. Making it even more confusing, there are two products available that are called sweet potato flour: one is orange and the other is white and starchy. The latter product, which is a straight starch, is what I use in my recipes and refer to as sweet potato starch. This starch works exactly the same as starch made from white potatoes, and the two can be used interchangeably.

arrowroot starch

Arrowroot starch is very similar to and can be substituted for tapioca starch. I do not call for arrowroot starch in any of the recipes in this book for one reason: cost. Tapioca starch is much less expensive and equally effective.

substitutions

All of the starches can be exchanged fairly well. Just keep in mind that your baked goods will be fluffier if you use potato starch or sweet potato starch/flour. Tapioca and arrowroot starch give less lift to recipes and instead make them chewy. But in a pinch, all of the starches will exchange well enough that your recipes may still turn out.

brands to buy

Bob's Red Mill carries great potato starch, tapioca starch, and arrowroot starch. You can buy the white, starchy type of sweet potato flour that I use at most Asian markets or online from Barry Farm Foods (barryfarm.com) for a reasonable price.

storage

Starches, being low in fat and refined, never go bad! Keep them in sealed bags or containers for as long as you wish. If you have space in the freezer, they can be stored there as well.

Sweeteners

Sugar is more than a sweetener when it's used in baked goods. It's an important ingredient that provides moisture, structure, and browning. There are many types of sweeteners on the market today. They come in two forms: liquid and granulated. Liquid sweeteners are, as their name implies, liquid in nature. Granulated sugars are crystallized. These different sweeteners come at a variety of price points, and each one offers its own health benefits. In this book, I use only the healthier varieties that are unrefined and unprocessed.

coconut palm sugar

Coconut palm sugar is made from the sap of the coconut tree. The taste is similar to brown sugar with a hint of molasses. It is sometimes called coconut sugar or, incorrectly, palm sugar. The latter is made from the sap of various palm trees, such as the Palmyra palm, date palm, or sugar date palm, depending on the region.

Baking tips. Use coconut palm sugar in recipes to which you wish to give a warm brown sugar flavor. Keep in mind that it will give your baked goods a light golden brown tint. Coconut palm sugar does not add as much moisture as white sugar; therefore, you may need to add a little extra liquid to balance your recipes for baked goods.

Substitutions. Granulated maple sugar substitutes beautifully for coconut palm sugar.

Brands to buy. Wholesome Sweeteners, Nutiva, Big Tree Farms, Navitas Naturals

maple syrup / sugar

As their names imply, maple syrup and granulated maple sugar are made from the sap that comes from maple trees. I love to use the granulated form as a cup-for-cup replacement for white sugar because it's lighter in color than the other Paleo-friendly granulated sweeteners, and it has a mild enough flavor that it won't take over a recipe. I use it in my Angell Food Cake (page 314) because it allows for a beautiful light cake and a white color!

Baking tips. Use granulated maple sugar in recipes for which you would typically use granulated white sugar. Maple syrup can be used in a baked good to help it hold together. I use Grade A maple syrup.

Substitutions. Honey or coconut nectar can be substituted fairly successfully for maple syrup. They aren't perfect substitutions, as each has a different thickness and therefore affects recipes differently. However, they are close enough that you can typically swap them with good results. Coconut palm sugar can be substituted for granulated maple sugar. If you use coconut palm sugar, your baked good will end up a little darker in color.

Brands to buy. For granulated maple sugar, I recommend Coombs Family Farm, Crown Maple, and Barry Farm Foods. Maple syrup is much easier to find, and I have been pleased with all of the organic grade A brands that I have purchased.

honey

There is a big difference between raw honey, which you can often find locally, and the processed honey you find at the grocery store. The former is a natural sweetener full of vitamins and minerals. The latter is devoid of nutritional value and may contain high-fructose corn syrup.

Baking tips. It's great to use raw honey as the sweetener in a dough that is crumbly because it will act like glue and hold the dough together. Honey adds a lot of moisture. For this reason, it's better suited to coconut flour recipes; almond flour already contains a lot of moisture.

Substitutions. Coconut nectar can generally be exchanged successfully with honey. If you can get your hands on some granulated honey, it could sub for coconut palm sugar or granulated maple sugar.

Brands to buy. The best honey to purchase is local raw honey, which has the side benefit of giving relief to those with pollen allergies.

coconut nectar

Like coconut palm sugar, coconut nectar is made from the sap of the coconut tree. It is lower on the glycemic index than white sugar. It's a syrup that is similar to honey in thickness but darker in color and a few notches less sweet.

Baking tips. Use coconut nectar in baked goods that you wish to be only moderately sweet. Due to the fact that coconut nectar is as thick as honey, it works well as "glue" in baked goods to give them a nice chewy texture. I find that it works well in cookie recipes.

Substitutions. Coconut nectar can be used as a replacement for honey in baked goods but has a milder, less sweet flavor. If you have a strong sweet tooth, it might not be the best sweetener for your palate. However, if you don't need your cookies to be super-sweet, it is a great option. Use a 1:1 ratio when using coconut nectar to replace other liquid sweeteners.

Brand to buy. Coconut Secret

Chocolate and Cocoa Powder

chocolate bars and chips

For all of the recipes in this book, any brand of chocolate bar or chocolate chips will work. I prefer using semisweet chocolate. If you are looking for dairy-free chocolate chips, I recommend the Enjoy Life brand.

cocoa powder

You will see two types of cocoa powder in stores:

Dutch cocoa powder—This type of cocoa powder is typically darker in color and richer in flavor. It is the type that I use in my recipes unless otherwise noted. My favorite product is Hershey's Special Dark, which has a delicious flavor and a beautiful dark color, and is very cost-effective. However, it is not sustainably sourced, which may be an issue for some people.

Standard cocoa powder—Standard cocoa powder has a milder flavor and a lighter color. Use it when you want a medium brown color, like the color of milk chocolate.

Leaveners

yeast

Working with yeast can seem intimidating, but once you get the hang of a few simple concepts, it's like riding a bike. The process is the same in all of my recipes.

Mix the yeast with lukewarm water and a little sugar to help it grow. The temperature of the water should be roughly 90 degrees. The water should be slightly warmer than your finger but should not come close to burning you. If the water is too hot, it will kill the yeast; if the water is too cold, it won't activate the yeast. If you've gotten the correct temperature, your yeast will start to bubble up within a few minutes. If this doesn't happen, either your water temperature is wrong or your yeast is dead. Try playing around with this process before you take on a bread recipe.

I use only one brand of yeast throughout this book: Red Star Quick Rise Yeast. I typically buy this instant yeast in a jar at Walmart. This type of yeast, which may be labeled "quick-rise," "rapid-rise," or "fast-acting," allows the majority of the breads in this book to proof within 30 minutes.

It's best to store yeast in the fridge to keep it fresh and ready to go at any time. This yeast will keep for years if stored in the fridge after it has been opened.

The beauty of gluten-free baking is that the steps of rising and proofing the dough are rolled into one, allowing you to have freshly baked bread in half the time required to make traditional grain-based breads. I have designed all of the recipes in this book to be as fast to make as possible.

baking soda

I use Bob's Red Mill brand of baking soda in all my recipes that call for baking soda. Like baking powder, it is used to create a rise in baked goods, but it is different from baking powder in that when soda is combined with wet ingredients, the reaction is *immediate;* therefore, recipes that contain it need to be baked right away. So be sure to preheat the oven before starting any recipe containing baking soda.

In order for baking soda to be activated, it needs an acidic ingredient, such as citrus juice or vinegar. For Paleo applications, apple cider vinegar is the best choice of vinegar.

baking powder

I use Bob's Red Mill double-acting, aluminum-free baking powder in all of my recipes. It tastes much better than baking powders made with aluminum. Double-acting baking powder produces bubbles immediately when the ingredients are mixed, but most of the rising occurs after being put into the hot oven. While the "double-acting" action is not required for the majority of my recipes, it does provide a nice cushion to help assure that the baked goods will puff up in the oven. If you can't find Bob's double-acting, any other type of baking powder will work.

When baking recipes call for baking powder, it's best to mix it into the dry ingredients thoroughly before adding the wet ingredients to ensure that it is evenly distributed throughout the dough or batter.

BAKING

Tutorials

Gram Weights versus Cups

In my recipes, you will see both gram weights and cups. This is for a very specific reason: Gram weights are 100 percent accurate, and cups are not. How you fill your cup will vary slightly from the way I fill mine, which means that my recipe could turn out very different from yours. For this reason, I highly recommend that you pick up a baking scale and use the gram measurements when they are provided. Using gram weights is most essential with flour, which is why you will see a gram measurement every time a flour is included in a baking recipe. But for all of the batters and doughs in this book, particularly those in the bread and pastry recipes, I recommend using gram weights for most of the ingredients, including liquids and fats. That said, I do not include gram weights for small amounts, such as those measured in teaspoons and tablespoons, because I have found that not all scales read the small amounts the same way. So, although you can dispense with measuring cups once you buy a baking scale, you should keep your measuring spoons handy for the recipes in this book.

how to use a baking scale

Simply place your bowl directly on the scale. Turn it on and click the "tare" button to zero the weight. Then add your first ingredient. When have the correct gram amount for the first ingredient, tare the scale back to zero and repeat this process until you have worked your way through all of the ingredients with gram weights. For accuracy and efficiency, I use this method to measure both dry and wet ingredients for doughs and batters.

how to measure flour

Though weighing ingredients is the best method for accuracy, not everyone has a scale. The second best option to ensure consistency is for you to use the same method of measuring flour that I use. I use the "scoop and level" method, which results in a packed cup of flour. To get a packed cup, dip your dry measuring cup into the bag of flour and level off the top of the cup with your fingers or a knife. I use this technique every time I fill a cup with flour.

how to measure liquids in cups

If you don't own a scale and are measuring liquids in cups, make sure to use a liquid measuring cup, ideally a 2-cup measuring cup. For consistency, this is what I used throughout these recipes. This may sound strange, but I've noticed that 1 cup of liquid measured in a 2-cup measuring cup does not have the same volume, and thus gram weight, as 1 cup of liquid measured in a 1-cup measuring cup (the 1-cup measuring cup holds more!).

How to Beat Eggs

whisked

Beat the eggs with a fork or whisk until the yolks and whites are well combined, about 1 minute.

frothy

Beat the eggs with a hand-held electric mixer or stand mixer on high speed. The eggs will increase in volume, the texture will go from liquid to thick and foamy, and the eggs will become light yellow in color. This takes about 5 minutes.

soft peaks

Beat the egg whites only with a hand-held electric mixer or stand mixer on medium speed until they are thick and white. To test for soft peaks, lift the beaters or whisk from the whites; if ready, the peaks should fold down. For best results, make sure that the bowl and beaters or whisk are free of oil and that the egg whites contain no traces of yolk. Even a trace of oil, fat, or yolk will prevent the whites from reaching full volume. A metal or glass bowl works best; avoid using plastic.

stiff peaks

Once the whites are soft peaks, continue beating on high speed until the volume increases further and the whites become thicker. To test for stiff peaks, lift the beaters or whisk from the whites; if ready, the peaks should stand straight up, and the whites should not move at all when the bowl is tilted.

How to Cut In Butter or Shortening

Begin with slightly chilled butter (firm, but not rock hard). Cut the butter into approximately ½-inch cubes so that it is easier to incorporate when added to the flour or starch. Using a pastry cutter or two forks, work the butter into the flour until the butter and flour come together into pea-sized pieces.

You can use an equal amount of room-temperature shortening or chilled bacon fat in place of the butter. These two options will obviously yield different flavors, so substitute depending on the flavor profile you are looking for.

How to Get Coconut Cream from Canned Full-Fat Coconut Milk

Not all cans of full-fat coconut milk are created equal. Some have more coconut cream in them than others! Do not buy cans labeled "light" when you are trying to get a good amount of cream. If you compare labels, snag the can with the highest amount of fat! I recommend experimenting with different brands to find out which one yields the most cream.

Trader Joe's occasionally sells entire cans of coconut cream—*only* cream, with no coconut water mixed in. If you ever come across that product, stock up!

To get coconut cream from canned milk:

1. Place a can(s) of full-fat coconut milk upright in the refrigerator overnight. Proper chilling time is crucial, as this is what causes the coconut cream to separate, leaving coconut water below it.

2. Once completely chilled, the coconut cream will have solidified at the top and separated from the water. Carefully scoop out the cream, leaving the water in the can. The leftover coconut water is perfectly good to use; feel free to refrigerate it and drink it later!

How to Make Powdered Sugar

1. Begin with your choice of granulated sugar. Depending on the type you use, your powdered sugar will be lighter or darker in color, which will affect the appearance of your baked goods.

   - Pure cane sugar is very light in color, almost white.

   - Maple sugar is also light in color, but darker than pure cane sugar. It is a great option if you want a lighter color for Paleo baking options.

   - Coconut palm sugar is the darkest in color, similar to traditional brown sugar.

   - Organic/non-GMO xylitol can also be used. Although not technically Paleo because it needs to be processed in order to be made, it is a great sugar-free option.

2. Place the sugar in a coffee grinder, spice grinder, blender, or food processor (small or large, depending on quantity) and blend on high speed until the sugar becomes light and fluffy. This process typically takes about 3 minutes but can vary depending on your equipment.

How to Use the "Hot Box" Proofing Method

The process of rising and proofing grain-free dough is a little different from the process used when working with dough for gluten-based bread. When making bread with gluten-based flours, rising and proofing are typically accomplished in two steps (though sometimes a second rise is required): First the dough is allowed to rise, and then it is formed into the shape it will take when baked and allowed to "proof" before being baked. One of the pluses of gluten-free baking is that these two steps—rising and proofing—occur at the same time, significantly decreasing the total time required to get fresh-baked bread on the table.

I've experimented with a ton of different proofing methods and settled on one that outperforms all the others.

When preheated and then turned off, the oven can act as the perfect "hot box" to get a quick rise (generally about 30 minutes). You'll find that my process is the same for many of my yeast-based recipes. I typically preheat the oven while I'm preparing the bread dough. Then, when the dough is in its appropriate shape or pan, I turn off the oven and place the dough in the oven, leaving the oven door open a crack so that the hot air can escape. After 15 minutes, I shut the oven door to trap the remaining heat. It's important to leave the oven door open for the first 15 minutes, or the bread will get too hot and begin to bake rather than proof. (When proofing the pretzels, however, which have a shorter total proof time, the oven door is left open the entire time.)

It's pretty standard bread-making practice to cover the bread with a towel while the dough is rising. I do it, but I've found that grain-free breads (particularly those made with rice flour) sometimes like to stick to the towel as they puff up. This won't ruin the bread as long as you remove the towel carefully, but it may leave the top looking slightly imperfect. If you don't want to risk that, try using oiled plastic wrap instead! Here's what to do:

Cut a piece of plastic wrap slightly bigger than the pan or tray you are using. Place the piece of plastic wrap flat on the counter and drizzle a little oil on it. With a paper towel, spread the oil so that the entire surface is lightly coated. Carefully place the plastic wrap over the dough in the pan with the oiled side touching the dough. The oil will prevent the dough from sticking to the plastic wrap. Loosely cover the dough with the plastic wrap so that the dough has room to expand. Cut off any extra plastic wrap before placing the dough in the oven so it does not touch the oven racks.

After your bread has spent time rising, remove it from the oven and preheat the oven. Remove the towel or plastic wrap. Follow the baking times and directions in the recipes for further instruction. Just be sure not to place the proofed dough in the oven to bake until the oven has come to temperature.

TEN THINGS
to Know Before You Bake!

1. Buy a baking scale. It's the only way to be sure that the recipes in this book will turn out perfect every time! Truth is, once you start using a scale, you'll probably prefer it. Bread can be finicky, and scooping out a cup of flour heavier or lighter than I do will make a difference in how a recipe turns out, especially if it contains yeast.

2. Take the time to read through the ingredients list and instructions carefully before you begin a recipe. This step will help you be prepared timing-wise. Several of my recipes, such as the sandwiches, French toast, biscuits and gravy, and croutons, call for homemade breads, rolls, or biscuits that must be prepared before the recipe in which they are utilized can be made.

3. Follow the recipes as they are written. Experiment with substitutions at your own risk! Baking is a science, and if you change one ingredient, the recipe may not turn out. Remember that I have created the recipes in this book to be free of as many allergens as possible. If you wish to make substitutions, see my suggestions in the Ingredients & Substitutions section (pages 13 to 21).

4. Because I use xanthan gum and guar gum in some recipes, you may notice that they are slightly gummy when piping hot. But once they cool down a little, the texture will be perfect.

5. When working with almond flour, you typically need to mix it for longer than you would expect. Almond flour contains a lot of fat and moisture, and it will begin to release that moisture into the dough. If a dough seems crumbly and isn't coming together as you expected, get your hands into the dough and knead—you'll be amazed to see that the dough starts to change!

6. Ovens can vary a little in temperature. Therefore, I recommend that you keep an eye on your baked goods in the last five minutes or so of baking to make sure that they don't become overdone.

7. Always preheat your oven fully before placing a pan in the oven. In most cases, I like to turn the oven on just before I begin mixing together the ingredients.

8. There are recipes for different skill levels throughout this book. If you are new to baking, try one of the yeast-free breads first because they are simpler.

9. The day after making your bread, warm it up before eating it. Grain-free breads tend to dry out and lose their soft, fluffy texture, but a quick preheating will bring them back to life. Pop your bread in the microwave for a minute or less, or warm it up in a 350-degree oven.

10. Have fun, and don't forget to share your creations online using the hashtag #EveryLastCrumb so that I can see them, too!

CHAPTER 1
Classic Breads

PREP TIME: 45 minutes, including proofing time
COOK TIME: 1 hour
YIELD: One 8½-by-4½-inch loaf

DAIRY *free*, **EGG** *free*, **NUT** *free*, **GRAIN** *free*, **COCONUT** *free*

basic sandwich bread

Before jumping into this recipe, I suggest that you read through it once or twice. Most of my recipes are basic; however, making bread is not. Now, don't get scared; you can do it! It just takes a few more steps and requires precise measurements. You will love the results, and it's worth all the effort!

ingredients

9 large egg whites

104 grams water (about ½ cup)

3 packets gelatin (3 tablespoons)

1 tablespoon instant yeast

91 grams lukewarm water (about ¼ cup plus 3 tablespoons)

3 tablespoons coconut palm sugar

251 grams potato starch or sweet potato starch (about 1½ cups)

165 grams coconut flour (about 1 cup plus 2 tablespoons)

2 tablespoons double-acting, aluminum-free baking powder

1 tablespoon plus 1½ teaspoons xanthan gum or guar gum

1 teaspoon kosher salt

190 grams Spectrum vegetable shortening (about 1 cup)

Oil of choice, for the work surface

notes

This bread tastes best slightly warm, so I like to heat up leftovers briefly before serving. Be sure to try toasting it as well!

directions

1. Preheat the oven to 350 degrees to warm it up as a "hot box" for the dough to proof. Line an 8½-by-4½-inch loaf pan with parchment paper.

2. Drop the egg whites into the bowl of a stand mixer (or a mixing bowl). Set aside.

3. In a small, microwave-safe bowl, heat the water for the gelatin in the microwave until it's almost boiling. Whisk in the gelatin with a fork until fully dissolved. Set aside.

4. In another small bowl, mix together the yeast, lukewarm water, and sugar. Set aside.

5. In another mixing bowl, whisk the potato starch, coconut flour, baking powder, xanthan gum, and salt. Add the shortening and mix until it is completely blended throughout the starch mixture. Set aside.

6. Using the whisk attachment on your stand mixer or a hand-held electric mixer, whip the egg whites on high speed until soft peaks form; this will take just under a minute. Pour in the gelatin mixture and beat for another 10 to 15 seconds. Then add the yeast mixture and beat for another 10 seconds.

7. Slowly add the flour mixture to the egg whites while beating on low speed. Once all the flour is in, beat on high speed until a sticky dough comes together, about 1 minute.

8. Lightly oil your work surface and use a spatula to drop the dough onto the oiled surface.

9. Oil your hands and pound the dough a little with your palms to beat out any big crevices. Then roll it around to form it into a loaf shape that will fit into the loaf pan.

10. It's time to proof the dough! Place the dough in the pan and cover with a towel (or a piece of plastic wrap, following the method described on page 27). Turn off the oven and place the dough in the warm oven to proof for a total of 30 minutes. Leave the oven door open a crack for the first 15 minutes, and then close the door for the last 15 minutes.

11. After 30 minutes of proofing, remove the pan from the oven. Preheat the oven to 375 degrees.

12. When the oven is fully preheated, remove the cover from the dough and place the pan in the oven on the middle rack. Bake for 20 minutes, and then gently tent it with foil so the crust doesn't get too dark. (Do not press down on the foil, as the bread may continue to rise during baking.) Return the pan to the oven and bake for 40 more minutes, until a toothpick inserted into the center comes out clean and the bread is golden brown.

13. Allow the bread to cool before slicing. Store the cooled bread in a sealed bag at room temperature (not in the fridge), or freeze for later.

PREP TIME: 45 minutes
COOK TIME: 1 hour
YIELD: One 8½-by-4½-inch loaf

DAIRY *free,* **EGG** *free,* **NUT** *free,*
GRAIN *free,* **COCONUT** *free*

yeast-free basic sandwich bread

Making bread is an advanced skill that requires exact measurements. Everyone measures a cup a bit differently, so I highly recommend getting a scale. In the realm of bread-making, however, this particular recipe is pretty basic, so it's a great starting place for beginners.

ingredients

9 large egg whites

174 grams water (about ¾ cup)

3 packets gelatin (3 tablespoons)

165 grams coconut flour (about 1 cup plus 2 tablespoons)

251 grams potato starch or sweet potato starch (about 1½ cups)

1 tablespoon plus 1½ teaspoons xanthan gum or guar gum

2 tablespoons double-acting, aluminum-free baking powder

1 teaspoon kosher salt

3 tablespoons coconut palm sugar

190 grams Spectrum vegetable shortening (about 1 cup)

2 tablespoons apple cider vinegar

Oil of choice, for the work surface

notes

If you want your bread crust softer, gently tent it with foil after the first 20 minutes of baking. Don't press the foil down hard, as the bread will continue to rise for at least the next 20 to 30 minutes of baking.

This bread tastes best slightly warm, so I like to heat up leftovers briefly before serving. Try toasting it as well!

directions

1. Preheat the oven to 400 degrees. Line an 8½-by-4½-inch loaf pan with parchment paper.

2. Drop the egg whites into the bowl of a stand mixer (or a mixing bowl). Set aside.

3. In a small, microwave-safe bowl, heat the water for the gelatin in the microwave until it's almost boiling. Whisk in the gelatin with a fork until fully dissolved. Set aside.

4. In a mixing bowl, whisk the coconut flour, potato starch, xanthan gum, baking powder, and salt until blended, and then add the sugar. Add the shortening and mix until it is completely blended throughout the flour mixture.

5. Using the whisk attachment on your stand mixer or a hand-held electric mixer, whisk the egg whites on high speed until soft peaks form; this will take just under a minute. Pour in the gelatin mixture and beat for another 10 to 15 seconds.

6. Slowly add the flour mixture to the egg whites while beating on low speed. Once all the flour is in, beat on high speed until a sticky dough comes together, about 1 minute.

7. Pour in the vinegar and beat for another 20 seconds.

8. Lightly oil your work surface and use a spatula to drop the dough onto the oiled surface.

9. Oil your hands and pound the dough a little with your palms to beat out any big crevices. Then roll it around to form it into a loaf shape that will fit into the loaf pan. Don't spend too much time doing this— the quicker you get the dough into the oven, the better!

10. Put the dough in the prepared pan and place it on the middle rack of the preheated oven. Bake for 20 minutes, and then reduce the heat to 375 degrees and bake for another 40 minutes.

11. Allow the bread to cool completely before slicing. Waiting makes a huge difference in how it will slice! (If you slice it too early, it will be gooey on the inside at first.) Store the cooled bread in a sealed bag at room temperature (not in the fridge), or freeze for later use.

PREP TIME: 10 to 15 minutes
COOK TIME: 48 to 50 minutes
YIELD: One 8½-by-4½-inch loaf

DAIRY *free*, **EGG** *free*, **NUT** *free*,
GRAIN *free*, **COCONUT** *free*

low-carb honey "wheat" bread

Think you can no longer enjoy bread because you're on a carb-restricted diet? Think again! This egg and almond butter–based bread is the perfect alternative to traditional or gluten-free bread if you are on a low-carb diet. It tastes just like honey wheat bread...minus the wheat!

ingredients

4 large eggs

431 grams almond butter (about 1½ cups)

84 grams raw honey (about ¼ cup)

2 tablespoons lemon juice

2 teaspoons vanilla extract

1 teaspoon ground cinnamon

¾ teaspoons baking soda

¼ teaspoon kosher salt

directions

1. Preheat the oven to 375 degrees. Line an 8½-by-4½-inch loaf pan with parchment paper.

2. In the bowl of a stand mixer, using the whisk attachment, mix the eggs on medium speed until they are whipped and fluffy, about 3 minutes.

3. Add the remaining ingredients and mix on medium speed for another 2 to 3 minutes, until smooth and fully blended.

4. Pour the batter into the prepared loaf pan and bake for 48 to 50 minutes, until firm to the touch and a deep, dark, golden brown color. Halfway through baking, cover loosely with foil to avoid overbrowning.

5. Store the cooled bread in a sealed bag at room temperature (not in the fridge), or freeze for later use.

PREP TIME: 45 minutes, including proofing time
COOK TIME: 25 minutes
YIELD: One 8½-by-4½-inch loaf

DAIRY *free*, **EGG** *free*, **NUT** *free*,
GRAIN *free*, **COCONUT** *free*

egg-free rice flour bread

For those of you who tolerate rice well, I created this delicious sandwich bread free of eggs. This crusty yet soft loaf works beautifully toasted, or you can make it into Croutons (page 152) or even Classic French Toast (page 210).

ingredients

330 grams lukewarm water (about 1½ cups)

84 grams raw honey (about ¼ cup)

1 tablespoon instant yeast

320 grams superfine white rice flour (about 2 cups)

132 grams potato starch or sweet potato starch (about ¾ cup)

1 tablespoon double-acting, aluminum-free baking powder

1¾ teaspoons xanthan gum or guar gum

½ teaspoon kosher salt

56 grams mild-flavored oil (about ¼ cup), plus more for the pan

2 teaspoons apple cider vinegar

notes

My goal is to give you options! Though not grain-free, this recipe is free of eggs. It is perfect for slicing up to make sandwiches.

directions

1. Preheat the oven to 375 degrees to warm it up as a "hot box" for the dough to proof. Oil an 8½-by-4½-inch loaf pan.

2. In a small bowl, mix together the lukewarm water, honey, and yeast. Set aside.

3. In the bowl of a stand mixer, using the whisk attachment, mix the rice flour, potato starch, baking powder, xanthan gum, and salt until blended.

4. Add the oil, vinegar, and yeast mixture and mix until a dough comes together. Pour the dough into the prepared loaf pan.

5. Cut a piece of plastic wrap slightly bigger than the pan. Place the piece of plastic wrap flat on your work surface and drizzle a little oil on it. With a paper towel, spread the oil so the entire surface is lightly coated. Carefully place the plastic wrap over the dough in the pan with the oiled side touching the dough. (The oil will prevent the dough from sticking to the plastic wrap.) Loosely cover the dough with the plastic wrap so the dough has room to expand. Cut off any extra plastic wrap before placing the pan in the oven so it does not touch the oven racks. You may also proof the dough by covering it with a clean towel; however, the dough is likely to stick to the towel.

6. Turn off the oven and place the dough in the warm oven to proof for a total of 30 minutes. Leave the oven door open a crack for the first 15 minutes, and then close the door for the last 15 minutes.

7. After 30 minutes of proofing, remove the pan from the oven. Preheat the oven to 375 degrees.

8. When the oven is fully preheated, remove the plastic wrap from the dough and place the pan in the oven. Bake for 25 minutes, until a toothpick inserted comes out clean and the bread is a light golden brown color.

9. Store the cooled bread in a sealed bag at room temperature (not in the fridge), or freeze for later use.

PREP TIME: 45 minutes, including proofing time
COOK TIME: 18 minutes
YIELD: 4 buns

DAIRY *free*, **EGG** *free*, **NUT** *free*, **GRAIN** *free*, **COCONUT** *free*

hamburger buns

These hamburger buns taste incredible. They keep well in a sealed bag and can be frozen. If you make them in advance, I suggest toasting them before using. See Step 6 below to adapt the texture to your preference.

ingredients

5 large egg whites

108 grams blanched almond flour (about ¾ cup)

132 grams tapioca starch (about 1 cup), plus more for the work surface (if crusty buns are desired)

1½ teaspoons xanthan gum or guar gum

1 tablespoon double-acting, aluminum-free baking powder

¼ teaspoon kosher salt

48 grams Spectrum vegetable shortening (about ¼ cup)

2 tablespoons apple cider vinegar

notes

Baking ring molds, also called English muffin rings, are not necessary, but they will create perfectly round buns. If you do not have ring molds, simply shape the buns as described in Step 6 and place them a few inches apart on the lined baking sheet.

directions

1. Preheat the oven to 375 degrees. Line a baking sheet with parchment paper. Spray the insides of four 4-inch ring molds with nonstick spray and place them on the baking sheet (see Notes).

2. In the bowl of a stand mixer, using the whisk attachment, whip the egg whites until frothy, about 1 minute.

3. In a separate bowl, whisk the almond flour, tapioca starch, xanthan gum, baking powder, and salt until blended.

4. Add the flour mixture to the egg whites and beat until combined. Add the shortening and vinegar and mix until combined.

5. Divide the dough into 4 equal portions.

6. If you would like buns with a harder, crunchier exterior, spread some starch over your work surface and roll the dough into round buns, 4 inches in diameter; I like to smack my dough so that the creases smooth out. If you would like buns with a softer crust, oil your hands and shape the dough into 4-inch-round buns without rolling the dough in starch.

7. Place the buns in the ring molds and brush them with water.

8. Bake for 18 minutes, until golden brown and firm to the touch. Allow to cool for 20 minutes before removing the ring molds.

9. Store leftover buns at room temperature in a sealed container, or freeze for later use.

PREP TIME: 15 minutes
COOK TIME: 20 minutes
YIELD: 6 buns

DAIRY *free*, EGG *free*, NUT *free*,
GRAIN *free*, COCONUT *free*

low-carb hamburger buns

These hamburger buns are incredible. Every time I make them, I'm shocked by how perfect they are, especially being low-carb. They have a beautiful soft crust, and they're just as soft on the inside, but also super airy and slightly chewy. Plus, no yeast! If you can't find baking ring molds, feel free to use mini springform pans instead.

ingredients

4 large eggs

431 grams cashew butter or almond butter (about 1½ cups)

84 grams raw honey (about ¼ cup)

2 tablespoons lemon juice or apple cider vinegar

2 teaspoons vanilla extract

¾ teaspoon baking soda

¼ teaspoon kosher salt

directions

1. Preheat the oven to 375 degrees. Line a baking sheet with parchment paper. Spray the insides of six 4-inch ring molds with nonstick spray and place them on the baking sheet (see Notes).

2. In a large bowl, using a hand-held electric mixer, whip the eggs until frothy and fluffy, about 2 minutes.

3. Stir in the remaining ingredients and mix well, until the batter is smooth and thoroughly combined.

4. Pour the batter into the ring molds, filling each about halfway.

5. Bake for 20 minutes, until a toothpick inserted comes out clean. Allow to cool for 20 minutes before removing the ring molds.

6. Store leftover buns at room temperature in a sealed container, or freeze for later use.

notes

If you don't have enough ring molds or mini springform pans to bake all 6 buns at once, divide the recipe in half and make the second batch of dough while the first batch is in the oven. Baking soda reacts quickly when added to liquid, and you want that reaction to happen in the oven, not on your kitchen counter.

PREP TIME: 40 minutes, including proofing time
COOK TIME: 20 minutes
YIELD: 8 buns

DAIRY free, **EGG** free, **NUT** free, **GRAIN** free, **COCONUT** free

hot dog buns

Grain-free hot dog buns? You got it! The question is, what will you put on top? I'm all about topping my hot dogs with Chili (page 272).

ingredients

126 grams raw honey (about ¼ cup plus 2 tablespoons)

2 teaspoons instant yeast

7 large egg whites

216 grams blanched almond flour (about 1½ cups)

132 grams tapioca starch (about 1 cup), plus more for the work surface

166 grams potato starch or sweet potato starch (about 1 cup)

2½ teaspoons xanthan gum or guar gum

1 tablespoon double-acting, aluminum-free baking powder

½ teaspoon kosher salt

128 grams Spectrum vegetable shortening (about ¾ cup)

2 tablespoons apple cider vinegar

Melted salted butter, ghee, or mild-flavored oil, for brushing the buns

notes

Like with most gluten-free baked goods, these buns have the best texture when they are slightly warm.

directions

1. Preheat the oven to 350 degrees to warm it up as a "hot box" for the dough to proof. Line a rimmed baking sheet with parchment paper.

2. In a microwave-safe bowl, heat the honey for 5 to 10 seconds, just until it is lukewarm. (Be careful! It heats up very quickly.) Stir in the yeast and set aside.

3. In the bowl of a stand mixer, using the whisk attachment, whip the egg whites until frothy, about 1 minute.

4. In a separate bowl, whisk the almond flour, starches, xanthan gum, baking powder, and salt until blended.

5. Working in batches, slowly add the flour mixture to the egg whites while mixing on low speed for about 30 seconds.

6. Add the yeast mixture, shortening, and vinegar and mix on low speed. When the ingredients are combined, increase the speed to high and continue mixing until a dough comes together.

7. It's time to shape the buns! Sprinkle some tapioca starch on your work surface. Scoop about ¾ cup of dough from the bowl and drop it onto the dusted work surface.

8. Using your hands, roll the dough into a hot dog bun shape about 6 inches long. Place on the prepared baking sheet. Repeat with the rest of the dough, spacing the buns about 1 inch apart on the pan, because they will rise and expand.

9. Liberally brush the buns with water. Turn off the oven and place the buns, uncovered, in the warm oven to proof for a total of 30 minutes. Leave the oven door open a crack for the first 15 minutes, and then close the door for the last 15 minutes.

10. After 30 minutes of proofing, remove the pan from the oven and brush the buns with melted butter. Preheat the oven to 375 degrees.

11. When the oven is fully preheated, place the pan on the middle rack of the oven and bake for 20 minutes, until firm to the touch and golden brown.

12. When cool enough to handle, cut slits in the buns so you can fill them with hot dogs! Store leftover buns at room temperature in a sealed container, or freeze for later use.

PREP TIME: 45 minutes, including proofing time
COOK TIME: 23 minutes
YIELD: 12 rolls

DAIRY *free*, EGG *free*, NUT *free*,
GRAIN *free*, COCONUT *free*

parker house dinner rolls

These delicious dinner rolls are fluffy, airy, and just slightly sweet. Brushing them with butter and keeping them covered as they cool ensures that they will have a soft crust.

ingredients

2 teaspoons instant yeast

126 grams raw honey (about ¼ cup plus 2 tablespoons)

7 large egg whites

216 grams blanched almond flour (about 1½ cups)

132 grams tapioca starch (about 1 cup), plus more for the work surface

166 grams potato starch or sweet potato starch (about 1 cup)

2½ teaspoons xanthan gum or guar gum

1 tablespoon double-acting, aluminum-free baking powder

½ teaspoon kosher salt

128 grams Spectrum vegetable shortening (about ¾ cup)

2 tablespoons apple cider vinegar

Melted salted butter, ghee, or mild-flavored oil, for brushing the rolls

directions

1. Preheat the oven to 375 degrees to warm it up as a "hot box" for the dough to proof. Oil an 8-inch square baking pan.

2. In a microwave-safe bowl, heat the honey for 5 to 10 seconds, just until it is lukewarm. (Be careful! It heats up very quickly.) Stir in the yeast and set aside.

3. In the bowl of a stand mixer, using the whisk attachment, whip the egg whites until frothy, about 1 minute.

4. In a separate bowl, whisk the almond flour, starches, xanthan gum, baking powder, and salt until blended.

5. Working in batches, slowly add the flour mixture to the egg whites while mixing on low speed until well combined.

6. Add the yeast mixture, shortening, and vinegar and mix on medium-high speed until a dough comes together.

7. It's time to shape the rolls! Sprinkle some tapioca starch on your work surface. Scoop about ⅓ cup of dough from the bowl and drop it onto the dusted work surface.

8. Using your hands, form the dough into a roll shape and place it on the prepared baking sheet. Repeat with the rest of the dough. If you find that you have extra space in the pan, use some foil to fill in the gap; you want the rolls to be touching.

9. Liberally brush the rolls with water and cover with a towel. Turn off the oven and place the rolls in the warm oven to proof for a total of 30 minutes. Leave the oven door open a crack for the first 15 minutes, and then close the door for the last 15 minutes.

10. After 30 minutes of proofing, remove the pan from the oven, carefully take off the towel, and brush the rolls with water again. Preheat the oven to 375 degrees.

11. When the oven is fully preheated, bake the rolls for 23 minutes, until firm to the touch and golden brown, brushing with melted butter halfway through baking. In the last 3 to 5 minutes, cover the pan with foil if you find that the rolls are getting too dark.

12. Remove from the oven and allow to cool in the pan, covered with foil. Store leftover rolls at room temperature in a sealed container, or freeze for later use.

PREP TIME: 45 minutes, including proofing time
COOK TIME: 25 to 28 minutes
YIELD: Two 9- to 10-inch loaves

DAIRY *free*, EGG *free*, NUT *free*, GRAIN *free*, COCONUT *free*

baguettes

This recipe was by far the most difficult one in this book to figure out. It took sixteen trial runs! But the finished recipe is worth all that work. This bread is fluffy on the inside and crusty on the outside, just as a baguette should be. I highly recommend picking up a baguette pan, as it will make all the difference in how the crust turns out.

ingredients

60 grams lukewarm water (about ¼ cup)

2 teaspoons instant yeast

1 tablespoon coconut palm sugar

108 grams water (about ½ cup)

2 packets gelatin (2 tablespoons)

3 large egg whites

108 grams coconut flour (about ½ cup plus 2 tablespoons)

126 grams potato starch or sweet potato starch (about ⅔ cup plus 2 teaspoons)

33 grams tapioca starch (about ¼ cup)

2¾ teaspoons xanthan gum or guar gum

1 tablespoon double-acting, aluminum-free baking powder

¼ teaspoon kosher salt

60 grams Spectrum vegetable shortening (about ¼ cup plus 1 tablespoon)

2 tablespoons apple cider vinegar

directions

1. Preheat the oven to 350 degrees to warm it up as a "hot box" for the dough to proof. Have a baguette pan on hand, or line a baking sheet with parchment paper.

2. In a small bowl, mix together the lukewarm water, yeast, and sugar. Set aside.

3. In a microwave-safe bowl, whisk together the water and gelatin. Microwave for 30 seconds; set aside.

4. In the bowl of a stand mixer, using the whisk attachment, whip the egg whites until frothy.

5. In a separate bowl, whisk the coconut flour, starches, xanthan gum, baking powder, and salt until blended.

6. Add the flour mixture to the egg whites and mix on low speed. When fully combined, add the shortening, vinegar, yeast mixture, and gelatin mixture. Mix on high speed for a few minutes until the dough holds together and is slightly tacky.

7. Divide the dough into 2 equal portions. Roll out each portion into a log about 9 to 10 inches long. Make crosswise slits on the tops of the baguettes, about ¼ inch deep and 1 inch apart.

8. Place the loaves in the baguette pan or on the prepared baking sheet. Brush the loaves liberally with water and cover with a kitchen towel.

9. Turn off the oven and place the covered baguettes in the warm oven to proof for a total of 30 minutes. Leave the oven door open a crack for the first 15 minutes, and then close the door for the last 15 minutes.

10. Meanwhile, bring a kettle of water to a boil.

11. After 30 minutes of proofing, remove the baguettes from the oven and carefully remove the towel. Preheat the oven to 400 degrees.

12. Once the water in the kettle is rapidly boiling, pour the water into an oven-safe baking dish and place in the oven on the bottom rack.

13. Brush the baguettes liberally with water and place them in the hot oven on the rack above the water. Bake for 25 to 28 minutes, until beautifully golden and firm to the touch.

14. Remove and enjoy! Store the baguettes at room temperature in a sealed container, or freeze for later use.

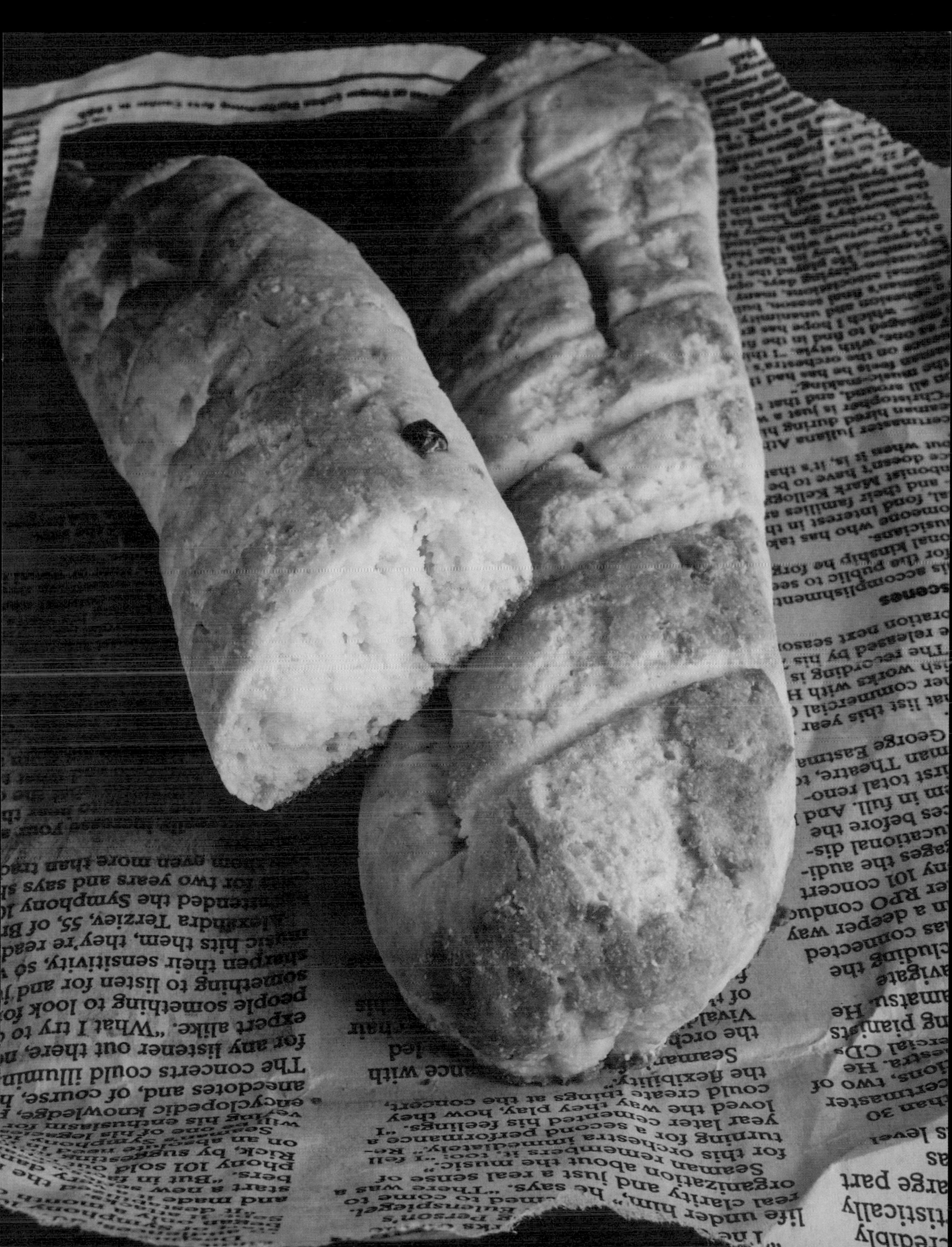

PREP TIME: 15 minutes
COOK TIME: 30 to 35 minutes
YIELD: 1 large tray

DAIRY *free*, **EGG** *free*, **NUT** *free*, **GRAIN** *free*, **COCONUT** *free*

all-purpose flatbread

This flatbread is very versatile. You can mix and match the spices as you desire. I love eating it with cream cheese and cucumbers for a light snack, or dipping it in pizza sauce!

ingredients

44 grams (about a scant ¼ cup) plus 2 teaspoons olive oil, divided, plus more for brushing the bread

¼ medium onion, diced (approximately ½ cup)

1 teaspoon garlic powder

178 grams blanched almond flour (about 1¼ cups)

112 grams tapioca starch (about ¾ cup plus 1½ tablespoons)

2½ teaspoons xanthan gum or guar gum

1 tablespoon plus 1 teaspoon double-acting, aluminum-free baking powder

½ teaspoon kosher salt

315 grams water (about a scant 1½ cups)

directions

1. Preheat the oven to 400 degrees. Line a rimmed baking sheet with parchment paper.

2. Heat 2 teaspoons of the olive oil in a small skillet over medium-low heat. Add the onion and sauté until softened, about 3 minutes. Add the garlic powder and cook for 1 minute. Set aside.

3. In a large bowl, whisk the almond flour, tapioca starch, xanthan gum, baking powder, and salt with a fork until blended.

4. In a medium-sized bowl, whisk together the water and the remaining 44 grams of olive oil. Pour into the dry ingredients, stirring constantly until mixed. (This is not your typical bread dough; the consistency will be closer to batter.)

5. Stir in the onion and garlic powder mixture.

6. Spoon the dough onto the prepared baking sheet. Using the back of the spoon, spread the dough evenly across the surface of the pan to the edges (it should be about ¾ inch thick). Brush with olive oil.

7. Bake for 30 to 35 minutes, until firm to the touch and lightly golden brown.

8. Let cool in the pan, and then cut into squares or rectangles. This bread is best when eaten fresh out of the oven. Leftovers can be stored in an airtight container in the fridge or frozen for later use.

PREP TIME: 40 minutes, including proofing time
COOK TIME: 27 to 30 minutes
YIELD: 1 loaf

• • • • • • • • • • • • • • •

DAIRY *free*, **EGG** *free*, **NUT** *free*, **GRAIN** *free*, **COCONUT** *free*

round loaf

• •

There is no greater joy than seeing a big loaf of crusty bread rising in the oven, filling the kitchen with its aroma. This recipe is one to master. It may seem complicated at first, but it's worth the extra effort. Before beginning, I like to pull out three separate bowls: one for the eggs, one for the gelatin mixture, and one for the yeast mixture. I save time by allowing the yeast to grow while I work on the other parts of the bread.

ingredients

4 large egg whites

2 packets gelatin (2 tablespoons)

108 grams water (about ½ cup)

1 tablespoon instant yeast

27 grams lukewarm water (about 2 tablespoons)

3½ tablespoons coconut palm sugar

108 grams coconut flour (about ½ cup plus 2 tablespoons)

126 grams potato starch or sweet potato starch (about ⅔ cup plus 2 teaspoons)

33 grams tapioca starch (about ¼ cup), plus more for the work surface

3 teaspoons xanthan gum or guar gum

1 teaspoon double-acting, aluminum-free baking powder

¼ teaspoon kosher salt

98 grams Spectrum vegetable shortening (about ½ cup plus 2 tablespoons)

2 tablespoons apple cider vinegar

notes

For even better-tasting bread with a beautiful crust, place a water bath on the rack below the bread while it is baking. You can do this by heating up some water and pouring it into an oven-safe casserole dish. Place the water bath in the oven right before you place the proofed dough in the oven to bake.

This bread tastes best slightly warm, so be sure to heat up leftovers briefly before serving.

directions

1. Preheat the oven to 350 degrees to warm it up as a "hot box" for the dough to proof. Line a baking sheet with parchment paper.

2. Drop the egg whites into the bowl of a stand mixer (or a mixing bowl). Set aside.

3. In a small, microwave-safe bowl, whisk together the gelatin and water. Heat in the microwave for a minute until very hot but not quite boiling. Set aside.

4. In another small bowl, mix together the yeast, lukewarm water, and sugar. Set aside.

5. In another mixing bowl, whisk the coconut flour, starches, xanthan gum, baking powder, and salt until blended. Add the shortening and thoroughly mix it in. Set aside.

6. Using the whisk attachment on your stand mixer (or a hand-held electric mixer), whisk the egg whites on high speed until frothy; this will take just under a minute. Pour in the gelatin mixture and beat for another 10 to 15 seconds. Then add the yeast mixture and beat for another 10 seconds.

7. Begin slowly pouring the flour mixture into the stand mixer while it's mixing on low. Once all the flour is in, beat on high speed for about a minute, until a dough comes together.

8. Lightly dust your work surface with tapioca starch. Drop the dough onto the dusted work surface and sprinkle it with just enough starch to prevent it from sticking.

9. Pound the dough a little with your palms to beat out any big crevices. Then roll it around to form it into a round loaf shape. Place the loaf on the prepared baking sheet and brush it liberally with water.

10. It's time to proof the dough! Cover the loaf with a towel. Turn off the oven and place the dough on the middle rack to proof for 30 minutes. Keep the door open a crack for the first 15 minutes, and then close the door for the last 15 minutes. Halfway through the proofing time, brush the dough with more water if it has started to dry out.

11. After 30 minutes of proofing, remove the pan from the oven. Preheat the oven to 400 degrees.

12. When the oven is fully preheated, remove the towel and return the loaf to the oven, placing it on the middle rack. Bake for 27 to 30 minutes, until firm to the touch and golden brown.

13. Allow the bread to cool before slicing. Store at room temperature in a sealed bag.

CHAPTER 2

Specialty Breads

PREP TIME: 10 minutes
COOK TIME: 2 to 4 minutes per lavash
YIELD: 8 to 12 lavash

. . . .

DAIRY *free*, **EGG** *free*, **NUT** *free*,
GRAIN *free*, COCONUT *free*

grain-free lavash

. . . .

When making this lavash, it's important to roll out the dough as thin as possible. This makes the cooking time quick. I typically double this recipe and freeze half for later, because lavash make the perfect flexible wraps to stuff with lunchmeat and veggies!

ingredients

315 grams hot water (about a scant 1½ cups)

17½ grams whole psyllium husks (about 3½ tablespoons) (see Notes)

138 grams coconut flour (about ¾ cup plus 1 tablespoon)

54 grams tapioca starch (about ⅓ cup plus 1½ tablespoons)

1 teaspoon kosher salt

4 cloves garlic, minced, or 2 teaspoons garlic powder

Oil of choice, for the pan

directions

1. In a bowl, mix together the hot water and psyllium husks until thickened. Pour into a food processor.

2. To the food processor, add the coconut flour, tapioca starch, salt, and garlic and process until fully combined.

3. Grab a handful of dough and place it between 2 sheets of parchment paper or wax paper. Using the edges of the paper as a guide, roll the dough into a very thin rectangle, about the thickness of a tortilla.

4. Heat a drizzle of oil in a large nonstick skillet over medium-low heat. Cook the lavash for 1 to 2 minutes per side. Repeat until all of the dough has been used.

5. Store leftover lavash in a sealed bag or container at room temperature, or freeze for later use.

notes

Whole psyllium husks can be found in most health food stores in the supplement aisle. Be sure to purchase only whole psyllium husks; any other variety will not work quite the same in this recipe.

PREP TIME: 10 minutes
COOK TIME: 2 to 4 minutes per lavash
YIELD: 8 to 12 lavash

DAIRY *free*, EGG *free*, NUT *free*, GRAIN *free*, COCONUT *free*

grain-free spinach lavash

Here's a second version of lavash for you spinach lovers! The cheese is 100 percent optional; it can be left out and the bread will still taste fantastic.

ingredients

273 grams hot water (about 1¼ cups)

20 grams whole psyllium husks (about ¼ cup) (see Notes)

30 grams thawed frozen spinach (about 1 very packed cup)

115 grams coconut flour (about ⅔ cup)

45 grams tapioca starch (about ⅓ cup)

1 teaspoon kosher salt

4 cloves garlic, minced, or 2 teaspoons garlic powder

¼ cup finely grated hard cheese, such as Pecorino Romano or Parmesan (optional)

Oil of choice, for the pan

directions

1. In a bowl, mix together the hot water and psyllium husks until thickened. Pour into a food processor.

2. To the food processor, add the spinach, coconut flour, tapioca starch, salt, garlic, and cheese (if using) and process until fully combined.

3. Grab a handful of dough and place it between 2 sheets of parchment or wax paper. Using the edges of the paper as a guide, roll the dough into a very thin rectangle, about the thickness of a tortilla.

4. Heat a large nonstick skillet over medium-low heat with a drizzle of oil. Cook the lavash for 1 to 2 minutes per side. Repeat until all the dough has been used.

5. Store leftover lavash in a sealed bag or container at room temperature, or freeze for later use.

notes

Whole psyllium husks can be found in most health food stores in the supplement aisle. Be sure to purchase only whole psyllium husks; any other variety will not work quite the same in this recipe.

PREP TIME: 15 minutes
COOK TIME: 24 minutes
YIELD: 4 large pieces

DAIRY *free*, **EGG** *free*, **NUT** *free*, **GRAIN** *free*, **COCONUT** *free*

naan

I love Indian food more than anything else in this world. This Naan recipe is very adaptable: You can sub in different spices to make it to your liking. Use this flatbread to soak up the delicious sauces in your favorite curries!

There are two ways to make naan: in a skillet on the stovetop or in the oven. I have come to prefer the skillet method, as it gives the classic look of naan with the golden brown marks on the surface.

ingredients

4 large eggs

25 grams whole psyllium husks (about ¼ cup plus 1 tablespoon) (see Notes)

175 grams (about ¾ cup) plain yogurt (dairy or nondairy) or cream from 1 to 2 cans full-fat coconut milk (see tutorial, page 26)

56 grams mild-flavored oil, melted salted butter, or melted ghee (about ¼ cup), plus more for the pan

165 grams coconut flour (about 1 cup plus 2 tablespoons)

132 grams tapioca starch (about 1 cup)

1½ teaspoons double-acting, aluminum-free baking powder

1 tablespoon garlic powder, garlic paste, or minced garlic (optional)

½ teaspoon kosher salt

1 teaspoon apple cider vinegar

notes

Whole psyllium husks can be found in most health food stores in the supplement aisle. Be sure to purchase only whole psyllium husks; any other variety will not work quite the same in this recipe.

directions

1. Lightly oil a baking sheet to use as a holding area for the formed Naan before they go into the skillet. Have on hand a large skillet with a lid.

2. In the bowl of a stand mixer, using the whisk attachment (or in a mixing bowl with a hand-held electric mixer), beat the eggs on medium speed for about 30 seconds. Add the psyllium husks, yogurt, and oil. Beat for an additional minute. Add the coconut flour, tapioca starch, baking powder, garlic powder, and salt and mix until well combined. The batter should be semi-thick and very sticky. *Note:* If you use garlic powder instead of garlic paste, you may want to add an extra tablespoon of yogurt.

3. Stir in the vinegar quickly using a spatula.

4. Oil your hands liberally and divide the dough into 4 roughly equal portions. Keeping your hands well oiled, shape a piece of dough into a ball and then plop it onto the oiled baking sheet. Using your palms, press the dough until it is between ¼ and ½ inch thick. Leave it slightly uneven to make it look authentic. Repeat with the other 3 pieces of dough.

5. Place the skillet over medium heat and coat the bottom with a little oil. Allow it to heat up for a minute or so, and then place a shaped Naan in the pan. Cover and cook for roughly 3 minutes on each side, until cooked through. (You will know it's done when the dough springs back slightly when you poke it with your finger.) Remove from the skillet and set aside.

6. Repeat with the other 3 shaped pieces of dough.

7. To enjoy Naan with the perfect texture, allow the breads to rest for 5 minutes or so after removing them from the skillet. (If you eat them as soon as they're done, hot from the skillet, the texture may be a little gummy.) Store in a sealed bag or container at room temperature, or freeze and then heat up at a later date.

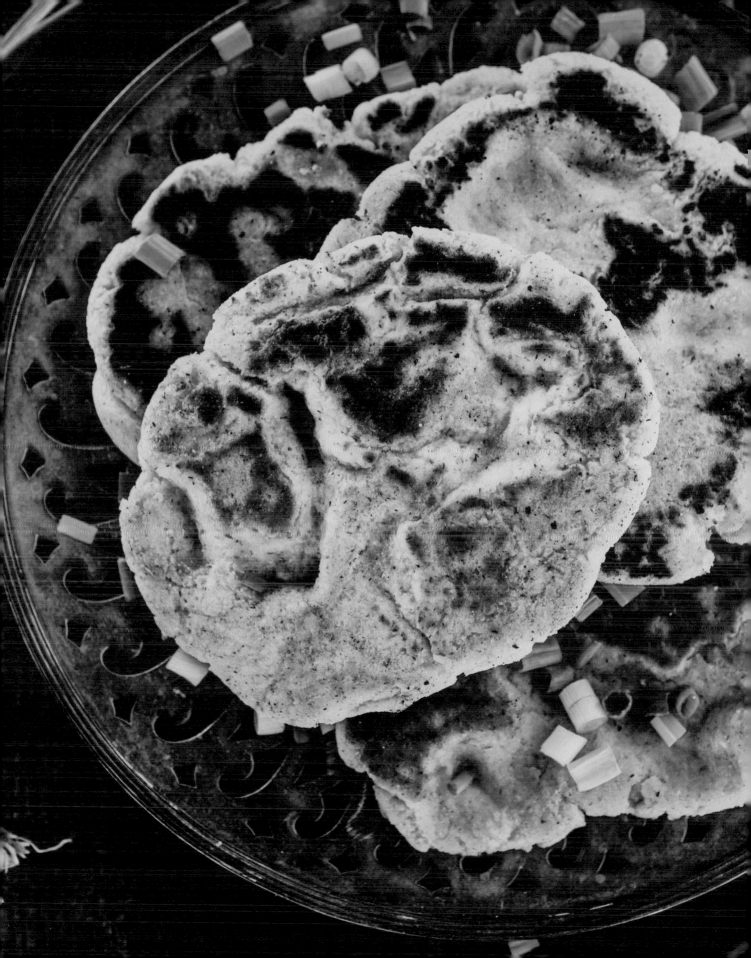

irish soda bread

This bread gets its rise from baking soda and baking powder. Its texture is somewhere between a loaf of bread and a biscuit. Be sure to make yourself a loaf on St. Patrick's Day!

ingredients

200 grams blanched almond flour (about 1½ cups)

78 grams tapioca, potato, or sweet potato starch (about ½ cup plus 1½ tablespoons), plus more for dusting the dough (see Notes)

2 teaspoons baking soda

½ teaspoon double-acting, aluminum-free baking powder

¼ teaspoon kosher salt

¼ teaspoon caraway seeds

1 tablespoon coconut palm sugar

½ cup raisins

3 large eggs

2 teaspoons apple cider vinegar

notes

If using potato or sweet potato starch and measuring with a cup, use a scant ½ cup.

directions

1. Preheat the oven to 350 degrees. Line a pie pan or small baking sheet with parchment paper.

2. In a large bowl, whisk the almond flour, tapioca starch, baking soda, baking powder, and salt until blended. Add the caraway seeds, sugar, and raisins and whisk again until blended.

3. In a small bowl, whisk together the eggs and vinegar. Pour into the flour mixture and stir until a dough comes together.

4. Plop the dough into the prepared pie pan. Dust the top and sides with tapioca or potato starch and form it into a round mound that is roughly 1½ to 2 inches tall and about 6 inches in diameter. Using a knife, score the top of the dough, about ½ inch deep, to make the classic cross shape.

5. Quickly place the pan in the oven and bake for 40 minutes. When done, the bread should be nice and hard to the touch and lightly golden.

6. Store in a sealed bag or container at room temperature, or freeze for later use.

PREP TIME: 10 minutes
COOK TIME: 19 to 26 minutes
YIELD: 4 arepas

DAIRY *free*, EGG *free*, NUT *free*, GRAIN *free*, COCONUT *free*

ingredients

Almond flour version:

72 grams blanched almond flour (about ½ cup)

33 grams tapioca starch (about ¼ cup)

132 grams potato starch or sweet potato starch (about ¾ cup)

2 teaspoons double-acting, aluminum-free baking powder

1¼ teaspoons xanthan gum or guar gum

¼ teaspoon kosher salt

½ cup water

2 tablespoons oil of choice, plus more for the pan

1 teaspoon apple cider vinegar

PREP TIME: 10 minutes
COOK TIME: 14 to 22 minutes
YIELD: 6 arepas

DAIRY *free*, EGG *free*, NUT *free*, GRAIN *free*, COCONUT *free*

ingredients

Coconut flour version:

84 grams coconut flour (about ½ cup)

33 grams tapioca starch (about ¼ cup)

132 grams potato starch or sweet potato starch (about ¾ cup)

1 tablespoon double-acting, aluminum-free baking powder

1¼ teaspoons xanthan gum or guar gum

½ teaspoon kosher salt

64 grams Spectrum vegetable shortening (about ⅓ cup)

220 grams water (about 1 cup)

2 teaspoons apple cider vinegar

Oil of choice, for the pan

arepas

My dear friend Juli Bauer from Paleomg.com introduced me to arepas. I tracked down our local food truck, "Hello Arepa," and the moment I took a bite an addiction formed. I had to Paleoize that sandwich bread ASAP. An arepa tastes similar to an English muffin but is thinner and crustier on the outside. It is cooked in a two-step process: first in a skillet to give it a nice golden brown color, and then in the oven to finish. Because I adore both the taste of arepas and the simplicity of making them (no proofing necessary!), I created two versions to share with you: one made with almond flour and the other made with coconut flour. So, whichever flour you prefer to work with, there is an option for you. Plus, both recipes are egg-free!

directions (almond flour version)

1. Preheat the oven to 350 degrees.
2. In a mixing bowl, whisk the almond flour, starches, baking powder, xanthan gum, and salt until blended.
3. Add the water, oil, and vinegar and mix until fully incorporated. The xanthan gum may take a while to thicken, so mix thoroughly!
4. Place a skillet over medium heat. Add a few drops of oil to prevent the dough from sticking.
5. While the skillet is heating up, oil your hands and divide the dough into 4 equal portions. Shape each portion into a thin disc about 4 inches in diameter and a little less than ⅛ inch thick.
6. Cook two at a time for 1 to 2 minutes per side, until golden brown.
7. Remove the Arepas from the skillet and place on a baking sheet. Repeat with the remaining dough.
8. Bake for 15 to 18 minutes, until firm to the touch and cooked through.

directions (coconut flour version)

1. Preheat the oven to 350 degrees.
2. In a mixing bowl, whisk the coconut flour, starches, baking powder, xanthan gum, and salt until blended.
3. Add the shortening and mix thoroughly.
4. Add the water and vinegar and mix until fully incorporated. The xanthan gum may take a while to thicken, so mix thoroughly!
5. Place a skillet over medium-high heat. Add a few drops of oil to the pan to prevent the dough from sticking.
6. While the skillet is heating up, oil your hands and divide the dough into 6 equal portions. Shape each portion into a thin disc about 5 inches in diameter and a little less than ⅛ inch thick.
7. Cook two at a time for 1 to 2 minutes per side, just to brown the outside.
8. Remove the Arepas from the skillet and place on a baking sheet. Repeat with the remaining dough.
9. Bake for 8 to 10 minutes, until firm to the touch and cooked through.

PREP TIME: 10 minutes
COOK TIME: 19 to 21 minutes
YIELD: 8 to 10 muffins

DAIRY *free*, EGG *free*, NUT *free*, GRAIN *free*, COCONUT *free*

honey "cornbread" muffins

Cornbread without corn: That's the Paleo way. I promise you'll love these Honey "Cornbread" Muffins so much that you won't miss the corn for a second!

ingredients

120 grams Spectrum vegetable shortening (about ¾ cup)

210 grams raw honey (about ½ cup plus 2 tablespoons)

120 grams milk (dairy or nondairy) (about ½ cup plus 2 teaspoons)

3 large eggs

126 grams coconut flour (about ¾ cup)

88 grams potato starch or sweet potato starch (about ½ cup)

66 grams tapioca starch (about ½ cup)

1 tablespoon double-acting, aluminum-free baking powder

1 teaspoon xanthan gum or guar gum

¾ teaspoon kosher salt

directions

1. Preheat the oven to 350 degrees. Line 8 to 10 cups of a muffin pan with cupcake liners.

2. In the bowl of a stand mixer, using the whisk attachment, mix together the shortening, honey, milk, and eggs until well combined.

3. In a separate bowl, whisk the coconut flour, starches, baking powder, xanthan gum, and salt until blended.

4. With the mixer on low speed, slowly add the flour mixture to the egg mixture until all of it has been incorporated. Turn the mixer to medium-high speed and continue to mix until the batter is thoroughly blended.

5. Spoon the batter into the lined cups, filling each about three-quarters full.

6. Bake for 19 to 21 minutes, until a toothpick inserted comes out clean.

7. Store in a sealed bag or container at room temperature, or freeze for later use.

PREP TIME: 15 minutes
COOK TIME: 46 to 48 minutes
YIELD: 6 rolls

DAIRY free, **EGG** free, **NUT** free, **GRAIN** free, **COCONUT** free

pretzel rolls

These beautiful rolls taste great as the buns for just about any sandwich filling. They are best eaten fresh from the oven!

ingredients

10 cups water

⅔ cup baking soda

Pretzel dough:

3 large eggs

193 grams lukewarm water (about ¾ cup plus 2 tablespoons)

2 tablespoons potato flour

129 grams coconut flour (about ¾ cup)

162 grams potato starch or sweet potato starch (about 1 cup)

66 grams tapioca starch (about ½ cup)

1½ teaspoons xanthan gum or guar gum

1 teaspoon double-acting, aluminum-free baking powder

½ teaspoon kosher salt

60 grams Spectrum vegetable shortening (¼ cup plus 1 tablespoon)

Egg wash:

1 large egg

1 tablespoon water

Coarse sea salt, for topping the rolls

directions

1. Preheat the oven to 375 degrees. Line a baking sheet with parchment paper.

2. In a large pot, bring the 10 cups water and baking soda to a boil while you prepare the dough.

3. In a bowl of a stand mixer, whip the eggs until frothy.

4. Add the lukewarm water, flours, starches, xanthan gum, baking powder, salt, and shortening and, using the whisk attachment, mix on high speed until a well-combined dough forms.

5. Oil your hands and divide the dough into 6 equal portions. Shape each portion into a round roll.

6. Using a knife, score the top of each roll to create a crisscross shape.

7. Carefully place one roll at a time into the boiling water. Boil for 30 seconds, flipping halfway through if the dough is not fully submerged. Place the boiled pretzel roll on the prepared baking sheet. Repeat with the rest of the rolls.

8. In a small bowl, whisk together the egg and water for the egg wash. Brush the rolls with the egg wash and top with coarse sea salt.

9. Bake for 40 minutes, until golden brown. Then broil on high for 3 to 5 minutes to give the rolls a nice, lightly toasted brown color.

10. Store leftover rolls in a sealed bag or container at room temperature, or freeze for later use.

CHAPTER 3
Breakfast Breads and Pastries

PREP TIME: 30 minutes
RESTING TIME: 3 to 3½ hours
COOK TIME: 12 to 14 minutes
YIELD: 10 to 12 croissants

DAIRY *free*, EGG *free*, **NUT** *free*,
GRAIN *free*, COCONUT *free*

croissants

Holy cow, was this recipe a tricky one to figure out! And let me warn you: Making croissants is for the advanced and patient baker. You'll need almost an entire day to make these delicious flaky pastries, though much of that time is unattended.

This recipe requires the use of butter. The only possible substitution would be goat's milk butter. I have included only gram weights and measuring spoon amounts, as precise measurements are essential for these to turn out; one small change and the recipe will be thrown off. Be sure to follow the directions closely. Be prepared watch a few YouTube croissant tutorials to get a general idea of the process. And be sure to use potato flour for this recipe (see page 17 for more information).

ingredients

Yeast mixture:

240 grams lukewarm milk or water

2 tablespoons raw honey

1 tablespoon instant yeast

Croissant dough:

165 grams tapioca starch, plus more for the work surface

88 grams potato starch or sweet potato starch

84 grams coconut flour

1½ tablespoons potato flour

2 teaspoons xanthan gum or guar gum

½ teaspoon double-acting, aluminum-free baking powder

½ teaspoon kosher salt

50 grams Spectrum vegetable shortening

2 large eggs

224 grams salted butter, frozen (1 cup/2 sticks)

Egg wash:

1 large egg

1 tablespoon water or milk

directions

1. In a small bowl, mix together the lukewarm milk, yeast, and honey. Set aside to let it get frothy.

2. In the bowl of a stand mixer, using the whisk attachment, mix the starches, flours, xanthan gum, baking powder, and salt until blended. Add the shortening and mix until you can no longer see clumps of shortening.

3. Add the eggs and yeast mixture. (*Note:* If the yeast mixture has not become frothy, then your yeast is old and shouldn't be used. Try again using a new container of yeast.) Beat the mixture on high speed for 2 to 3 minutes, until the dough holds together and is sticking slightly to the sides of the mixing bowl. It will thicken as the xanthan gum is activated.

4. Lightly dust a 2-foot-long sheet of parchment paper with tapioca starch. Place the dough on the dusted parchment and set aside while you prepare the butter.

5. Using a food processor with a grating blade, grate the butter. Place the pile of grated butter on an 8-inch square piece of plastic wrap. Close the plastic wrap around the butter and, pressing down lightly, form it into a 5-inch square that is ¼ inch thick. Don't press down too hard—you want it to be loosely packed. Do this quickly. The square shape does not have to be exact.

6. Using a rolling pin, roll the dough on the sheet of parchment paper into a 20-by-10-inch rectangle. Unwrap the butter and place it in the center of the rectangle. Using the parchment as your guide, gently lift the short ends of the rectangle of dough over the butter, overlapping the ends slightly.

(directions continue on page 74)

7. Pick up the dough, sprinkle the surface of the parchment paper with starch again, and flip the dough over so that its long side is facing the length of the parchment paper. Gently roll it out into a 20-by-10-inch rectangle, using as much starch as needed to keep the dough from sticking to the parchment. Again, fold the short ends in, overlapping them slightly. Pick up the dough, dust the surface, and flip it seam side down so that its long side is facing the length of the parchment paper. Roll out into a rectangle. Repeat the process for a third time: Fold the short ends in, pick up the dough, dust the surface, flip it seam side down so that its long side is facing the length of the parchment paper, and roll it out into a 20-by-10-inch rectangle.

8. It's time to chill the dough! To keep it from drying out in the fridge, wet 3 pieces of paper towel, wring them out, and then wrap the dough in the damp paper towels. Then wrap the covered dough in parchment paper and place it in the fridge for 45 minutes to 1 hour to chill and keep the butter semi-firm. (The difference in timing depends on the time of year you make the croissants: If making them in the summer, chill for a full hour; in the winter, 45 minutes will do.)

9. Place the chilled rectangle of dough on a dusted piece of parchment paper. Fold in the short ends, overlapping them by 1 inch, and gently roll it out into a 20-by-10-inch rectangle, using as much starch as needed to keep the dough from sticking to the parchment. Following the instructions in Step 7, repeat the process of turning the dough, redusting the parchment, rolling it out, and turning in the sides 3 more times, again using as much starch as needed to keep the dough from sticking to the parchment. After the third turn, wrap the dough in the damp paper towels and parchment paper again and place in the fridge for another 45 minutes to 1 hour.

10. Repeat this process a third time! Then place in the fridge for 1½ hours.

11. When it's time to remove the dough from the fridge, turn on the oven to 350 degrees to create a "hot box" for proofing the croissants. Line a baking sheet with parchment paper. Take the dough out of the fridge.

12. Lightly oil a 30-inch-long sheet of parchment paper. Roll out the dough on the oiled parchment paper into a rectangle that is about ¼ inch thick. Using a pizza cutter, cut triangles that are about 3½ inches wide at the base. Photo 1 (opposite) shows the general method for cutting the triangles tip to base, but with smaller triangles for mini croissants. You will end up with 10 to 12 triangles.

13. Cut a ½-inch slit in the center of the base of each triangle (photo 2). Then, starting at the base (photo 3) and using the parchment to help you lift the dough, gently roll the dough into a croissant shape (photo 4).

14. Repeat with the remaining triangles, placing the rolled-up croissants on the prepared baking sheet, about 1½ inches apart. Turn off the oven. Place the tray of croissants in the warm oven and allow to proof, with the door left slightly open, for 15 minutes. Close the oven door and allow to proof for an additional 15 minutes. During this time, the croissants will puff up slightly.

15. After 30 minutes of proofing, remove the tray from the oven. Preheat the oven to 400 degrees.

16. In a small bowl, whisk together the egg and water for the egg wash. Lightly brush each croissant with the egg wash.

17. Once the oven is fully preheated, bake the croissants for 12 to 14 minutes, until lightly golden brown and firm to the touch. Store at room temperature in a sealed container.

notes

If at any point you find that the butter is melting and you can see it coming through the dough, quickly stick the dough back in the fridge. You want to keep the butter semi-firm at all times; otherwise, it will become part of the dough rather than being its own buttery layer. These buttery layers are what create flaky pastries.

These croissants are best the day they are made! As they sit out, the potato flour will make them harden. If that happens, pop them in the microwave for 30 seconds to soften them slightly.

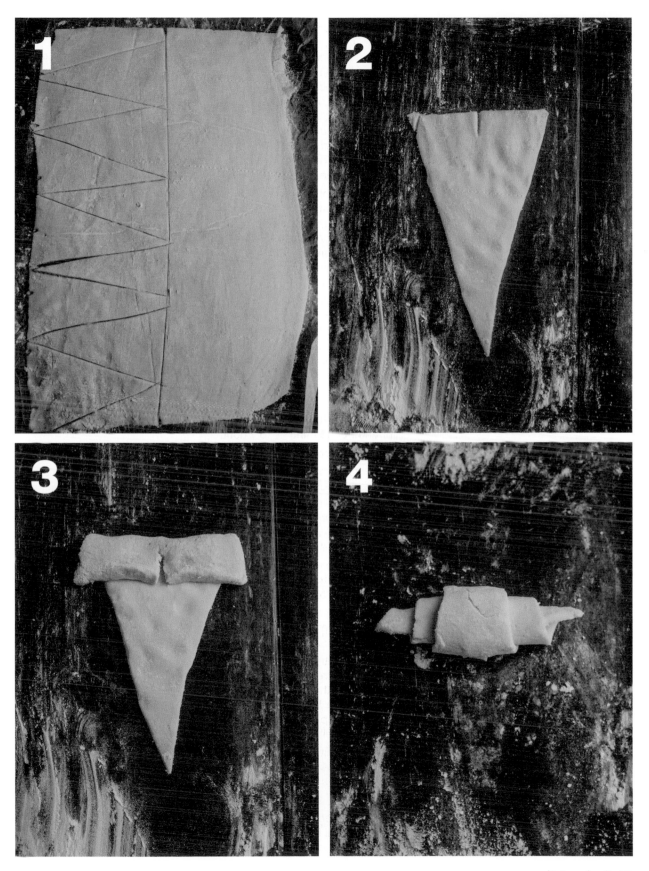

PREP TIME: 30 minutes
RESTING TIME: 3 to 3½ hours
COOK TIME: 12 to 14 minutes
YIELD: 10 to 12 croissants

DAIRY *free*, EGG *free*, NUT *free*,
GRAIN *free*, COCONUT *free*

chocolate croissants

The process of making pain au chocolat, a French chocolate-filled pastry, is almost identical to my basic croissant recipe. In this chocolate version, you simply place a piece of chocolate in the croissant dough before rolling it up! While using solid chocolate is traditional, feel free to melt the chocolate in the microwave for about a minute and then spread some on the croissant dough before rolling them up. Just be sure that the chocolate isn't scalding hot. Let it cool down to almost room temperature first!

ingredients

1 batch Croissant dough (page 72), prepared through Step 12

12 (3-inch) chocolate sticks or ½ cup chopped chocolate chips

Egg wash:

1 large egg

1 tablespoon water or milk

notes

These croissants are best the day they are made! As they sit out, the potato flour will make them harden. If that happens, pop them in the microwave for 30 seconds to soften them slightly.

directions

1. Preheat the oven to 350 degrees to create a "hot box" for the croissants to proof. Line a baking sheet with parchment paper.

2. As directed in Step 13 of the Croissants recipe, cut a ½-inch slit in the center of the base of each dough triangle, but before rolling, place a chocolate stick at the base of each triangle. If using chocolate chips, place about ½ to 1 tablespoon of chopped chocolate chips across the base of each triangle. Or, as noted above, you can melt the chocolate and spread about 1 tablespoon over the top of the dough triangle before rolling it up.

3. Starting at the base, and using the parchment paper to help you lift the dough, roll the dough up and over the chocolate into a croissant shape. Repeat with the remaining triangles, placing the rolled-up croissants on the prepared baking sheet, about 1½ inches apart.

4. Turn off the oven. Place the tray of croissants in the warm oven and allow to proof, with the door left slightly open, for 15 minutes. Close the oven door and allow to proof for an additional 15 minutes. During this time, the croissants will puff up slightly.

5. After 30 minutes of proofing, remove the tray from the oven. Preheat the oven to 400 degrees.

6. In a small bowl, whisk together the egg and water to make the egg wash. Lightly brush each croissant with the egg wash.

7. Once the oven is fully preheated, bake the croissants for 12 to 14 minutes, until lightly golden brown and firm to the touch. Store at room temperature in a sealed container.

PREP TIME: 45 minutes
RESTING TIME: 3½ hours
COOK TIME: 12 to 14 minutes
YIELD: 10 to 12 small Danish

DAIRY *free*, EGG *free*, **NUT** *free*,
GRAIN *free*, COCONUT *free*

danish

This delicious Danish recipe is based on my Croissant recipe. Just like with the Chocolate Croissants (page 76), you will want to prepare the Croissant dough to Step 10 on page 74. The difference with this recipe is the way the Croissant dough is cut. To keep things simple, I like to cut my Danish pastries into squares, add a small spoonful of filling, then fold the sides together and put them in the oven to proof. Just like the plain Croissants and Chocolate Croissants, this recipe is for those who have patience, because it will take you all day to make these pastries!

ingredients

1 batch Croissant dough (page 72), prepared through Step 10

Jelly filling:

½ cup jelly of choice

or

Cream cheese filling:

½ cup cream cheese, softened

1½ tablespoons maple syrup

½ teaspoon pumpkin spice blend

Egg wash:

1 large egg

1 tablespoon water or milk

notes

To get lovely fluted edges on your Danish, as pictured, use a fluted wheel pastry cutter to cut the dough into squares.

These Danish are best the day they are made. As they sit out, the potato flour will make them harden. If that happens, pop them in the microwave for 30 seconds to soften them slightly.

directions

1. Preheat the oven to 350 degrees to create a "hot box" for the Danish to proof. Line a baking sheet with parchment paper.

2. Lightly oil two 2-foot-long sheets of parchment paper. Place the chilled dough on one of the oiled sheets of parchment and place the other oiled sheet on top, oiled side down. Roll out the dough into a large rectangle that is about ¼ inch thick.

3. Using a ruler and pizza cutter, mark off (by scoring the dough) every 3 inches on each side of the dough as guides. Then, using your ruler as a straightedge, cut the dough into 3-inch squares. You should end up with 10 to 12 squares.

4. If using the cream cheese filling, mix together the cream cheese, maple syrup, and pumpkin spice blend in a small bowl.

5. Place 2 teaspoons of filling in the center of each dough square. Then fold 2 opposite corners of the square in toward the center, allowing the edges to overlap slightly. Press down gently to seal the edges. (You don't need to press too hard, as the pastry will not spread much during proofing and baking.)

6. Place the pastries seam side up on the prepared baking sheet, 1 inch apart.

7. Turn off the oven. Place the tray of Danish in the warm oven to proof for a total of 30 minutes. Leave the door slightly open for the first 15 minutes, and then close the oven door for the last 15 minutes. During this time, the Danish will puff up slightly.

8. After 30 minutes of proofing, remove the tray from the oven. Preheat the oven to 400 degrees.

9. In a small bowl, whisk together the egg and water to make the egg wash. Lightly brush each Danish with the egg wash.

10. Once the oven is fully preheated, bake the Danish for 12 to 14 minutes, until lightly golden brown and firm to the touch. Store at room temperature in a sealed container.

PREP TIME: 25 minutes, including proofing time
COOK TIME: 20 minutes
YIELD: 4 English muffins

DAIRY *free*, EGG *free*, NUT *free*, GRAIN *free*, COCONUT *free*

english muffins

Before I went gluten-free, English muffins were my favorite breakfast. Since finding a grain-free English muffin at the grocery store is out of the question, I had to create a recipe of my own. You'll love making these— you don't even need to turn on your oven!

ingredients

207 grams lukewarm water (about a scant 1 cup)

1 tablespoon instant yeast

2 teaspoons coconut palm sugar

127 grams potato starch or sweet potato starch (about ⅔ cup plus 2 teaspoons)

72 grams coconut flour (about ⅓ cup plus 2 tablespoons)

30 grams tapioca starch (about ¼ cup)

¾ teaspoon xanthan gum or guar gum

½ teaspoon kosher salt

64 grams Spectrum vegetable shortening (about ⅓ cup)

notes

You can create your own English muffin rings by folding aluminum foil over itself. Use metal paper clips to hold them together.

If you find that your English Muffins are not fully cooked through, lower the heat and cook them longer. You can continue to cook a muffin in the skillet even if it has been cut open.

directions

1. In a small bowl, mix together the lukewarm water, yeast, and sugar. Set aside.

2. In a mixing bowl, combine the potato starch, coconut flour, tapioca starch, xanthan gum, and salt.

3. Stir the yeast mixture and shortening into the dry ingredients and mix until fully incorporated and a dough forms. The dough will be fairly wet and sticky.

4. Oil a large skillet and the inside of each of 4 English muffin rings (see Notes). Place the rings in the skillet.

5. Divide the dough into 4 equal portions and place a portion in each ring. Brush the tops liberally with water.

6. Cover the skillet and place over low heat for 1 minute. Turn off the heat, keeping the English Muffins covered, and allow them to rise for 15 to 18 minutes.

7. Turn the burner back on to medium-low heat. Keeping the lid on the skillet, cook the English Muffins for 10 minutes. Remove the lid and flip the English Muffins.

8. Cover and cook for another 5 to 6 minutes, until golden brown on the bottom. Remove the rings.

9. Cover the skillet and cook for another 10 minutes.

10. Remove the finished English Muffins from the skillet and let cool completely before breaking open with a fork and toasting. Store extras at room temperature in a sealed container, or freeze for another day.

PREP TIME: 45 minutes, including proofing time
COOK TIME: 23 to 25 minutes
YIELD: 5 or 6 bagels

DAIRY *free*, EGG *free*, NUT *free*, GRAIN *free*, COCONUT *free*

grain-free bagels

These bagels are the real deal. The texture will take you back to your gluten-eating days. Just like traditional bagels, they are boiled before being baked. They are fun to prepare and are perfect to make ahead and freeze. You could even use this dough to make bagel dogs!

ingredients

Bagel dough:

256 grams lukewarm water (about 1 cup plus 2½ tablespoons)

1 tablespoon instant yeast

1 tablespoon coconut palm sugar

108 grams coconut flour (about ½ cup plus 2 tablespoons)

129 grams potato starch or sweet potato starch (about ⅔ cup plus 1 tablespoon)

2 tablespoons potato flour

1 tablespoon xanthan gum or guar gum

2 teaspoons double-acting, aluminum-free baking powder

⅛ teaspoon kosher salt

48 grams Spectrum vegetable shortening (about ¼ cup)

2 large eggs

Egg wash:

1 large egg

1 tablespoon water

Topping(s) of choice, such as coarse sea salt, sesame seeds, or dried onions (optional)

directions

1. Preheat the oven to 375 degrees to warm it up as a "hot box" for the bagels to proof. Line a baking sheet with parchment paper.

2. In a small bowl, mix together the lukewarm water, yeast, and sugar. Set aside for 10 minutes while you prepare the rest of the ingredients.

3. In the bowl of a stand mixer, using the whisk attachment, mix the coconut flour, potato starch, potato flour, xanthan gum, baking powder, and salt until blended.

4. Add the shortening, eggs, and yeast mixture. Mix on high speed for a few minutes until a slightly tacky dough has formed.

5. Oil your hands and divide the dough into 5 or 6 equal portions. Roll each portion between your hands to form a ball, and then use a well-oiled thumb to create a hole in the center. Make the hole large (as I did in the photo), because when the dough rises, the hole will close in quite a bit! Re-oil your hands as needed to keep the dough from sticking.

6. Place the shaped bagels on the prepared baking sheet. Cover with a kitchen towel.

7. Turn off the oven and place the covered baking sheet in the warm oven to proof for a total of 30 minutes. Leave the oven door open a crack for the first 15 minutes, and then close the door for the last 15 minutes.

8. Meanwhile, bring a large pot of water to a boil.

9. After 30 minutes of proofing, remove the bagels from the oven. Preheat the oven to 375 degrees.

10. It's time to boil the bagels! Using a large spoon, gently drop a bagel into the rapidly boiling water for 12 to 14 seconds. Flip it once halfway through the boiling time. Remove and place on the baking sheet. *Note:* Be careful not to leave the bagels in the water for longer than 14 seconds, or they may start to get soggy and fall apart.

11. After boiling all the bagels, whisk together the egg and water in a small bowl to make the egg wash. Paint a little egg wash over each bagel and then add any toppings, if using.

12. Bake the bagels for 23 to 25 minutes, until beautifully golden and firm to the touch.

13. Remove from the oven and enjoy! Store in a sealed bag or container, or freeze for another day.

PREP TIME: 15 minutes
COOK TIME: 50 to 55 minutes
YIELD: 8 to 10 mini bagels

DAIRY *free*, **EGG** *free*, **NUT** *free*,
GRAIN *free*, **COCONUT** *free*

yeast-free mini bagels

Not everyone likes to work with yeast, so I created a yeast-free recipe for mini bagels. Be sure to try the super-simple recipes for Pizza Bagel Bites (page 230) and Bagel Chips (page 196), which use these bite-sized bagels as a base.

ingredients

Bagel dough:

108 grams coconut flour (about ½ cup plus 2 tablespoons)

129 grams potato starch or sweet potato starch (about ⅔ cup plus 1 tablespoon)

2 tablespoons potato flour

1 tablespoon plus ½ teaspoon xanthan gum or guar gum

1 tablespoon double-acting, aluminum-free baking powder

¼ teaspoon kosher salt

265 grams water (about 1 cup plus 3 tablespoons)

60 grams Spectrum vegetable shortening (about ¼ cup plus 1 tablespoon)

3 large eggs

1 tablespoon apple cider vinegar

Egg wash:

1 large egg

1 tablespoon water

Topping(s) of choice, such as coarse sea salt, sesame seeds, or dried onions (optional)

directions

1. Preheat the oven to 350 degrees. Line a baking sheet with parchment paper.

2. In the bowl of a stand mixer, using the whisk attachment, mix the coconut flour, potato starch, potato flour, xanthan gum, baking powder, and salt until blended.

3. Add the water, shortening, eggs, and vinegar and mix on high speed for a few minutes, until a slightly tacky dough has formed.

4. Oil your hands and divide the dough into 8 to 10 equal portions. Roll each portion between your hands to form a ball, and then use a well-oiled thumb to create a hole in the center. Make the hole large, because when the dough rises in the oven, the hole will close in quite a bit! Place the shaped bagels on the prepared baking sheet.

5. In a small bowl, whisk together the egg and tablespoon of water to make the egg wash. Paint a little egg wash over each bagel and then add any toppings, if using. Reserve the leftover egg wash.

6. Bake the bagels for 50 to 55 minutes, until beautifully golden and firm to the touch. Brush them with additional egg wash halfway through baking.

7. Remove from the oven and enjoy! Store in a sealed bag or container, or freeze for another day.

DAIRY *free*, EGG *free*, NUT *free*,
GRAIN *free*, COCONUT *free*

cinnamon raisin bagels

These bagels are free of both yeast and eggs. Yes, you heard me right! They are made with a combination of chestnut flour and rice flour for those who can't have almond flour or coconut flour. You'll love their classic chewy texture!

ingredients

143 grams potato starch or sweet potato starch (about ¾ cup plus 1 tablespoon)

80 grams chestnut flour (about ½ cup)

80 grams superfine white rice flour (about ½ cup)

2 tablespoons potato flour

1 tablespoon ground cinnamon

2 teaspoons xanthan gum or guar gum

2 teaspoons double-acting, aluminum-free baking powder

¾ teaspoon kosher salt

60 grams Spectrum vegetable shortening (about ¼ cup plus 1 tablespoon)

51 grams coconut palm sugar (about ⅓ cup)

1 tablespoon apple cider vinegar

½ cup raisins

214 grams water (about 1 cup)

Oil of choice, for brushing the bagels

directions

1. Preheat the oven to 350 degrees. Line a baking sheet with parchment paper.

2. In the bowl of a stand mixer, using the whisk attachment, mix the potato starch, flours, cinnamon, xanthan gum, baking powder, and salt until blended.

3. Add the shortening, sugar, vinegar, raisins, and water and mix on high speed for a few minutes, until a slightly tacky dough has formed.

4. Oil your hands and divide the dough into 4 or 5 equal portions. Roll each portion between your hands to form a ball, and then use a well-oiled thumb to create a hole in the center. Make the hole large, because when the dough rises in the oven, the hole will close in quite a bit! Place the shaped bagels on the prepared baking sheet.

5. Brush a little oil on the tops of the bagels.

6. Bake for 45 minutes, until beautifully golden and firm to the touch.

7. Remove from the oven and enjoy! Store in a sealed bag or container, or freeze for another day.

PREP TIME: 45 minutes, including proofing time
COOK TIME: 30 minutes
YIELD: One 8½-by-4½-inch loaf

DAIRY *free*, EGG *free*, NUT *free*, GRAIN *free*, COCONUT *free*

egg-free cinnamon raisin bread

A thick slice of toasted cinnamon raisin bread with a smear of butter may be one of my favorite things to eat. This bread is so soft thanks to the addition of chestnut flour.

ingredients

330 grams lukewarm water (about 1½ cups)

128 grams raw honey (about ¼ cup plus 2 tablespoons)

1 tablespoon instant yeast

120 grams superfine white rice flour (about ¾ cup)

132 grams potato starch or sweet potato starch (about ¾ cup)

80 grams chestnut flour (about ½ cup)

1 tablespoon double-acting, aluminum-free baking powder

2 teaspoons xanthan gum or guar gum

½ teaspoon kosher salt

2 teaspoons apple cider vinegar

56 grams oil of choice (about ¼ cup)

1 cup raisins

1 tablespoon ground cinnamon

directions

1. Preheat the oven to 375 degrees to warm it up as a "hot box" for the dough to proof. Oil an 8½-by-4½-inch loaf pan.

2. In a small bowl, mix together the lukewarm water, honey, and yeast. Set aside.

3. In the bowl of a stand mixer, using the whisk attachment, mix the rice flour, potato starch, chestnut flour, baking powder, xanthan gum, and salt until blended.

4. Add the vinegar, oil, and yeast mixture and mix until a batter forms.

5. Fold in the raisins and cinnamon by hand.

6. Pour the batter into the prepared loaf pan and cover with a piece of plastic wrap, following the method described on page 27.

7. Turn off the oven and place the bread in the warm oven to proof for a total of 30 minutes. Leave the oven door open a crack for the first 15 minutes, and then close the door for the last 15 minutes.

8. After 30 minutes of proofing, remove the pan from the oven. Preheat the oven to 375 degrees.

9. When the oven is fully preheated, carefully remove the plastic wrap and return the pan to the oven. Bake for 25 minutes, and then cover with foil and bake for an additional 5 minutes, until firm to the touch.

PREP TIME: 40 minutes, including proofing time
COOK TIME: 12 to 16 minutes
YIELD: 8 donuts

DAIRY *free*, **EGG** *free*, **NUT** *free*,
GRAIN *free*, **COCONUT** *free*

donuts

Donuts can be finicky, but they are so worth the extra effort. You have to be precise when measuring each ingredient, because more or less of a starch or liquid could throw everything off. Once you master them, though, they are a cinch! You can use a round biscuit cutter or donut cutter to shape them.

ingredients

55 grams lukewarm water (about ¼ cup)

2 teaspoons instant yeast

1 tablespoon coconut palm sugar

77 grams coconut flour (about ⅓ cup plus 2 tablespoons)

91 grams potato starch or sweet potato starch (about ½ cup), plus more for the work surface

42 grams tapioca starch (about ⅓ cup)

1 teaspoon xanthan gum or guar gum

2 teaspoons double-acting, aluminum-free baking powder

2 teaspoons potato flour

½ teaspoon kosher salt

120 grams powdered coconut palm sugar or maple sugar (about 1 cup) (see tutorial, page 26)

60 grams Spectrum vegetable shortening (about ¼ cup plus 1 tablespoon)

3 large eggs

Oil of choice, for frying

Powdered sugar, for dusting the fried donuts (optional; see Notes)

directions

1. Preheat the oven to 375 degrees to warm it up as a "hot box" for the dough to proof. Line a baking sheet with parchment paper.

2. In a small bowl, mix together the lukewarm water, yeast, and sugar. Set aside.

3. In the bowl of a stand mixer, using the whisk attachment, mix the coconut flour, starches, xanthan gum, baking powder, potato flour, and salt until blended. Add the powdered sugar, shortening, and eggs. Pour in the yeast mixture and mix on high speed for 1 to 2 minutes. The dough will thicken some (the xanthan gum and potato flour will take a minute to activate). When sufficiently mixed, the dough will be thick and sticky.

4. Dust your work surface with tapioca starch. Plop the dough onto the dusted surface and pat it into a round about 1½ inches thick. Using a starch-dusted biscuit cutter or glass, cut the dough into 8 circles.

5. Place the dough rounds on the prepared baking sheet and brush each with a little water. Cover the baking sheet with a towel.

6. Turn off the oven and place the covered pan in the warm oven to proof for a total of 30 minutes. Leave the oven door open a crack for the first 15 minutes, and then close the door for the last 15 minutes.

7. Meanwhile, heat a few inches of oil in a heavy-bottomed saucepan or skillet over low heat to 350 degrees. (The pot only needs to be large enough to fry one donut at a time.)

8. After 30 minutes of proofing, remove the pan from the oven. Fry the donuts one by one in the hot oil until golden, about 1½ to 2 minutes. I keep my heat pretty low, just high enough that the oil bubbles gently when a donut is added. If the oil is too hot, the donuts will brown on the outside before they fully cook on the inside. Make sure to flip them a few times so they cook evenly.

9. If you want powdered donuts, toss them in powdered sugar while still warm. Place the donuts on a cooling rack to cool. Eat the donuts within 2 days, and store them in a sealed container or bag.

notes

Love powdered sugar on your donuts? Make your own by using granulated maple sugar or coconut palm sugar, following the tutorial on page 26. You can even make a mixture of cinnamon and sugar and then toss the hot donuts into the cinnamon sugar in a bowl or brown bag. For a fun, fruit-based powdered coating, throw some freeze-dried fruit into a blender and process until powdery, and use that instead of (or mixed with) the powdered sugar!

PREP TIME: 45 minutes, including proofing time
COOK TIME: 35 to 40 minutes
YIELD: 9 rolls

DAIRY *free*, EGG *free*, NUT *free*, GRAIN *free*, COCONUT *free*

cinnamon rolls

Ooey, gooey, sticky, fluffy, sugary cinnamon rolls—that's what these are. They don't taste grain-free; they taste like a dream come true! You'll love them.

ingredients

1 tablespoon oil or melted butter, plus more for the work surface

Dough:

122 grams applesauce (about ½ cup)

1 tablespoon instant yeast

126 grams coconut flour (about ¾ cup)

82 grams tapioca starch or arrowroot starch (about ½ cup plus 1½ tablespoons)

1 tablespoon double-acting, aluminum-free baking powder

1 teaspoon xanthan gum or guar gum

¼ teaspoon kosher salt

120 grams granulated maple sugar (about ¾ cup)

100 grams Spectrum vegetable shortening (about ½ cup plus 2 tablespoons)

3 large eggs

1 tablespoon melted salted butter, melted ghee, or mild-flavored oil, for brushing the rolls

Cinnamon filling:

2 tablespoons melted salted butter, melted ghee, or mild-flavored oil

¾ cup coconut palm sugar

2 teaspoons ground cinnamon

Glaze:

1 cup granulated maple sugar or coconut palm sugar

1 tablespoon plus 2 teaspoons milk (dairy or nondairy) or water

1 teaspoon vanilla extract

directions

1. Preheat the oven on to 375 degrees to warm it up as a "hot box" for the rolls to proof. Line an 8-inch square baking pan (or a pan of similar size) with parchment paper. Drizzle the oil or melted butter into the pan and spread it evenly across the parchment with a paper towel. Set aside.

2. In a small microwaveable bowl, heat the applesauce in the microwave for 10 to 20 seconds just until it's lukewarm (but not hot). The yeast needs this warm temperature to activate! Stir in the yeast. Set aside and let it proof.

3. In the bowl of a stand mixer, using the whisk attachment, mix the coconut flour, tapioca starch, baking powder, xanthan gum, and salt until blended.

4. Add the sugar and shortening and mix until the shortening is evenly incorporated into the flour mixture.

5. Add the eggs and yeast mixture, which should have started to bubble up a little. Mix on high speed for roughly 1 to 2 minutes, until a dough comes together. The dough will thicken as it's mixed.

6. Place a large sheet of parchment paper on the countertop and lightly oil it.

7. Place the dough on the parchment. Oil your hands and shape the dough into a rectangle that is roughly 14 by 10 inches and about ½ inch thick.

8. Onto the dough, spread the filling ingredients: Start with the melted butter, and then sprinkle on the sugar and cinnamon.

9. Turn the parchment paper so that the long side of the dough is facing you. Starting at the bottom, using the parchment paper as a guide, roll the dough into a cylinder, with the seam on the bottom.

10. Using unflavored dental floss or a sharp knife (floss gives a cleaner cut), cut the dough crosswise into 9 rolls. Place them in the prepared pan.

11. Drizzle the tablespoon of melted butter on top of the cinnamon rolls and cover the pan with a towel.

12. It's time to proof the rolls! Turn off the oven and slide the covered pan into the warm oven to proof for a total of 30 minutes. Leave the door open a crack for the first 15 minutes, and then close the door for the last 15 minutes.

13. After 30 minutes of proofing, take the rolls out of the oven and remove the towel. Brush the tops of the rolls with 1 tablespoon of water. Cover with foil and place on top of the stove.

14. Preheat the oven to 375 degrees. When the oven is fully preheated, bake the rolls for 35 to 40 minutes, leaving the foil on the entire time. But you can peek under the foil toward the end to check the color. If the rolls are starting to look a bit brown around the edges, they are done. Remove from the oven and allow to cool in the pan.

15. While the rolls are cooling, make the glaze: Place the sugar in a coffee grinder or spice grinder and grind until you have a powder. Place the powdered sugar in a small bowl and mix it with the milk and vanilla.

16. Once the rolls have cooled, drizzle the glaze over the top. Store leftovers at room temperature, or freeze for another day.

CHAPTER 4

Biscuits and Scones — Sweet and Savory

PREP TIME: 15 minutes
COOK TIME: 18 minutes
YIELD: 6 biscuits

DAIRY *free*, **EGG** *free*, **NUT** *free*,
GRAIN *free*, **COCONUT** *free*

classic biscuits

Biscuits require a little bit more attention than other kinds of baked goods. Don't get me wrong, biscuits are quick to make—just be sure to follow the directions. I like to mix the dry ingredients together, cut in the fat, and add the egg and lemon juice last, mixing everything together very briefly. These biscuits cook up fairly quickly and are best eaten fresh out of the oven, but also are tasty reheated the next day!

ingredients

220 grams blanched almond flour (about 1½ cups)

89 grams potato starch or sweet potato starch (about ½ cup), plus more for the work surface

¾ teaspoon baking soda

¾ teaspoon kosher salt

112 grams (½ cup/1 stick) semi-chilled salted butter or 88 grams (½ cup plus 1 tablespoon) room-temperature Spectrum vegetable shortening

2 large eggs

¾ teaspoon lemon juice or apple cider vinegar

directions

1. Preheat the oven to 350 degrees. Line a baking sheet with parchment paper.

2. In a large bowl, whisk the almond flour, potato starch, baking soda, and salt until well blended.

3. Cut the butter into the flour mixture until small pea-sized clumps form.

4. In a small bowl, whisk together the eggs and lemon juice. Pour into the flour mixture and mix briefly and gently, just until the dough comes together. It may feel a little wet.

5. Dust a sheet of parchment paper or clean work surface with potato starch. Gently pat the dough into a disc shape, about 1½ inches thick. Cut into biscuits using a biscuit cutter or glass, using as much starch as needed to prevent sticking. Gather up the leftover dough, gently reshape it, and cut out more biscuits until all the dough has been used. You should end up with 6 biscuits.

6. Place the biscuits 1 inch apart on the prepared baking sheet. Bake for 18 minutes, until firm to the touch and lightly golden brown. Serve warm.

PREP TIME: 15 minutes
COOK TIME: 18 minutes
YIELD: 5 or 6 biscuits

DAIRY *free*, EGG *free*, NUT *free*,
GRAIN *free*, COCONUT *free*

egg-free biscuits

I often get requests for an egg-free version of my wildly popular biscuit recipe. After much trial and error, I figured out a way to make it happen. These biscuits are a little on the crumbly side but will hold up well enough to be enjoyed!

ingredients

3 tablespoons milk (dairy or nondairy)

1½ tablespoons lemon juice

119 grams blanched almond flour (about ¾ cup plus 1 tablespoon)

171 grams potato starch or sweet potato starch (about 1 cup), plus more for the work surface

¾ teaspoon baking soda

½ teaspoon kosher salt

¼ teaspoon xanthan gum or guar gum (optional; see Notes)

168 grams (¾ cup/1½ sticks) semi-chilled salted butter, or 144 grams (¾ cup plus 2 tablespoons) chilled bacon fat or room-temperature Spectrum vegetable shortening

directions

1. Preheat the oven to 350 degrees. Line a baking sheet with parchment paper.

2. In a measuring cup, combine the milk and lemon juice to "sour." Set aside.

3. In a large bowl, whisk the almond flour, potato starch, baking soda, salt, and xanthan gum, if using, until well blended.

4. Cut the butter into the flour mixture until small pea-sized clumps form. Pour in the soured milk and mix briefly and gently, just until the dough comes together.

5. Dust a sheet of parchment paper or clean work surface with potato starch. Gently pat the dough into a disc shape, about 1½ inches thick. Cut into biscuits using a biscuit cutter or glass, using as much starch as needed to prevent sticking. Gather up the leftover dough, gently reshape it, and cut out more biscuits until all the dough has been used. You should end up with 5 or 6 biscuits.

6. Place the biscuits 1 inch apart on the prepared baking sheet. Bake for 18 minutes, until firm to the touch and lightly golden brown. Serve warm.

notes

The xanthan gum in this recipe is optional, but it makes the biscuits a little fluffier and helps prevent them from being too crumbly.

PREP TIME: 15 minutes
COOK TIME: 18 minutes
YIELD: 4 or 5 biscuits

DAIRY *free*, EGG *free*, NUT *free*,
GRAIN *free*, COCONUT *free*

egg-free rosemary garlic biscuits

I can't eat eggs, so I was so thrilled to be able to create not one but two biscuit recipes that do not use eggs! The flavor of these biscuits will make your taste buds happy.

ingredients

119 grams blanched almond flour (about ¾ cup plus 1 tablespoon)

106 grams tapioca starch (about ¾ cup plus 2 teaspoons), plus more for the work surface

1 teaspoon double-acting, aluminum-free baking powder

¼ teaspoon kosher salt

¼ teaspoon xanthan gum or guar gum (optional; see Notes)

1 teaspoon dried ground rosemary

1 teaspoon garlic powder

112 grams (½ cup/1 stick) semi-chilled salted butter, or 88 grams (½ cup plus 1 tablespoon) chilled bacon fat or room-temperature Spectrum vegetable shortening

2 tablespoons hot water (see Notes)

1 tablespoon apple cider vinegar

directions

1. Preheat the oven to 350 degrees. Line a baking sheet with parchment paper.

2. In a large bowl, whisk the almond flour, tapioca starch, baking powder, salt, xanthan gum (if using), rosemary, and garlic powder until well blended.

3. Cut the butter into the flour mixture until small pea-sized clumps form. Pour in the hot water and vinegar and mix briefly and gently, just until the dough comes together.

4. Dust a sheet of parchment paper or clean work surface with tapioca starch. Gently pat the dough into a disc shape, about 1½ inches thick. Cut into biscuits using a biscuit cutter or glass, using as much starch as needed to prevent sticking. Gather up the leftover dough, gently reshape it, and cut out more biscuits until all the dough has been used. You should end up with 4 or 5 biscuits.

5. Place the biscuits 1 to 2 inches apart on the prepared baking sheet. Bake for 18 minutes, until firm to the touch and lightly golden brown. Serve warm.

notes

If you want these biscuits to be less crumbly, replace the water with 1 large egg, whisked.

The xanthan gum in this recipe is optional, but it makes the biscuits a little fluffier.

PREP TIME: 15 minutes
COOK TIME: 18 to 19 minutes
YIELD: 5 or 6 biscuits

DAIRY *free*, EGG *free*, NUT *free*,
GRAIN *free*, COCONUT *free*

chocolate biscuits

These chocolate biscuits are super-moist and rich! Try pairing them with fresh raspberries and Coconut Whipped Topping (page 318) for a fun twist on classic strawberry shortcake.

ingredients

223 grams potato starch or sweet potato starch (about 1¼ cups plus 1 tablespoon), plus more for the work surface

112 grams plantain flour (about ¾ cup) (see Notes)

70 grams cocoa powder (about ¾ cup)

256 grams coconut palm sugar (about 1½ cups plus 1½ tablespoons)

1 teaspoon double-acting, aluminum-free baking powder

1 teaspoon kosher salt

½ teaspoon xanthan gum or guar gum

224 grams (1 cup/2 sticks) semi-chilled salted butter or 183 grams (a scant 1 cup) room-temperature Spectrum vegetable shortening

1 large egg

169 grams applesauce (about ¾ cup)

50 grams strong brewed coffee, cooled (about ¼ cup)

1 teaspoon vanilla extract

directions

1. Preheat the oven to 400 degrees. Line a baking sheet with parchment paper.

2. In a large bowl, whisk the potato starch, plantain flour, cocoa powder, sugar, baking powder, salt, and xanthan gum until well blended.

3. Cut the butter into the flour mixture until small pea-sized clumps form.

4. In a separate bowl, combine the egg, applesauce, coffee, and vanilla. Beat slightly to break up the egg.

5. Add the wet ingredients to the flour-butter mixture and mix briefly and gently, just until the dough comes together.

6. Dust a sheet of parchment paper or clean work surface with potato starch to prevent the dough from sticking. Gently shape the dough into a disc shape, about 1½ inches thick. Cut into biscuits using a biscuit cutter or glass, using extra starch as needed to prevent sticking. Gather up the leftover dough, gently reshape it, and cut out more biscuits until all the dough has been used. You should end up with 5 or 6 biscuits.

7. Place the biscuits 1 inch apart on the parchment-lined baking sheet. Bake for 18 to 19 minutes, until firm to the touch and lightly golden. Serve warm.

notes

I buy my plantain flour online from Barry Farm Foods (barryfarm.com).

PREP TIME: 30 minutes
COOK TIME: 35 to 38 minutes
YIELD: 3 to 4 servings

DAIRY *free*, EGG *free*, NUT *free*,
GRAIN *free*, COCONUT *free*

biscuits and sawmill gravy

Soft, buttery biscuits smothered in creamy sausage gravy...need I say more? You must make this recipe! The caramelized onion takes the flavor of the gravy over the top.

ingredients

2 tablespoons salted butter or ghee

1 medium onion, finely chopped

2 sausage links

1½ tablespoons tapioca, potato, sweet potato, or arrowroot starch

⅓ cup blanched almond flour, plus more if needed

½ teaspoon garlic powder

½ teaspoon black pepper

1¼ cups chicken broth

1 tablespoon heavy cream or coconut cream (from a can of coconut milk; see tutorial, page 26)

Kosher salt

1 batch Classic Biscuits (page 96) or Egg-Free Biscuits (page 98)

directions

1. In a medium saucepan, melt the butter over medium-low heat. Add the onion and cook until caramelized (it will have a beautiful golden brown color and be very soft), about 20 minutes.

2. Meanwhile, cook the sausage: Remove the sausage from its casings and crumble it into a skillet over medium heat. Cook until browned, stirring to break up clumps. When fully cooked, remove the sausage with a slotted spoon and set aside.

3. Once the onion is caramelized, add the starch, almond flour, garlic powder, and pepper and stir for 1 minute.

4. Add the chicken broth and cream and whisk constantly over medium heat until the gravy begins to thicken. If you want thicker gravy, add 2 to 3 more tablespoons of almond flour. The gravy will thicken a bit as it cools.

5. When the gravy has reached the desired consistency, add the browned sausage.

6. Season with salt to taste, spoon over split biscuits, and then devour!

notes

If you like your gravy to have a smoother texture, use an immersion blender or food processor to process the mixture until smooth. Do this step *before* you add the sausage to the gravy.

If this gravy gets too thick after you package it up and refrigerate it, you can add a little water or cream to thin it.

PREP TIME: 20 minutes
COOK TIME: 35 to 38 minutes
YIELD: 6 servings

DAIRY *free*, **EGG** *free*, **NUT** *free*,
GRAIN *free*, **COCONUT** *free*

biscuit pot pie

I am in love with this recipe. It is out-of-this-world delicious and pretty simple to prepare. This pot pie can be made with my Classic Biscuits, Egg-Free Biscuits, or Egg-Free Rosemary Garlic Biscuits—it's your choice!

ingredients

3 tablespoons salted butter, ghee, or mild-flavored oil

2 medium onions, finely chopped

1 cup chopped carrots

1 cup chopped celery

1 pound boneless, skinless chicken thighs, cut into bite-sized pieces

½ teaspoon black pepper

2½ tablespoons arrowroot, tapioca, potato, or sweet potato starch

½ cup blanched almond flour

2 cups frozen peas

1½ cups chicken broth

1 teaspoon garlic powder

½ cup heavy cream, coconut cream (from a can of coconut milk; see tutorial, page 26), or milk (dairy or nondairy)

Kosher salt

1 batch Classic Biscuit dough (page 96), Egg-Free Biscuit dough (page 98), or Egg-Free Rosemary Garlic Biscuit dough (page 100)

directions

1. Preheat the oven to 350 degrees.

2. In a large skillet over medium-low heat, melt the butter. Add the onions, carrots, and celery and cook until softened.

3. Add the chicken and cook until you no longer can see pink in the meat. Add the pepper, starch, and almond flour and stir constantly for 1 minute.

4. Add the peas, chicken broth, garlic powder, cream, and salt to taste and bring to a boil. Cook until the liquid has thickened and all the vegetables are cooked through.

5. Pour the mixture into a 2½-quart casserole dish.

6. Roll out the biscuit dough to about ¼ inch thick. Cut out rounds using a biscuit cutter or glass, using extra starch as needed to prevent sticking. Gather up the leftover dough, gently reshape it, and cut out more biscuits until all the dough has been used.

7. Arrange the biscuits on top of the gravy in the casserole dish. Bake for 35 to 38 minutes, until the biscuits are cooked through and lightly browned.

PREP TIME: 20 minutes
COOK TIME: 27 to 30 minutes
YIELD: 10 cupcakes

DAIRY *free*, EGG *free*, NUT *free*,
GRAIN *free*, COCONUT *free*

monkey bread "cupcakes"

Monkey bread is a dream to make and to eat. You take biscuit dough, roll it in cinnamon and sugar, and then drown it with caramel sauce! After you bake it, you pull out one delicious piece at a time to eat. This version creates individual cupcake-sized monkey bread treats.

ingredients

Dough:

40 grams coconut palm sugar (about ¼ cup)

288 grams blanched almond flour (about 2 cups)

88 grams potato starch or sweet potato starch (about ½ cup)

2 teaspoons baking soda

¼ teaspoon kosher salt

112 grams (½ cup/1 stick) semi-chilled salted butter or 88 grams (½ cup plus 1 tablespoon) room-temperature Spectrum vegetable shortening

2 large eggs

Cinnamon sugar coating:

½ cup granulated maple sugar

2 teaspoons ground cinnamon

2 tablespoons melted salted butter or ghee

Caramel sauce:

¼ cup (½ stick) salted butter, ghee, or mild-flavored oil

½ cup granulated maple sugar

2 tablespoons coconut cream (from a can of coconut milk; see tutorial, page 26) or heavy cream

directions

1. Set an oven rack in the middle position and preheat the oven to 350 degrees. Line 10 cups of a muffin tin with cupcake liners.

2. Make the dough: In a large bowl, whisk the sugar, almond flour, potato starch, baking soda, and salt until well blended.

3. Cut the butter into the flour mixture until small pea-sized clumps form.

4. In a separate bowl, whisk the eggs. Pour the eggs into the flour-butter mixture and mix briefly and gently, just until the dough comes together.

5. Make the coating: In a small bowl or plastic bag, mix together the sugar and cinnamon. You will roll the biscuit dough in this mixture.

6. Take a heaping teaspoon of dough and gently roll it into a ball. Roll the ball in the bowl of cinnamon sugar (or shake it in the plastic bag) until it is fully covered in cinnamon sugar. Place the sugar-coated ball in a lined muffin cup.

7. Continue this process, placing a total of 3 or 4 sugar-coated balls in each cup, until all 10 cups are filled with sugar-coated balls. Press down gently to help assure that the balls stick together.

8. Brush the top of each mound of dough balls with the melted butter.

9. Place the pan on the middle rack in the oven and bake for 27 to 30 minutes, until golden brown.

10. While the monkey bread is baking, make the caramel sauce: Combine the butter, sugar, and cream in a heavy-bottomed saucepan over medium heat. Cook just until the sugar has melted and the sauce has started to gently boil. (The sauce should be thin; this will take only a few minutes.) Remove from the heat and set aside.

11. As soon as the cupcakes come out of the oven, pour the caramel sauce evenly over them, letting it seep into all the nooks and crannies. Remove from the pan when cool enough to handle.

12. Serve warm or at room temperature. Store leftovers at room temperature in a sealed bag or container for up to several days.

PREP TIME: 1 hour 20 minutes, including time for berries to macerate
COOK TIME: 18 minutes
YIELD: 6 to 8 servings

DAIRY *free*, **EGG** *free*, **NUT** *free*, **GRAIN** *free*, **COCONUT** *free*

strawberry shortcake

Strawberry shortcake is my family's favorite thing to make as soon as local strawberries start becoming available. We often make a huge batch and enjoy it on my parents' sailboat. It's one of those fresh, delicious desserts that is impossible to screw up. If you plan to serve your shortcake with homemade whipped topping, be sure to chill your cans of coconut the night before!

ingredients

Strawberry topping:

2 pounds strawberries, hulled and sliced

¼ cup granulated maple sugar or coconut palm sugar

2 teaspoons lemon juice

⅛ teaspoon kosher salt

1 batch Classic Biscuit dough (page 96) or Egg-Free Biscuit dough (page 98)

1 batch Coconut Whipped Topping (page 318; optional)

directions

1. Prepare the strawberry topping: In a bowl, combine the strawberries, sugar, lemon juice, and salt. Let sit in the refrigerator for 1 hour to develop the flavor.

2. While the strawberries are macerating, bake the biscuits according to instructions. Let cool.

3. While the biscuits are cooling, making the Coconut Whipped Topping.

4. It's time to assemble the shortcakes! Cut the biscuits in half, spoon on the strawberry topping, and top with the Coconut Whipped Topping, if using.

PREP TIME: 20 minutes
COOK TIME: 27 to 30 minutes
YIELD: 10 cupcakes

DAIRY free, **EGG** free, **NUT** free, **GRAIN** free, **COCONUT** free

strawberry shortcake monkey bread "cupcakes"

These little "cupcakes" are so much fun to make! There's only one catch: The strawberries have to be worked into the dough balls just before you roll them in the sugar and pop them in the oven; otherwise, they will make for a mushy dough. I suggest reading through the directions for this recipe once or twice before getting started.

ingredients

Dough:

288 grams blanched almond flour (about 2 cups)

88 grams potato, sweet potato, or tapioca starch (about ½ cup) (see Notes)

2 teaspoons double-acting, aluminum-free baking powder

¼ teaspoon kosher salt

112 grams (½ cup/1 stick) salted butter, semi-chilled, or 88 grams (½ cup plus 1 tablespoon) Spectrum vegetable shortening, room temperature

2 large eggs

1 cup finely diced fresh strawberries

Coating:

1 cup granulated maple sugar

Glaze:

½ cup granulated maple sugar

2½ to 3 teaspoons water or milk

notes

Either potato/sweet potato starch or tapioca starch will work in this recipe, but if you have potato/sweet potato starch, use it. It gives a better texture. If using tapioca starch and measuring with a cup, use ½ cup plus 3 tablespoons.

directions

1. Preheat the oven to 350 degrees. Line 10 cups of a muffin tin with cupcake liners.

2. Make the dough: In a large bowl, whisk the almond flour, potato starch, baking powder, and salt until well blended.

3. Cut the butter into the flour mixture until small pea-sized clumps form.

4. Beat the eggs in a separate bowl. Then pour the eggs into the flour-butter mixture and mix ever so gently, just until the dough holds together.

5. Take a heaping teaspoon of dough and roll it between your hands with a small pinch of strawberries, pressing the strawberries into the dough. (*Note:* To keep the dough from becoming wet and mushy, you will mix in the strawberries one dough ball at a time rather than add them all at once to the entire quantity of dough.)

6. Place 1 cup of granulated maple sugar in a small bowl. Roll the strawberry-stuffed dough ball in the sugar and place the sugar-coated ball in a lined muffin cup.

7. Continue this process, placing a total of 3 or 4 sugar-crusted balls in each cup, until all 10 cups are filled with sugar-crusted balls. Press down gently to help assure that the balls stick together.

8. Bake for 27 to 30 minutes, until slightly golden and firm to the touch.

9. While the monkey bread is baking, make the glaze: Place ½ cup of granulated maple sugar in a coffee grinder or spice grinder and grind it into a powder. Place the powdered sugar in a small bowl. Slowly pour in the water while stirring. Add only as much water as you need to attain a perfect thickness for drizzling. The glaze should be a little less runny than honey.

10. As soon as the cupcakes come out of the oven, drizzle the glaze evenly over them, letting it seep into all the nooks and crannies. Remove from the pan when cool enough to handle.

11. Serve warm or at room temperature. Store leftovers at room temperature in a sealed bag or container for up to several days.

PREP TIME: 10 minutes
COOK TIME: 35 to 40 minutes
YIELD: 4 sandwiches

DAIRY *free,* **EGG** *free,* **NUT** *free,*
GRAIN *free,* **COCONUT** *free*

"fried" chicken breakfast biscuit sandwiches

This is the king of all breakfast sandwiches. I pretty much pulled out all the stops when putting together each layer: a biscuit with a fried chicken cutlet, my Sawmill Gravy (page 104), and a fried egg. If it was healthy to do so, I would live on this sandwich alone!

ingredients

Wet coating for the chicken:

¼ cup medium-hot hot sauce, such as Frank's RedHot Original

5 tablespoons salted butter, ghee, or mild-flavored oil

1 tablespoon tapioca, arrowroot, potato, or sweet potato starch

¼ cup plus 1 tablespoon milk (dairy or nondairy)

Breading for the chicken:

½ cup tapioca, arrowroot, potato, or sweet potato starch

½ cup blanched almond flour

1 teaspoon black pepper

½ teaspoon kosher salt

1 pound boneless, skinless chicken cutlets, cut into 4 equal portions

Melted coconut oil or other mild-flavored oil, for drizzling the chicken

4 large eggs

2 teaspoons coconut oil or other mild-flavored oil, for frying the eggs

1 batch Sawmill Gravy (page 104)

4 Classic Biscuits (page 96), Egg-Free Biscuits (page 98), or Egg-Free Rosemary Garlic Biscuits (page 100)

directions

1. Preheat the oven to 400 degrees. Line a rimmed baking sheet with foil.

2. Make the chicken cutlets: In a microwave-safe bowl, combine the ingredients for the wet coating and heat in the microwave until thickened, 1 to 2 minutes. You can also do this on the stovetop in a saucepan over medium heat. If using the microwave, whisk vigorously as soon as you remove the bowl. If using a saucepan, whisk continually while it thickens, and then pour into a bowl.

3. In another bowl, combine the breading ingredients.

4. Drop the chicken cutlets into the wet coating and then heavily dredge in the breading mixture. Place the coated chicken cutlets on the prepared baking sheet. Repeat until all the chicken cutlets have been coated. Drizzle the chicken with coconut oil.

5. Bake for 35 to 40 minutes, until golden brown and cooked through.

6. About 5 minutes before the chicken is done, fry the eggs: Heat the coconut oil in a large skillet over medium heat. Carefully crack the eggs into the skillet and cook until the whites are set and the yolks are cooked to your liking. If cooking the eggs sunny side up, cover the pan with a lid while cooking.

7. It's time to assemble your sandwiches! Cut the biscuits in half. On the bottom half, place a chicken cutlet and a fried egg. Smother with gravy and then top with the other half of the biscuit.

PREP TIME: 15 minutes
COOK TIME: 38 to 40 minutes
YIELD: 6 scones

DAIRY *free,* **EGG** *free,* **NUT** *free,* **GRAIN** *free,* **COCONUT** *free*

cherry chocolate chip scones

This grain-free scone recipe will make you throw out every other scone recipe you have ever tried. I know that is bold to say, but trust me on this one. If you prefer another fruit in your scones, feel free to swap out the cherries. For fun, try melting an extra ½ cup of chocolate chips in the microwave for 1 minute and then drizzle the melted chocolate over the finished scones, as pictured.

ingredients

220 grams blanched almond flour (about 1½ cups)

89 grams potato starch or sweet potato starch (about ½ cup), plus more for the work surface

½ teaspoon baking soda

½ teaspoon kosher salt

112 grams (½ cup/1 stick) semi-chilled salted butter or 88 grams (½ cup plus 1 tablespoon) room-temperature Spectrum vegetable shortening

80 grams granulated maple sugar (about ½ cup)

2 large eggs

¾ teaspoon apple cider vinegar or lemon juice

½ cup chocolate chips

1 cup cherries, fresh or frozen, pitted and halved

2 tablespoons (or more) tapioca starch, for dusting the cherries

directions

1. Preheat the oven to 350 degrees.

2. In a large bowl, whisk the almond flour, potato starch, baking soda, and salt until well blended.

3. Cut the butter into the flour mixture until small pea-sized clumps form.

4. In a small bowl, whisk together the sugar, eggs, and vinegar. Pour into the flour-butter mixture and mix briefly and gently, just until the dough comes together. It may feel a little wet.

5. Stir in the chocolate chips.

6. In a bowl, toss the cherries with the tapioca starch. Fold the cherries into the dough.

7. Dust a sheet of parchment paper with potato starch. Place the dough on the dusted parchment and gently pat it into a circle, about 6 inches in diameter and 2 inches thick.

8. Transfer the parchment paper to a baking sheet. Bake for 38 to 40 minutes, until firm to the touch and golden brown. Cover with foil halfway through baking to prevent it from becoming too dark.

9. Allow to cool on the pan. When completely cool, slice into 6 wedges and serve. Store at room temperature in a sealed bag or container, or freeze for up to 3 months.

PREP TIME: 15 minutes
COOK TIME: 38 to 40 minutes
YIELD: 6 scones

DAIRY *free*, EGG *free*, NUT *free*,
GRAIN *free*, COCONUT *free*

gingerbread scones

'Tis the season for gingerbread...any season you choose! These delightfully fluffy and cakelike scones are absolutely perfect to make for breakfast on Christmas morning, or just a typical Sunday morning. Any day feels like the holiday season when you bake up a batch of these!

ingredients

288 grams blanched almond flour (about 2 cups)

88 grams potato starch or sweet potato starch (about ½ cup), plus more for the pan and dough

2 teaspoons ginger powder

2 teaspoons ground nutmeg

2 teaspoons ground allspice

½ teaspoon baking soda

Grated zest of 1 orange

112 grams (½ cup/1 stick) semi-chilled salted butter or 88 grams (½ cup plus 1 tablespoon) room-temperature Spectrum vegetable shortening

120 grams coconut palm sugar (about ¾ cup)

1 tablespoon molasses

¾ teaspoon orange juice or lemon juice

2 large eggs

directions

1. Preheat the oven to 350 degrees. Line a baking sheet with parchment paper and dust it with potato starch.

2. In a mixing bowl, whisk the almond flour, potato starch, ginger, nutmeg, allspice, and baking soda until blended. Add the orange zest and stir to mix through.

3. Cut the butter into the flour mixture until small pea-sized clumps form.

4. In a separate small bowl, whisk together the sugar, molasses, orange juice, and eggs. Pour the wet ingredients into the flour-butter mixture and mix until well combined.

5. Shape the dough into a ball and place it on the prepared baking sheet. Pat out the dough into a circle, about 6 inches in diameter and 2 inches thick. Pat the top and sides with potato starch.

6. Bake for 38 to 40 minutes, until firm to the touch and golden brown. Cover with foil halfway through baking to prevent it from burning.

7. Allow to cool on the pan. When completely cool, slice into 6 wedges and serve. Store at room temperature in a sealed bag or container, or freeze for up to 3 months.

variations

Glazed Gingerbread Scones

In a small bowl, mix together 1 cup powdered coconut palm sugar, 2 tablespoons water, and 1 teaspoon orange oil/extract or vanilla extract until well combined. Drizzle the glaze over the cooled and cut scones, as pictured. (See the tutorial "How to Make Powdered Sugar" on page 26.)

Crackle-Top Gingerbread Scones

Sprinkle 1 tablespoon coconut palm sugar on the dough before baking. This will give the scones a molasses cookie–style crust.

CHAPTER 5
Quick Breads and Muffins

PREP TIME: 20 to 25 minutes
COOK TIME: 25 to 26 minutes
YIELD: 8 or 9 muffins

DAIRY *free*, **EGG** *free*, **NUT** *free*,
GRAIN *free*, **COCONUT** *free*

caramel apple muffins

Chestnut flour has amazing cake flour qualities. It's what allows these muffins to be egg-free without being dense, and to be gluten-free without being tough. It's nothing short of magical!

ingredients

Muffin batter:

158 grams chestnut flour (about 1 cup)

2 teaspoons double-acting, aluminum-free baking powder

½ teaspoon xanthan gum or guar gum (optional; see Notes)

1 teaspoon ground cinnamon

Pinch of kosher salt

240 grams milk (dairy or nondairy) (about 1 cup plus 1½ tablespoons)

120 grams finely chopped apples (no need to peel) (about 1 cup)

167 grams coconut palm sugar (about 1 cup)

52 grams applesauce (about a scant ¼ cup)

48 grams melted salted butter, melted ghee, or mild-flavored oil (about a scant ¼ cup)

2 teaspoons apple cider vinegar

1 teaspoon vanilla extract

Caramel topping:

¼ cup (½ stick) salted butter or ghee

½ cup coconut palm sugar

1 tablespoon heavy cream or coconut cream (from a can of coconut milk; see tutorial, page 26)

Pinch of kosher salt

directions

1. Preheat the oven to 350 degrees. Line 8 or 9 cups of a muffin tin with cupcake liners or grease them with nonstick spray.

2. Make the muffin batter: In a large bowl, whisk the chestnut flour, baking powder, xanthan gum (if using), cinnamon, and salt until well blended. Add the rest of the batter ingredients and stir until smooth.

3. Pour the batter into the prepared muffin cups, filling them three-quarters full. Bake for 25 to 26 minutes, until a toothpick inserted comes out clean.

4. While muffins are baking, make the caramel topping: Combine the ingredients for the topping in a saucepan over medium-high heat and stir constantly until thick. This will take just a few minutes.

5. Remove the muffins from the oven and drizzle on the caramel. Store at room temperature in a sealed bag or container, or freeze for another day.

notes

Feel free to throw some chopped raw walnuts or pecans into the batter!

The xanthan gum or guar gum helps give the muffins a better shape and helps them hold together really well. Without the xanthan gum, they still taste great, but they may end up a little crumbly.

PREP TIME: 20 to 25 minutes
COOK TIME: 20 to 22 minutes
YIELD: 8 muffins

DAIRY *free*, **EGG** *free*, **NUT** *free*,
GRAIN *free*, **COCONUT** *free*

coffee cake muffins

Scrumptious, mesmerizing, and worthy of your next brunch, these muffins are a spin on my popular coffee cake. They will truly make you the envy of all your friends.

ingredients

Crumb topping:

½ cup blanched almond flour

3 tablespoons potato starch or sweet potato starch

¾ cup coconut palm sugar

3½ tablespoons melted salted butter or melted ghee

1½ teaspoons ground cinnamon

Coffee-flavored caramel (optional):

¼ cup (½ stick) salted butter or ghee

½ cup coconut palm sugar

1 tablespoon heavy cream or coconut cream (from a can of coconut milk; see tutorial, page 26)

1 tablespoon finely ground coffee

Pinch of kosher salt

Muffin batter:

180 grams blanched almond flour (about 1¼ cups)

132 grams potato starch or sweet potato starch (about ¾ cup)

1 teaspoon double-acting, aluminum-free baking powder

¼ teaspoon kosher salt

4 large eggs

174 grams coconut palm sugar or granulated maple sugar (about 1 cup plus 1½ tablespoons)

60 grams melted coconut oil or grapeseed oil (about ⅓ cup)

50 grams milk (dairy or nondairy) or water (about ¼ cup)

1 tablespoon vanilla extract

1 teaspoon lemon juice

directions

1. Preheat the oven to 350 degrees. Line 8 cups of a muffin tin with cupcake liners or grease them with nonstick spray.

2. Make the crumb topping: In a bowl, mix together the almond flour, potato starch, sugar, melted butter, and cinnamon with a fork until pea-sized clumps form. Set aside.

3. Make the coffee-flavored caramel, if using: Combine the ingredients for the caramel in a saucepan over medium-high heat, stirring. Bring to a boil and then reduce the heat to low. Continue to cook and stir until it thickens. This will take just a few minutes.

4. Make the muffin batter: In a bowl, whisk the almond flour, potato starch, baking powder, and salt until well blended. Add the rest of the batter ingredients and stir to combine.

5. Pour the batter into the prepared muffin cups, filling them three-quarters full. Sprinkle the crumb topping over the muffins.

6. Bake for 20 to 22 minutes, until the tops are lightly golden and a toothpick inserted comes out clean.

7. Drizzle the caramel over the top, if using. Store at room temperature in a sealed bag or container, or freeze for another day.

PREP TIME: 15 minutes
COOK TIME: 20 to 22 minutes
YIELD: 12 muffins

DAIRY *free*, **EGG** *free*, **NUT** *free*,
GRAIN *free*, **COCONUT** *free*

double chocolate chip muffins

Calling all chocolate lovers! This recipe is for you, and it's for breakfast, too! You'll love the rich flavor and texture of these muffins.

ingredients

72 grams coconut flour (about ⅓ cup plus 2 tablespoons)

88 grams potato starch or sweet potato starch (about ½ cup)

30 grams cocoa powder (about ⅓ cup)

1 tablespoon double-acting, aluminum-free baking powder

⅛ teaspoon kosher salt

4 large eggs

165 grams coconut palm sugar (about 1 cup)

120 grams milk (dairy or nondairy) (about ½ cup plus 2 teaspoons)

44 grams melted salted butter, melted ghee, or mild-flavored oil (about a scant ¼ cup)

1 teaspoon lemon juice

1 cup chocolate chips

directions

1. Preheat the oven to 350 degrees. Line a muffin tin with cupcake liners or grease it with nonstick spray.

2. In a bowl, whisk the coconut flour, potato starch, cocoa powder, baking powder, and salt until well blended. Add the eggs, sugar, milk, butter, and lemon juice and stir to combine. After the ingredients have come together into a smooth batter, stir in the chocolate chips.

3. Pour the batter into the prepared muffin cups, filling each about three-quarters full.

4. Bake for 20 to 22 minutes, until a toothpick inserted comes out clean.

5. Store at room temperature in a sealed bag or container, or freeze for another day.

PREP TIME: 15 minutes
COOK TIME: 30 minutes
YIELD: 12 muffins

DAIRY *free*, EGG *free*, NUT *free*,
GRAIN *free*, COCONUT *free*

blueberry muffins

There's nothing better than waking up to the smell of blueberry muffins. The lemon zest in this recipe really brings the blueberry flavor to life! These fluffy muffins are perfectly moist and will stand up to any gluten-based muffin you have eaten.

ingredients

180 grams blanched almond flour (about 1¼ cups)

132 grams potato starch or sweet potato starch (about ¾ cup)

1 teaspoon double-acting, aluminum-free baking powder

½ teaspoon kosher salt

174 grams granulated maple sugar or coconut palm sugar (about 1 cup plus 1½ tablespoons)

60 grams melted coconut oil or grapeseed oil (about ⅓ cup)

4 large eggs

Grated zest of 1 lemon

1 tablespoon vanilla extract

1 teaspoon lemon juice or apple cider vinegar

2 cups fresh or frozen blueberries

directions

1. Preheat the oven to 350 degrees. Line a muffin tin with cupcake liners or grease it with nonstick spray.

2. In a bowl, whisk the almond flour, potato starch, baking powder, and salt until well blended. Add the rest of the ingredients, except the blueberries, and stir to combine.

3. Fold in the blueberries.

4. Pour the batter into the prepared muffin cups, filling each about three-quarters full.

5. Bake for 30 minutes, until a toothpick inserted comes out clean.

6. Store at room temperature in a sealed bag or container, or freeze for another day.

PREP TIME: 15 to 20 minutes
COOK TIME: 20 to 22 minutes
YIELD: 11 or 12 muffins

DAIRY *free*, EGG *free*, NUT *free*, GRAIN *free*, COCONUT *free*

streusel peach pie muffins
with brown butter caramel glaze

Here's a true morning treat! The streusel crumb topping and caramel stack layers of deliciousness on top a fluffy peach muffin. For fun, try subbing sliced fresh pears in place of the frozen peaches.

ingredients

Crumb topping:

1½ tablespoons potato starch or sweet potato starch

¼ cup coconut flour

¼ cup coconut palm sugar

2 to 3 tablespoons melted salted butter, melted ghee, or mild-flavored oil

¾ teaspoon ground cinnamon

¼ teaspoon ginger powder

Pinch of kosher salt

Muffin batter:

72 grams coconut flour (about ⅓ cup plus 2 tablespoons)

72 grams tapioca starch (about ½ cup plus 1 tablespoon)

1 tablespoon double-acting, aluminum-free baking powder

⅛ teaspoon kosher salt

4 large eggs

120 grams coconut palm sugar or granulated maple sugar (about ¾ cup)

120 grams milk (dairy or nondairy) (about ½ cup plus 2 teaspoons)

44 grams melted salted butter, melted ghee, or mild-flavored oil (about a scant ¼ cup)

1 teaspoon lemon juice

1 cup sliced frozen peaches, cut into ½-inch pieces

Brown Butter Caramel Glaze:

¼ cup (½ stick) salted butter or ghee

½ cup coconut palm sugar

1 tablespoon heavy cream or coconut cream (from a can of coconut milk; see tutorial, page 26)

Pinch of kosher salt

directions

1. Preheat the oven to 350 degrees. Line a muffin tin with cupcake liners or grease it with nonstick spray.

2. Make the crumb topping: In a bowl, combine the ingredients for the topping, using 2 tablespoons of melted butter to start, as coconut flour tends to absorb liquid. Mix together with a fork until pea-sized clumps form. If needed, add another tablespoon of melted butter. Set aside.

3. Make the muffin batter: In a bowl, whisk the coconut flour, tapioca starch, baking powder, and salt until well blended. Add the rest of the batter ingredients, except for the peaches, and stir to combine.

4. Fold in the frozen peaches.

5. Pour the batter into the prepared muffin cups, filling each about three-quarters full. Sprinkle the crumb topping over the muffins.

6. Bake for 20 to 22 minutes, until a toothpick inserted comes out clean. Allow to cool in the pan.

7. While the muffins are cooling, make the glaze: Brown the butter in a saucepan over medium heat, about 7 minutes. Watch carefully, and stir constantly to keep the butter from burning.

8. Once the butter is browned, remove the pan from the heat. Add the sugar and stir until dissolved, and then stir in the cream and salt.

9. Drizzle the glaze over the cooled muffins and enjoy! Store at room temperature in a sealed bag or container, or freeze for another day.

PREP TIME: 15 to 20 minutes
COOK TIME: 22 to 24 minutes
YIELD: 9 muffins

DAIRY *free*, EGG *free*, NUT *free*,
GRAIN *free*, COCONUT *free*

banana nut muffins

I can't say enough good things about these muffins. They are soft, billowy, and utterly perfect. Plus, they are egg-free! I have to hide them in the bottom of my chest freezer to keep control of myself.

ingredients

Muffin batter:

158 grams chestnut flour (about 1 cup)

2 teaspoons double-acting, aluminum-free baking powder

1 teaspoon ground cinnamon

½ teaspoon xanthan gum or guar gum (optional)

Pinch of kosher salt

130 grams puréed yellow bananas (about ½ cup or 2 medium)

100 grams milk (dairy or nondairy) (about a scant ½ cup)

167 grams coconut palm sugar (about 1 cup)

45 grams raw pecans, chopped (about ½ cup), plus more for garnish, if desired

48 grams melted salted butter, melted ghee, or mild-flavored oil (about a scant ¼ cup)

1 teaspoon vanilla extract

2 teaspoons apple cider vinegar

Caramel sauce (optional):

¼ cup (½ stick) salted butter or ghee

½ cup coconut palm sugar

1 tablespoon heavy cream or coconut cream (from a can of coconut milk; see tutorial, page 26)

Pinch of kosher salt

directions

1. Preheat the oven to 350 degrees. Line 9 cups of a muffin tin with cupcake liners or grease them with nonstick spray.

2. Make the muffin batter: In a large bowl, whisk the chestnut flour, baking powder, cinnamon, xanthan gum, and salt until well blended. Add the rest of the batter ingredients and stir to combine.

3. Pour the batter into the prepared muffin cups, filling each about three-quarters full.

4. Bake for 22 to 24 minutes, until a toothpick inserted comes out clean.

5. Make the caramel sauce, if using: In a saucepan over medium heat, combine the butter, sugar, cream, and salt. Bring to a boil, stirring constantly, and then take the pan off the heat.

6. Drizzle the caramel sauce over the muffins, and top with chopped pecans, if desired. Store leftover muffins at room temperature in a sealed bag or container, or freeze for another day.

PREP TIME: 15 minutes
COOK TIME: 20 to 22 minutes
YIELD: 12 to 14 muffins

DAIRY *free*, EGG *free*, NUT *free*,
GRAIN *free*, COCONUT *free*

strawberry cream cheese muffins

These beautiful pink muffins burst with fresh strawberry flavor, and when you cut them open, the cream cheese filling adds a special touch.

ingredients

Muffin batter:

180 grams blanched almond flour (about 1¼ cups)

132 grams potato starch or sweet potato starch (about ¾ cup)

1 teaspoon double-acting, aluminum-free baking powder

¼ teaspoon kosher salt

4 large eggs

174 grams granulated maple sugar (about 1 cup plus 1½ tablespoons)

60 grams melted coconut oil or grapeseed oil (about ⅓ cup)

50 grams milk (dairy or nondairy) or water (about ¼ cup)

1 tablespoon vanilla extract

1 teaspoon lemon juice

1 (1.2-ounce) package freeze-dried strawberries, crushed into a powder in a coffee grinder or spice grinder

Filling:

1 (8-ounce) package cream cheese, softened

Garnishes (optional):

Strawberry jam

Coconut Whipped Topping (page 318)

directions

1. Preheat the oven to 350 degrees. Line a muffin tin with cupcake liners or grease it with nonstick spray. You will need to line or grease 2 cups of a second pan if you make 14 muffins.

2. Make the muffin batter: In a bowl, whisk the almond flour, potato starch, baking powder, and salt until well blended. Add the rest of the batter ingredients and stir to combine.

3. Using a spoon, drop a dollop of batter into each prepared muffin cup.

4. Place 1 tablespoon of the cream cheese in the center of each muffin. Use a spoon to drop in the cream cheese, or use a pastry bag to squeeze it in. Top the muffins with the remaining batter, filling each cup about three-quarters full.

5. Bake for 20 to 22 minutes, until a toothpick inserted comes out clean.

6. Let cool, and then top with a dollop of strawberry jam and/or Coconut Whipped Topping, if desired. Store leftover muffins at room temperature in a sealed bag or container, or freeze for another day.

PREP TIME: 15 to 20 minutes
COOK TIME: 20 to 22 minutes
YIELD: 11 or 12 muffins

DAIRY *free*, **EGG** *free*, **NUT** *free*,
GRAIN *free*, **COCONUT** *free*

ham and cheese morning muffins

Fluffy and loaded with ham and cheese, these muffins are fantastic to make ahead for busy mornings. You can freeze them and pull them out as you want. I add a pinch of cayenne to give them an extra punch, but that is completely optional!

ingredients

72 grams coconut flour (about ⅓ cup plus 2 tablespoons)

72 grams tapioca starch (about ½ cup plus 1 tablespoon)

1 tablespoon double-acting, aluminum-free baking powder

½ teaspoon garlic powder

¼ teaspoon black pepper

⅛ teaspoon kosher salt

Pinch of cayenne pepper (optional)

4 large eggs

120 grams milk (dairy or nondairy) (about ½ cup plus 2 teaspoons)

44 grams melted salted butter, melted ghee, or mild-flavored oil (about a scant ¼ cup)

1 teaspoon lemon juice

4 ounces deli ham, chopped

1 cup shredded cheddar cheese (dairy or nondairy)

directions

1. Preheat the oven to 350 degrees. Line a muffin tin with cupcake liners or grease it with nonstick spray.

2. In a large bowl, whisk the coconut flour, tapioca starch, baking powder, garlic powder, pepper, salt, and cayenne, if using, until well blended. Add the eggs, milk, melted butter, and lemon juice and stir to combine.

3. Fold in the ham and cheese.

4. Pour the batter into the prepared muffin cups, filling each about three-quarters full.

5. Bake for 22 to 24 minutes, until a toothpick inserted comes out clean.

6. Store leftover muffins at room temperature in a sealed bag or container, or freeze for another day.

PREP TIME: 15 minutes
COOK TIME: 1 hour 10 minutes
YIELD: One 8½-by-4½-inch loaf

DAIRY *free*, **EGG** *free*, **NUT** *free*,
GRAIN *free*, **COCONUT** *free*

lemon poppy seed bread

This is the perfect loaf to make on Saturday morning and lay out for everyone to pick at through the weekend. You'll love both the texture and the flavor of this quick bread. It tastes great on its own or drizzled with a glaze (see Cinnamon Rolls, page 92, for a glaze recipe).

ingredients

180 grams blanched almond flour (about 1¼ cups)

132 grams potato starch or sweet potato starch (about ¾ cup)

1 teaspoon double-acting, aluminum-free baking powder

¼ teaspoon kosher salt

4 large eggs

174 grams granulated maple sugar (about 1 cup plus 1½ tablespoons)

60 grams melted coconut oil or grapeseed oil (about ⅓ cup)

64 grams milk (dairy or nondairy) or water (about ¼ cup)

Grated zest of 1½ lemons

2 tablespoons lemon juice

1 tablespoon vanilla extract

1 tablespoon poppy seeds

1 batch glaze (from Cinnamon Rolls, page 92; optional)

directions

1. Preheat the oven to 350 degrees. Line an 8½-by-4½-inch loaf pan with parchment paper.

2. In a bowl, whisk the almond flour, potato starch, baking powder, and salt until well blended. Add the rest of the ingredients, except for the glaze, and stir to combine.

3. Pour the batter into the prepared loaf pan and cover with foil.

4. Bake for 50 minutes. Remove the foil and bake for another 20 minutes, until a toothpick inserted comes out clean.

5. Once cool, slice and drizzle with the glaze, if using. Store in a sealed bag or container, or freeze for another day.

PREP TIME: 20 minutes
COOK TIME: 1 hour
YIELD: One 8½-by-4½-inch loaf

DAIRY *free*, **EGG** *free*, **NUT** *free*,
GRAIN *free*, **COCONUT** *free*

orange cranberry bread

This quick bread pops with both flavor and color! I make it several times each year throughout the holiday season.

ingredients

72 grams coconut flour (about ⅓ cup plus 2 tablespoons)

72 grams tapioca starch (about ½ cup plus 1 tablespoon)

1 tablespoon double-acting, aluminum-free baking powder

⅛ teaspoon kosher salt

4 large eggs

Grated zest of 1 orange

110 grams granulated maple sugar (about a scant ¾ cup)

64 grams milk (dairy or nondairy) (about ¼ cup plus 2 teaspoons)

60 grams orange juice (about ¼ cup)

44 grams melted salted butter, melted ghee, or mild-flavored oil (about a scant ¼ cup)

¾ cup frozen cranberries

1 batch glaze (from Cinnamon Rolls, page 92; optional)

directions

1. Preheat the oven to 350 degrees. Line an 8½-by-4½-inch loaf pan with parchment paper.

2. In a bowl, whisk the coconut flour, tapioca starch, baking powder, and salt until well blended. Add the rest of the ingredients, except the cranberries, and stir to combine. Fold in the cranberries.

3. Pour the batter into the prepared loaf pan and cover with foil.

4. Bake for 50 minutes. Remove the foil and bake for another 10 minutes, until a toothpick inserted comes out clean. Let cool in the pan.

5. Drizzle with the glaze, if using. Store in a sealed bag or container, or freeze for another day.

CHAPTER 6
Breakfast and Brunch

PREP TIME: 15 minutes
COOK TIME: Varies
YIELD: 4 Belgian waffles or 8 to 10 regular waffles

ALMOND FLOUR VERSION:

DAIRY *free*, **EGG** *free*, **NUT** *free*, **GRAIN** *free*, **COCONUT** *free*

RICE FLOUR VERSION:

DAIRY *free*, **EGG** *free*, **NUT** *free*, **GRAIN** *free*, **COCONUT** *free*

extra-crispy paleo waffles

Get ready for a waffle that is crispy on the outside and soft on the inside. This recipe (and its variations) is famous; it's the most-often-made recipe from my website, BrittanyAngell.com. You may never care to try any other waffle recipe again! Because I didn't want anyone missing out, I created two versions, the first of which includes an egg-free, almond flour–free variation. Be sure to make a big batch and freeze them to have on hand for busy mornings. You might even try using them as the base of a sandwich.

ingredients

Almond flour version:

120 grams blanched almond flour (about ¾ cup plus 1 tablespoon)

70 grams tapioca starch (about ½ cup plus 1½ teaspoons)

2 teaspoons double-acting, aluminum-free baking powder

¼ teaspoon kosher salt

1 large egg

136 grams milk (dairy or nondairy) (about ½ cup plus 2 tablespoons)

60 grams mild-flavored oil, melted salted butter, or melted ghee (about ¼ cup plus 1 tablespoon), plus more for the waffle iron

2 tablespoons coconut palm sugar or granulated maple sugar

1 teaspoon lemon juice or apple cider vinegar

Egg-free rice flour version:

200 grams superfine white rice flour (about 1¼ cups)

1 teaspoon potato flour

88 grams potato starch or sweet potato starch (about ½ cup)

2 teaspoons double-acting, aluminum-free baking powder

¼ teaspoon kosher salt

275 grams milk (dairy or nondairy) (about 1¼ cups)

100 grams mild-flavored oil, melted salted butter, or melted ghee (about ½ cup), plus more for the waffle iron

2 tablespoons coconut palm sugar or granulated maple sugar

1½ teaspoons lemon juice or apple cider vinegar

directions (for both almond flour and rice flour versions)

1. Preheat a waffle iron. If you have the option, preheat to the medium setting.

2. In a bowl, whisk the flour(s), starch, baking powder, and salt until well blended. Add the remaining ingredients and stir to combine.

3. Lightly brush the heated waffle iron with oil. Following the manufacturer's guidelines for suggested quantity, ladle the batter into the oiled waffle iron and spread it evenly across the surface, leaving a ½-inch border. Cook, following the manufacturer's directions. When done, set the waffle aside on a baking sheet in a low oven to keep warm while you cook the remaining waffles.

4. Store leftover waffles in a sealed bag or container for up to 2 days, or freeze for later. They can be popped directly into the toaster oven from the freezer.

variation:

Egg-Free, Nut/Seed Flour–Based Waffles

Can't have almond flour or eggs? Another nut or seed flour, such as hazelnut flour or cashew flour, will work. Coconut flour, however, will not. Note that sunflower seed flour tends to turn green when used with baking powder; if you use it here, there's a strong possibility that the reaction could occur.

To make the almond flour version of these waffles egg- and almond flour–free, omit the egg, use the alternate nut or seed flour of your choice but increase the amount to 1¼ cups, and decrease the amount of milk to ½ cup. Keep the rest of the recipe the same. The batter will be pretty thick, and the finished waffles will be crispy on the outside and soft on the inside, but slightly gummy. I wasn't able to work completely around the gumminess without the egg, but they are still delicious.

PREP TIME: 15 minutes
COOK TIME: Varies
YIELD: 6 or 7 waffles

DAIRY *free*, EGG *free*, NUT *free*,
GRAIN *free*, COCONUT *free*

coconut flour waffles

This recipe strikes a balance on several counts! It creates perfectly textured waffles that are both lightly crispy and fluffy. These waffles are also a great breakfast option for those with nut allergies.

ingredients

5 large eggs

110 grams milk (dairy or nondairy) (about ½ cup)

74 grams melted salted butter or mild-flavored oil (about ½ cup plus 2 tablespoons)

100 grams granulated maple sugar or coconut palm sugar (about ½ cup plus 2 tablespoons)

132 grams potato starch (about ¾ cup)

84 grams coconut flour (about ½ cup)

1 tablespoon double-acting, aluminum-free baking powder

¼ teaspoon kosher salt

1 tablespoon lemon juice

1 tablespoon vanilla extract

Oil of choice, for the waffle iron

directions

1. Preheat a waffle iron. If you have the option, preheat to the medium setting.

2. In a blender or food processor, combine the eggs, milk, melted butter, and sugar. Blend until frothy, about 1 minute.

3. Add the potato starch, coconut flour, baking powder, salt, lemon juice, and vanilla. Blend until well combined, about 1 minute.

4. Lightly oil the preheated waffle iron. Following the manufacturer's guidelines for suggested quantity, ladle the batter into the oiled waffle iron and spread it evenly across the surface, leaving a ½-inch border. Cook, following the manufacturer's directions. When done, set the waffle aside on a baking sheet in a low oven to keep warm while you cook the remaining waffles.

5. Store leftover waffles in a sealed bag or container for up to 2 days, or freeze for later. They can be popped directly into the toaster oven from the freezer.

chocolate waffles
with strawberries

Chocolate and strawberries for breakfast…need I say more? This is a truly indulgent way to start your day. You deserve it every once in a while! For an extra-special treat, drizzle these waffles with melted chocolate.

ingredients

134 grams blanched almond flour (about ¾ cup plus 3 tablespoons)

68 grams tapioca starch (about ½ cup)

28 grams cocoa powder (about ¼ cup plus 1 tablespoon)

2 teaspoons double-acting, aluminum-free baking powder

½ teaspoon kosher salt

1 large egg

88 grams coconut palm sugar (about ½ cup plus 1 tablespoon)

100 grams milk (dairy or nondairy) (about a scant ½ cup)

60 grams mild-flavored oil, melted salted butter, or melted ghee (about ¼ cup plus 1 tablespoon), plus more for the waffle iron

1 tablespoon vanilla extract

1 teaspoon apple cider vinegar or lemon juice

Toppings:

Several fresh strawberries, sliced

½ cup chocolate chips, melted (optional)

directions

1. Preheat a waffle iron. If you have the option, preheat to the medium setting.

2. In a bowl, whisk the almond flour, tapioca starch, cocoa powder, baking powder, and salt until well blended. Add the rest of the ingredients for the waffles and stir to combine.

3. Lightly brush the heated waffle iron with oil. Following the manufacturer's guidelines for suggested quantity, ladle the batter into the oiled waffle iron and spread it evenly across the surface, leaving a ½-inch border. Cook, following the manufacturer's directions. When done, set the waffle aside on a baking sheet in a low oven to keep warm while you cook the remaining waffles.

4. Top the waffles with as many strawberries as you wish. If you want to take it a step further, drizzle melted chocolate over the top and add a dollop of Coconut Whipped Topping!

5. Store leftover waffles in a sealed bag or container for up to 2 days, or freeze for later. They can be popped directly into the toaster oven from the freezer.

strawberry waffles
with coconut whipped topping

The color of these waffles is pure fun! By using powdered freeze-dried strawberries, you get a bold burst of berry flavor, too. If strawberry isn't your thing, then feel free to make the powder from another freeze-dried fruit instead.

ingredients

1 (1.2-ounce) package freeze-dried strawberries

216 grams blanched almond flour (about 1½ cups)

88 grams potato starch or sweet potato starch (about ½ cup)

66 grams tapioca starch (about ½ cup)

2 teaspoons double-acting, aluminum-free baking powder

¾ teaspoon kosher salt

1 large egg

120 grams milk (dairy or nondairy) (about ½ cup plus 2 teaspoons)

126 grams raw honey or granulated maple sugar (about ¼ cup plus 2 tablespoons) (see Notes)

70 grams mild-flavored oil (about ¼ cup plus 1½ tablespoons), plus more for the waffle iron

1 teaspoon lemon juice

Natural red food coloring (optional)—the amount is up to you!

Toppings:

2 cups sliced fresh strawberries

1 batch Coconut Whipped Topping (page 318)

directions

1. Preheat a waffle iron. If you have the option, preheat to the medium setting.

2. Using a coffee grinder or spice grinder, grind the freeze-dried strawberries into a powder.

3. Place the powdered strawberries in a mixing bowl with the almond flour, starches, baking powder, and salt and whisk until well blended. Add the rest of the ingredients for the waffles and stir to combine. (Remember to add 3 tablespoons of water if you're using granulated maple sugar.)

4. Lightly brush the heated waffle iron with oil. Following the manufacturer's guidelines for suggested quantity, ladle the batter into the oiled waffle iron and spread it evenly across the surface, leaving a ½-inch border. Cook, following the manufacturer's directions. When done, set the waffle aside on a baking sheet in a low oven to keep warm while you cook the remaining waffles.

5. Serve topped with sliced strawberries, their juice, and Coconut Whipped Topping.

6. Store leftover waffles in a sealed bag or container for up to 2 days, or freeze for later. They can be popped directly into the toaster oven from the freezer.

notes

If you choose to use granulated maple sugar, you will need to add 3 tablespoons of water to the batter.

PREP TIME: 15 to 20 minutes
COOK TIME: 8 to 10 minutes
YIELD: 4 servings

DAIRY *free*, EGG *free*, NUT *free*,
GRAIN *free*, COCONUT *free*

classic french toast

Who doesn't love French toast? It's simple and delicious. If you aren't up for making a loaf of bread to use for this recipe, make some waffles instead. (Find recipes earlier in this chapter.) For a fancy brunch presentation, create a layered stack filled with Coconut Whipped Topping (page 318) and topped with melted chocolate and strawberries—or any fresh fruit you like!

ingredients

8 slices sandwich bread of choice, or 8 Extra-Crispy Paleo Waffles (page 144)

4 large eggs

⅔ cup milk (dairy or nondairy)

2 teaspoons ground cinnamon

Pinch of kosher salt

1 tablespoon salted butter, ghee, or mild-flavored oil, plus more if needed

Toppings (optional):

1 batch Coconut Whipped Topping (page 318)

½ cup chocolate chips, melted

Fresh fruit of choice

directions

1. If using waffles, lightly toast the waffles. (Gluten-free waffles tend to absorb a lot of moisture, so pretoasting will help keep them from getting too soggy when dipped in the batter.)

2. In a bowl, mix together the eggs, milk, cinnamon, and salt.

3. Heat the butter in a skillet over medium heat.

4. If using waffles, dunk one side in the egg mixture and place it in the skillet battered side down. (When making French toast with waffles, it's important not to dunk both sides, or it may end up a bit soggy!) If using bread, dunk both sides in the egg mixture before placing in the skillet.

5. When the underside is golden brown, pour some of the egg mixture on the top, unbattered side (if using waffles) and then flip. Cook for another 4 to 5 minutes, until lightly golden on both sides. Repeat with the remaining bread slices or waffles, adding more butter to the pan if needed. Set the cooked French toast aside on a baking sheet in a low oven to keep warm while you cook the remaining French toast.

6. If desired, serve with Coconut Whipped Topping, melted chocolate, and fresh fruit.

PREP TIME: 15 to 20 minutes
COOK TIME: 8 to 10 minutes
YIELD: 4 servings

DAIRY *free*, **EGG** *free*, **NUT** *free*,
GRAIN *free*, **COCONUT** *free*

egg-free banana french toast

If you need to avoid eggs (or if you just love the idea of banana French toast), this recipe is for you! Both are great reasons. Just like with the Classic French Toast recipe (page 152), either bread or waffles will do the job!

ingredients

8 slices egg-free bread of choice, or 8 egg-free waffles of choice (see Notes)

2 bananas, puréed

¾ cup milk (dairy or nondairy)

1½ teaspoons ground cinnamon

1 teaspoon vanilla extract

Pinch of kosher salt

1 tablespoon salted butter, ghee, or mild-flavored oil, plus more if needed

notes

Here's a list of the egg-free breads and waffles in this book: Egg-Free Rice Flour Bread (page 38), Egg-Free Cinnamon Raisin Bread (page 88), Egg-Free Rice Flour Waffles (page 144), and Egg-Free, Nut/Seed Flour–Based Waffles (page 144). The allergens in these breads and waffles vary.

directions

1. If using waffles, lightly toast the waffles. (Gluten-free waffles tend to absorb a lot of moisture, so pretoasting will help keep them from getting too soggy when dipped in the batter.)

2. In a bowl, mix together the bananas, milk, cinnamon, vanilla, and salt, mashing until the mixture is smooth.

3. Heat the butter in a skillet over medium heat.

4. If using waffles, dunk one side in the banana mixture and place it in the skillet battered side down. (When making French toast with waffles, it's important not to dunk both sides, or it may end up a bit soggy!) If using bread, dunk both sides in the banana mixture before placing in the skillet.

5. When the underside is golden brown, pour some of the banana mixture on the top, unbattered side (if using waffles) and then flip. Cook for another 4 to 5 minutes, until lightly golden on both sides. Repeat with the remaining bread slices or waffles, adding more butter to the pan if needed. Set the cooked French toast aside on a baking sheet in a low oven to keep warm while you cook the remaining French toast.

PREP TIME: 15 minutes
COOK TIME: 3 minutes per batch
YIELD: 10 to 12 pancakes

DAIRY *free,* **EGG** *free,* **NUT** *free,*
GRAIN *free,* **COCONUT** *free*

fluffy blueberry pancakes

These pancakes are the real deal! They are fluffy as can be, and the texture is spot-on—just like the Bisquick pancakes I used to love. Feel free to replace the blueberries with any other fruit, or even chocolate chips!

ingredients

5 large eggs

176 grams milk (dairy or nondairy) (about ¾ cup plus 2 teaspoons)

56 grams mild-flavored oil, melted salted butter, or melted ghee (about ¼ cup), plus more for the pan

78 grams coconut palm sugar or granulated maple sugar (about ½ cup)

84 grams coconut flour (about ½ cup)

88 grams potato, sweet potato, or tapioca starch (about ½ cup) (see Notes)

2 teaspoons lemon juice

⅛ teaspoon kosher salt

1 tablespoon double-acting, aluminum-free baking powder

1 cup (or more) fresh or frozen blueberries

directions

1. Place the eggs, milk, and oil in a blender or food processor and process on high speed until fluffy.

2. Add the rest of the ingredients, except the baking powder and blueberries, and process until smooth. Add the baking powder and process once more.

3. Stir in the blueberries. (Or you can just plop a few into each pancake as you make them.)

4. Lightly oil a nonstick skillet and place it over medium-low heat. Pour in ¼ cup of the batter and gently tap the pan so the batter spreads. Place a lid on top (it makes the pancakes fluffier) and cook for about 2 minutes. Flip and cook for about 1 minute on the second side, keeping the skillet covered the entire time.

5. Re-oil the pan with each new batch. Be careful not to turn the heat up too high, as the bottom will burn before the inside has enough time to cook, which will prevent you from getting a good, clean flip.

notes

These pancakes will turn out better if you use potato or sweet potato starch, but I included tapioca starch as an option for those needing to avoid nightshades. If using tapioca starch and measuring with a cup, use ½ cup plus 3 tablespoons.

pumpkin mug cakes

Mug cakes…all the fun with less mess! These are perfect for crisp fall evenings when you curl up on the couch with a good movie or book. This recipe makes three mini mug cakes that are equally perfect for breakfast. Feel free to stick the extras in the fridge, covered, for a quick meal in the morning. If you warm them up in the microwave the next day, they will be just as delicious.

ingredients

120 grams superfine white rice flour (about ¾ cup)

1 teaspoon double-acting, aluminum-free baking powder

1 teaspoon ground cinnamon

¼ teaspoon ground allspice

¼ teaspoon kosher salt

½ cup canned pumpkin puree

74 grams mild-flavored oil, melted salted butter, or melted ghee (about ¼ cup plus 2 tablespoons)

83 grams milk (dairy or nondairy) (about ¼ cup plus 2 tablespoons)

50 grams coconut palm sugar (about ¼ cup plus 1 tablespoon)

1 teaspoon vanilla extract

3 tablespoons mini chocolate chips

directions

1. In a bowl, whisk the rice flour, baking powder, cinnamon, allspice, and salt until well blended.

2. Add the rest of the ingredients, except the chocolate chips, and stir until well combined. Fold in the chocolate chips.

3. Divide the batter evenly among 3 standard-sized ramekins or mugs. Microwave each mug cake for 3½ to 4½ minutes or until it is firm and springs back to the touch.

PREP TIME: 15 minutes
COOK TIME: 12 to 28 minutes
YIELD: 12 to 14 crepes

DAIRY *free*, EGG *free*, NUT *free*,
GRAIN *free*, COCONUT *free*

basic vanilla crepes

Light, soft, and delicate, yet strong enough to hold up to your favorite stuffed crepe recipe...you will love these grain-free beauties. Fill them with fruit, chocolate, or anything you like.

ingredients

1 tablespoon oil of choice, plus more for the pan if needed

5 large eggs

179 grams milk (dairy or nondairy) (about ¾ cup plus 1 tablespoon)

1 teaspoon coconut oil or other mild-flavored oil

73½ grams coconut flour (about ¼ cup plus 3 tablespoons)

57 grams tapioca starch (about ⅓ cup plus 2 tablespoons)

3 tablespoons raw honey or maple syrup

1 tablespoon vanilla extract

⅛ teaspoon kosher salt

directions

1. Heat the oil in an 8-inch or larger skillet over medium-high heat. Place the remaining ingredients in a blender and blend on high speed for about 1 minute.

2. Pour about ¼ cup of the batter into the hot skillet and rotate the pan in a circular motion to thin out and evenly distribute the batter. Cook until you can flip the crepe without it breaking, about 30 seconds to 1 minute.

3. Flip and cook for an additional 30 seconds to 1 minute. Set aside.

4. Repeat Steps 1 to 3 with the remaining batter. If the crepes begin to stick, add a little more oil to the pan before pouring in the batter.

PREP TIME: 35 minutes
COOK TIME: 12 to 28 minutes
YIELD: 8 servings

DAIRY *free*, EGG *free*, **NUT** *free*,
GRAIN *free*, COCONUT *free*

layered gingerbread crepes
with orange-maple cream cheese filling

This recipe brings me right back to my childhood on Christmas morning, unwrapping gifts and playing with my new toys while my mom was in the kitchen baking and cooking. Make this amazing layered crepe cake for your loved ones for a little holiday cheer any day of the year! To give it an extra touch of elegance for your next brunch, top it with Coconut Whipped Topping (page 318) and Candied Oranges (page 330).

ingredients

Gingerbread crepes:

1 tablespoon coconut oil or other mild-flavored oil, plus more for the pan if needed

5 large eggs

179 grams milk (dairy or nondairy) (about ¾ cup plus 1 tablespoon)

73½ grams coconut flour (about ¼ cup plus 3 tablespoons)

70 grams tapioca starch (about ½ cup plus 1½ teaspoons)

3 tablespoons maple syrup

3 tablespoons molasses

1 tablespoon vanilla extract

¼ teaspoon kosher salt

½ teaspoon ginger powder

½ teaspoon ground cinnamon

½ teaspoon ground nutmeg

Orange-Maple Cream Cheese Filling:

2 (8-ounce) packages cream cheese, room temperature

½ cup plus 2 tablespoons pure maple syrup

1 teaspoon ground cinnamon

¼ teaspoon kosher salt

1 teaspoon orange extract

Toppings (optional):

1 batch Coconut Whipped Topping (page 318)

1 batch Candied Oranges (page 330)

directions

1. Heat the coconut oil in a skillet over medium-high heat. Place all of the crepe ingredients in a blender and blend on high speed for about 1 minute.

2. Pour about ¼ cup of the batter into the hot skillet. Rotate the pan in a circular motion to thin out and evenly distribute the batter. Cook until you can flip the crepe without it breaking, about 30 seconds to 1 minute.

3. Flip and let it cook for an additional 30 seconds to 1 minute. Set aside on a plate.

4. Repeat Steps 1 to 3 with the remaining batter. If the crepes begin to stick, add a little more oil to the pan before pouring the batter. Allow the crepes to cool completely before assembling the layered crepe cake.

5. While the crepes are cooling, make the filling: Place all of the filling ingredients in a bowl and, using a hand-held electric mixer on medium speed, beat until fluffy, 2 to 3 minutes.

6. Assemble the cake: Once the gingerbread crepes have fully cooled, place a crepe on the serving plate or platter. (When assembled, the cake is a bit wobbly due to its height.)

7. Fill a pastry bag or 1-gallon zip-top bag with the filling. If using a zip-top bag, snip off one corner (an ⅛-inch opening is ideal). Gently squeeze the bag and pipe a ring of filling around the outer edge of the first crepe that is about the thickness of the crepe, leaving just a little bit of the edge exposed.

8. Pipe more of the filling inside the ring. This part does not need to be as neat or as thick as the outer ring of filling because it will be covered by the crepe you place on top of it. Just be sure that the outer ring is a bit thicker and uniform because this is the part you will see!

9. Place another crepe on top of the first completed layer. Repeat the process of piping the filling and layering a crepe on top until you have used all of the crepes and filling. Do not pipe filling on top of the final, top crepe.

10. If you wish, top the fully assembled crepe cake with Coconut Whipped Topping, and garnish with as many Candied Oranges as you like!

CHAPTER 7
Burgers and Sandwiches

PREP TIME: 15 to 20 minutes
COOK TIME: 20 to 25 minutes
YIELD: 4 subs

DAIRY *free,* **EGG** *free,* **NUT** *free,*
GRAIN *free,* **COCONUT** *free*

meatball subs

Meatball Subs are the ultimate comfort food—at least that's what my Italian mamma thinks. I created this recipe for her. I kept things simple by calling for store-bought red sauce. Instead of using eggs and breadcrumbs in my meatballs, I threw in some almond flour, which does a beautiful job of adding moisture and binding the meat. Take note that in order to make these subs, you will need to bake a batch of Baguettes (page 48).

ingredients

Meatballs:

1 pound ground beef

1 teaspoon garlic powder

¼ cup blanched almond flour

1 tablespoon dried basil

½ teaspoon kosher salt

½ teaspoon black pepper

1 batch Baguettes (page 48)

1 (24-ounce) jar marinara sauce of choice

2 cups shredded mozzarella cheese (dairy or nondairy)

directions

1. Preheat the oven to 400 degrees.

2. In a bowl, combine the ingredients for the meatballs, mixing by hand. Scoop up 2 tablespoons of the mixture and shape into a meatball. Repeat with the remaining meat mixture.

3. Place the meatballs in a 2½-quart baking dish. Pour the marinara sauce over the meatballs.

4. Bake, uncovered, for 20 to 25 minutes, until the meatballs are cooked all the way through.

5. Assemble the subs: Cut the Baguettes in half crosswise and then in half lengthwise to create 4 sub-style rolls. Place 3 or 4 meatballs on a sub roll, cover with a large spoonful of marinara sauce, and top with a generous sprinkling of cheese. Repeat with the remaining ingredients to make 4 subs.

6. Broil the subs for 2 to 3 minutes to melt the cheese, and enjoy!

notes

If you wish to make this recipe dairy-free, you can use Daiya brand mozzarella cheese. If you choose to use this "cheese," you will need to cover your subs with foil before placing them in the oven. Daiya cheese tends to burn rather than melt under direct heat. The foil will allow the cheese to melt properly.

PREP TIME: 15 to 20 minutes
COOK TIME: 1 hour
YIELD: 4 sandwiches

DAIRY *free*, **EGG** *free*, **NUT** *free*,
GRAIN *free*, **COCONUT** *free*

italian beef combos
with au jus

My husband, Rich, is originally from Chicago, so it's no surprise that Italian beef is one of his favorite things. Whenever we visit his family, a trip to Portillo's is first on the agenda so that he can order combo-style beef sandwiches that also include an Italian sausage link, peppers, and onions. I was lucky enough to experience one before going gluten-free. It's been a longtime goal to re-create the recipe. Now we make these all the time!

ingredients

1 batch Baguettes (page 48)

Au Jus:

1 pound thinly sliced roast beef

1 medium onion, minced

2 cups beef broth

2 cups water

1½ teaspoons garlic powder

1 teaspoon onion powder

½ teaspoon dried ground thyme

Kosher salt and black pepper

1 cup sliced green bell peppers

1 cup sliced onions

Olive oil, for pan-frying

4 mild Italian sausages

directions

1. Cut the Baguettes in half crosswise and then in half lengthwise to create 4 sub-style rolls.

2. Prepare the Au Jus: In a soup pot, stir together the beef, onion, beef broth, water, garlic powder, onion powder, and thyme. Bring to a boil and then reduce the heat to maintain a simmer for about 1 hour while you prepare the other components. Once the meat is fully cooked, give the Au Jus a taste and then season with salt and pepper as needed.

3. In a little olive oil over medium heat, pan-fry the sliced peppers and onions for just a few minutes, until the peppers are browned and the onions are translucent.

4. Remove the peppers and onions from the pan and set aside. Place the sausages in the pan and cook until cooked through.

5. Assemble the sandwiches: Place a sausage in the center of each roll and then top with some beef and a heap of peppers and onions. Then dip the sandwiches into the Au Jus!

ginger-teriyaki bbq burgers
with guac

. . . .

This burger is both a mouthful to describe and to eat. It's totally worth it, though—the layers of flavor will blow you away! As with all of my sandwich recipes, you can mix and match whichever bread you like as the bun base, depending on your intolerances. If you want egg-free buns, I recommend using one of the arepa recipes from Chapter 2.

ingredients

Ginger-Teriyaki BBQ sauce:

1 batch Ginger-Teriyaki Sauce (page 354)

¼ cup barbecue sauce of choice

Guacamole:

¼ cup minced onion

2 avocados, pitted and peeled

¼ teaspoon ground cumin

1 tablespoon lime juice

¼ teaspoon cayenne pepper

2 tablespoons finely chopped fresh cilantro (optional)

Kosher salt and black pepper

Burgers:

¼ cup seeded and minced jalapeño peppers

¼ cup minced onion

1 pound ground beef

1 teaspoon kosher salt

1 teaspoon black pepper

1 teaspoon garlic powder

1 tablespoon coconut oil or other mild-flavored oil

Toppings (optional):

4 to 8 slices bacon

4 pineapple rings

4 slices cheddar cheese (dairy or nondairy; optional)

Lettuce leaves

Onion slices

Buns:

1 batch Hamburger Buns (page 40) or Arepas (page 64), sliced in half

directions

1. Make the sauce: In a bowl, mix together the Ginger-Teriyaki Sauce and the barbecue sauce; set aside.

2. Make the guacamole: In another bowl, combine the onion, avocados, cumin, lime juice, cayenne, and cilantro, if using. With a fork, mash the guacamole to the desired texture, and season to taste with salt and pepper. Place in the refrigerator while you prepare the burgers.

3. Make the burgers: Place the ingredients for the burgers in a large mixing bowl. Using your hands, mix the ingredients together until evenly combined. Shape into 4 equal-sized patties.

4. Heat the coconut oil in a large skillet over high heat.

5. Place the burger patties in the preheated skillet and cook, covered, for 3 to 5 minutes per side for a medium-done burger with a little pink in the center.

6. While the burgers cook, prepare the toppings, if using. Fry the bacon in a skillet over medium heat until crispy. Pan-fry the pineapple rings over medium-high heat until golden brown. Have the cheese, lettuce, and onion slices prepped and at hand.

7. It's time to assemble the burgers! Slather the buns with the sauce and stack the ingredients, topping each burger with a pineapple ring, if using. Serve the extra sauce on the side.

PREP TIME: 15 to 20 minutes
COOK TIME: 6 to 10 minutes
YIELD: 4 burgers

DAIRY *free*, **EGG** *free*, **NUT** *free*,
GRAIN *free*, **COCONUT** *free*

curry chicken burgers
with mango and guac

Tropical and oh so good! If you've never had mango on a burger, especially a delicious curry-flavored one, now is the time to try it. The guac sends the flavor combo over the top! For the buns, you have a choice: You can make either my Hamburger Buns (page 40) or, for an egg-free option, Arepas (page 64).

ingredients

Guacamole:

¼ cup minced onion

2 avocados, pitted and peeled

¼ teaspoon ground cumin

1 tablespoon lime juice

¼ teaspoon cayenne pepper

2 tablespoons finely chopped fresh cilantro (optional)

Kosher salt and black pepper

Burgers:

¼ cup minced jalapeño peppers, seeded if you want less heat (optional)

¼ cup minced onion

1 pound ground chicken

2 teaspoons curry powder

1 teaspoon garlic powder

1 teaspoon kosher salt

1 teaspoon black pepper

1 teaspoon turmeric powder

1 tablespoon coconut oil or other mild-flavored oil

Buns:

1 batch Hamburger Buns (page 40) or 4 Arepas (page 64), sliced in half

Toppings:

1 mango, sliced

Spinach leaves (optional)

½ red onion, sliced (optional)

directions

1. Make the guacamole: In a bowl, combine the onion, avocados, cumin, lime juice, cayenne, and cilantro, if using. With a fork, mash the guacamole to the desired texture, and season to taste with salt and pepper. Place in the refrigerator while you prepare the burgers.

2. Make the burgers: Place the ingredients for the burgers in a large mixing bowl. Using your hands, mix the ingredients together until evenly combined. Shape into 4 equal-sized patties.

3. Heat the coconut oil in a large skillet over medium-high heat.

4. Place the patties in preheated skillet and cook, covered, for 3 to 5 minutes per side, or until cooked through.

5. It's time to assemble the burgers! Don't forget to top them with mango slices and guacamole, along with the spinach leaves and onion slices, if using.

open-faced beef stroganoff mushroom burgers

This sandwich is so intense that you won't be able to pick it up. I say go big or go home! So get out your plate and your fork and get your taste buds ready for a magical journey. If you love beef stroganoff, you will love every layer of this deconstructed version.

ingredients

Shaved beef:

1 pound thinly sliced roast beef

1 medium onion, minced

2 cups beef broth

2 cups water

1½ teaspoons garlic powder

1 teaspoon onion powder

½ teaspoon dried thyme leaves

Kosher salt and black pepper to taste

Portobello "buns":

4 large portobello mushrooms

Olive oil, for drizzling the mushrooms

Kosher salt and black pepper

Stroganoff sauce:

1½ tablespoons salted butter, ghee, or mild-flavored oil

3 tablespoons red wine

¼ cup chicken broth

½ tablespoon plus 1 teaspoon tapioca starch

⅓ cup heavy cream or coconut cream (from a can of coconut milk; see tutorial, page 26)

½ cup plus 3½ tablespoons blanched almond flour

¼ teaspoon grated fresh ginger

¾ teaspoon dried thyme leaves

Kosher salt and black pepper to taste

Caramelized onions:

1 teaspoon coconut oil or other mild-flavored oil

1 small onion, sliced

4 slices Swiss cheese (optional)

directions

1. Preheat the oven to 400 degrees.

2. In a soup pot, combine the ingredients for the beef. Bring to a boil, reduce the heat to maintain a simmer, and cook until the liquid has reduced by half.

3. Prepare the portobellos: Remove the stems and spoon out the gills. Place them on a rimmed baking sheet. Drizzle them with olive oil and sprinkle them with salt and pepper. Bake for 10 minutes. Remove from the pan and let cool.

4. Meanwhile, begin the stroganoff sauce: Place the butter and red wine in a pan over low heat.

5. In a microwave-safe bowl, mix together the chicken broth and tapioca starch. Heat in the microwave for 30 seconds. Pour into the pan with the butter and wine and stir to combine.

6. Add the cream, almond flour, ginger, thyme, and salt and pepper. Simmer over medium heat for 3 to 5 minutes.

7. Make the caramelized onions: Heat the coconut oil in a skillet over medium-low heat. Cook the onion slices until slightly caramelized, about 8 minutes.

8. Assemble the burgers: On top of a portobello mushroom, place a slice of cheese (if using), a small pile of meat, and some of the stroganoff sauce. Top with caramelized onions. Eat with a knife and fork!

notes

If you don't want to make roast beef, you can substitute ground beef or thinly sliced steak and add it directly to the soup pot.

PREP TIME: 15 to 20 minutes
COOK TIME: 10 to 14 minutes
YIELD: 4 sandwiches

DAIRY *free*, **EGG** *free*, **NUT** *free*,
GRAIN *free*, **COCONUT** *free*

po-boys

These Po-Boys are ever so slightly spicy. For the bread, you can use either my Baguettes (page 48) or, for an egg-free option, my Arepas (page 64). To add an extra layer of deliciousness, I top my Po-Boys with Homemade Remoulade (page 352).

ingredients

1 batch Baguettes (page 48) or 4 Arepas (page 64)

Wet coating for the shrimp:

1 large egg

½ tablespoon water

Breading for the shrimp:

¼ cup blanched almond flour

¼ cup tapioca starch

1 teaspoon black pepper

½ teaspoon kosher salt

⅛ teaspoon cayenne pepper

¼ teaspoon paprika

⅛ teaspoon garlic powder

⅛ teaspoon onion powder

½ pound medium-sized shrimp, peeled and deveined

Melted coconut oil or other mild-flavored oil, for drizzling the shrimp

Toppings:

1 batch Homemade Remoulade (page 352)

Lettuce leaves

Tomato slices

directions

1. If using Baguettes, cut them in half crosswise and then in half lengthwise to create 4 sub-style rolls. If using Arepas, slice them in half.

2. Preheat the oven to 350 degrees.

3. In a bowl, combine the egg and water for the wet coating; set aside.

4. In a separate bowl, combine the breading ingredients.

5. Drop the shrimp into the wet coating and then heavily dredge in the breading mixture. You may need to drop the shrimp into the dry ingredients a second time to get a good coating.

6. Place the breaded shrimp on a rimmed baking sheet and drizzle with melted coconut oil.

7. Bake for 5 to 7 minutes, flip the shrimp over, and then cook for another 5 to 7 minutes, until lightly golden.

8. Assemble the sandwiches: Spread the Homemade Remoulade on the bread, and then add the cooked shrimp, lettuce leaves, and tomato slices.

PREP TIME: 20 to 25 minutes
COOK TIME: 37 to 43 minutes
YIELD: 5 sandwiches

DAIRY *free*, EGG *free*, NUT *free*,
GRAIN *free*, COCONUT *free*

chicken nugget–stuffed grilled cheese

As a kid, I used to live for chicken nugget day at school. I don't think I ever really grew out of that love! These nuggets have just a little spice and a serious crunch. What could be better than sticking them in a grilled cheese sandwich? For a more adult sandwich, try pairing this with my Ginger-Teriyaki BBQ Sauce (page 170). You should also try it with Bacon Jam (page 348)!

ingredients

Wet coating for the chicken:

½ cup plus 1 tablespoon milk (dairy or nondairy)

1 tablespoon lemon juice

5 tablespoons salted butter, ghee, or mild-flavored oil

1 tablespoon tapioca starch

Breading for the chicken:

⅓ cup blanched almond flour

⅓ cup superfine white rice flour

¼ cup tapioca starch

1 teaspoon black pepper

½ teaspoon kosher salt

¼ teaspoon cayenne pepper

½ teaspoon garlic powder

4 boneless, skinless chicken thighs (about 1 pound), cut into bite-sized pieces

Melted coconut oil or other mild-flavored oil, for drizzling the chicken

1 batch Basic Sandwich Bread (page 32), Yeast-Free Basic Sandwich Bread (page 34), Egg-Free Rice Flour Bread (page 38), or English Muffins (page 80), or 5 Arepas (page 64)

Butter, for the bread

10 to 15 slices cheddar cheese (dairy or nondairy)

directions

1. Preheat the oven to 400 degrees. Line a rimmed baking sheet with foil.

2. Make the wet coating: In a small bowl, combine the milk and lemon juice. Let sit for about 5 minutes to "sour."

3. Melt the butter in a saucepan over low heat. Add the tapioca starch and stir to combine. Pour in the soured milk and whisk continually until it thickens, 2 to 3 minutes. Remove the pan from the heat and let cool slightly.

4. In another bowl, mix together the ingredients for the breading.

5. Drop the chicken pieces one at a time into the wet coating and then heavily dredge in the breading mixture. Place the breaded chicken pieces on the prepared baking sheet and drizzle with melted coconut oil.

6. Bake for 35 to 40 minutes, until the chicken is opaque when cut into and there is no pinkness left in the meat.

7. Assemble the sandwiches: Cut the sandwich bread into 10 slices, or split the English Muffins or Arepas in half. Butter the outsides of the bread and fill each sandwich with 2 or 3 slices of cheese and 4 or 5 chicken nuggets.

8. Close the sandwiches and either grill using a panini press or toast in a skillet over medium heat, covered, until the cheese melts and the bread is golden.

PREP TIME: 20 minutes
COOK TIME: 24 minutes
YIELD: 2 sandwiches

DAIRY *free*, EGG *free*, NUT *free*,
GRAIN *free*, COCONUT *free*

"fried" fish sandwiches

Love fish Fridays? Now you can enjoy them again in sandwich form with a delicious, crispy fish that isn't actually fried (though you could never tell from taking a bite!).

ingredients

Wet coating for the fish:

1 tablespoon tapioca, arrowroot, or potato starch

½ cup plus 2½ tablespoons milk (dairy or nondairy)

5 tablespoons salted butter, ghee, or mild-flavored oil

Breading for the fish:

¼ cup tapioca, arrowroot, or potato starch

¼ cup blanched almond flour

½ teaspoon black pepper

¼ teaspoon kosher salt

⅛ teaspoon paprika

⅛ teaspoon cayenne pepper

¼ teaspoon garlic powder

1 (1-pound) haddock fillet

Melted coconut oil or other mild-flavored oil, for drizzling the fish

2 Hamburger Buns (page 40) or
1 Baguette (page 48)

1 batch Tartar Sauce (page 342)

Toppings (optional):

Lettuce leaves

Tomato slices

Onion slices

directions

1. Preheat the oven to 425 degrees. Line a rimmed baking sheet with foil.

2. Make the wet coating: In a bowl, combine the starch and milk and mix until no clumps remain.

3. Melt the butter in a saucepan over low heat. Add the starch-milk mixture and whisk continuously until it thickens into a slurry thick enough to cling to the fish. Pour into a pie pan or shallow dish.

4. While the coating mixture cools slightly, combine the ingredients for the breading in another bowl.

5. Cut the haddock fillet in half to yield 2 sandwich-sized pieces. Place each piece in the wet mixture and then heavily dredge in the breading mixture. Remove from the breading, place in the wet mixture again, and then again in the breading, coating each piece twice.

6. Place the breaded fish pieces on the prepared baking sheet and drizzle with melted coconut oil.

7. Bake for 20 minutes, until lightly golden and crispy and cooked through. For a little extra color and crunch, turn on the broiler to high and broil for 3 to 4 minutes or until golden brown.

8. Assemble the sandwiches: Cut 2 Hamburger Buns in half or 1 Baguette in half crosswise and then lengthwise. Spread on as much Tartar Sauce as you'd like. Add the fish and your favorite toppings and enjoy!

notes

For an egg-free option, these sandwiches can be made with the Arepas on page 64.

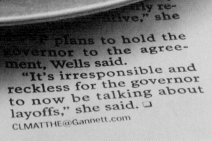

donut sandwiches
with roasted pear, brie, and balsamic

Pears, Brie cheese, and balsamic vinegar are a lethally delicious combo! Place on top of a hot homemade fried Donut (page 90), and you can't go wrong. This recipe is for the dairy-eating crowd.

ingredients

4 pears, quartered and cored

1 teaspoon lemon juice

¼ cup coconut palm sugar

1 tablespoon melted salted butter, melted ghee, or mild-flavored oil

4 Donuts (page 90), sliced in half

8 thick slices cow's or goat's milk Brie

Balsamic vinegar, for drizzling

directions

1. Preheat the oven to 375 degrees.

2. In a bowl, toss the pears with the lemon juice to prevent them from browning.

3. Place the pears on a rimmed baking sheet and sprinkle them with the sugar and melted butter.

4. Roast the pears for 30 minutes.

5. Assemble the sandwiches: Divide the roasted pears among the 4 Donuts and top with 2 Brie slices and a drizzle of balsamic vinegar.

PREP TIME: 10 minutes
COOK TIME: n/a
YIELD: 3 sandwiches

DAIRY *free*, EGG *free*, NUT *free*,
GRAIN *free*, COCONUT *free*

reina pepiada arepas

Ever eaten food from an arepa food truck? You'll get addicted quickly if you do. This version, filled with Cilantro-Avocado Mousse, shredded chicken, and chives, is one of the most popular items on the menu of our local food truck. Give this sandwich a go!

ingredients

1 batch Cilantro-Avocado Mousse (page 350; see Notes)

3 cups shredded cooked chicken

¼ cup chopped fresh chives or scallions

3 Arepas, sliced in half (page 64; see Notes)

directions

1. In a bowl, mix the mousse with the shredded chicken and chives until the chicken is evenly coated with the mousse.

2. Spread the filling evenly between the sliced Arepas and enjoy!

notes

When making the Cilantro-Avocado Mouse, increase the amount of lemon juice to 1 tablespoon and the amount of jalapeño pepper to 1 whole pepper.

If you prepare the Arepas the day before, you will need to heat them up slightly before assembling the sandwiches.

PREP TIME: 10 to 15 minutes
COOK TIME: n/a
YIELD: 3 sandwiches

DAIRY *free*, **EGG** *free*, **NUT** *free*, **GRAIN** *free*, **COCONUT** *free*

arepas with fried egg, feta, and hot sauce

While these arepas would be appropriate for dinner and are great at any time of the day, my husband and I love throwing them together for breakfast. You can't go wrong with a fried egg and feta cheese in the same bun!

ingredients

3 Arepas (page 64)

Salted butter or ghee, for the bread

1 teaspoon coconut oil, salted butter, or ghee, for the eggs

3 large eggs

¼ cup crumbled feta cheese or 3 slices cheese of choice (dairy or nondairy)

Sriracha Mayo (page 341) or hot sauce of choice, to taste

directions

1. Cut the Arepas in half, butter them, and toast them facedown in a skillet over medium-high heat.

2. In another skillet over medium heat, place the coconut oil. Cook the eggs sunny side up to your liking.

3. Place an egg on each halved Arepa and top with the cheese and Sriracha Mayo.

PREP TIME: 15 to 20 minutes
COOK TIME: 10 to 15 minutes
YIELD: 2 sandwiches

DAIRY *free,* **EGG** *free,* **NUT** *free,*
GRAIN *free,* **COCONUT** *free*

jibarito sandwiches

This sandwich, also known as a "jib," is a great option for those who are scared of baking bread. A fried plantain plays the role of bread in this delicious steak sandwich.

ingredients

Oil of choice, for frying

1 large green plantain, peeled and cut in half lengthwise

Pinch of cayenne pepper

Pinch of chili powder

Pinch of kosher salt

Pinch of black pepper

1 strip steak

Toppings (optional):

¼ onion, cut into rings

Lettuce leaves

2 tomato slices

2 slices cheese of choice (dairy or nondairy)

¼ cup Classic Mayo (page 340), Egg-Free Mayo (page 340), or Sriracha Mayo (page 341)

directions

1. Heat a thin layer of oil in a large skillet over medium heat.

2. Cook the plantain halves in the hot oil for 2 to 3 minutes (no need to flip them at this stage).

3. Remove the plantains from the skillet and place them between 2 cutting boards. Press to flatten.

4. Return the plantains to the skillet and cook for an additional 2 to 3 minutes per side, getting some color on both sides.

5. Remove the plantains from the heat and place on paper towels to drain. Return the skillet to medium heat.

6. In a small bowl, whisk together the cayenne, chili powder, salt, and pepper. Season both sides of the steak with the spice mixture.

7. Place the steak in the skillet and cook for 2 to 3 minutes per side or until done to your liking.

8. Remove the steak from the pan and let it cool while you cook the onion, if using. Heat 2 teaspoons of oil in the same skillet over medium-high heat. Add the onion rings and cook for 3 to 4 minutes, until softened.

9. Cut the plantain pieces in half crosswise, and slice the steak crosswise into strips.

10. Top a plantain piece with half of the steak, onion rings, lettuce, tomato slices, cheese, and mayo, if using. Top with another plantain piece to close. Repeat with the remaining plantain pieces and filling ingredients.

DAIRY *free*, **EGG** *free*, **NUT** *free*,
GRAIN *free*, **COCONUT** *free*

thanksgiving leftovers sandwiches

Every year I get so excited to make this sandwich. This year, however, is the first time I'll have the opportunity to stack my fillings tall and call it Paleo!

ingredients

1 tablespoon oil of choice, for cooking raw turkey (if needed)

1 pound raw turkey cutlet or breast or sliced cooked turkey

2 cups Sage Sausage Stuffing (page 264)

1 batch Sawmill Gravy (page 104)

1 batch Cranberry Sauce (page 356)

8 slices sandwich bread of choice (see Notes)

directions

1. If using raw turkey, heat the oil in a skillet over medium heat. Add the turkey and cook, covered, for a few minutes on each side or until the meat is cooked through and no longer pink in the center. The exact timing will depend on the thickness of the turkey. Once cooked, let it rest for a few minutes and then slice thinly.

2. To assemble the sandwiches, divide the turkey, stuffing, gravy, and Cranberry Sauce equally among the bread slices to make 4 sandwiches.

notes

Try any of the following breads for these sandwiches: Basic Sandwich Bread (page 32), Yeast-Free Basic Sandwich Bread (page 34), Low-Carb Honey "Wheat" Bread (page 36), or Egg-Free Rice Flour Bread (page 38).

CHAPTER 8
Crackers and Snacks

PREP TIME: 10 to 15 minutes
COOK TIME: 13 minutes
YIELD: 2 trays

DAIRY *free*, **EGG** *free*, **NUT** *free*,
GRAIN *free*, **COCONUT** *free*

lime tortilla chips

Super-simple and so delicious! Throw these chips together quickly and dip them in your favorite salsa. This recipe is dedicated to my sweet friend Hayley Mason Staley from PrimalPalate.com, who gave me the idea to make it.

ingredients

Chips:

264 grams blanched almond flour (about 1¾ cups plus 1 tablespoon)

2 large egg whites

1 teaspoon kosher salt

Grated zest of 4 limes

Lime salt (optional):

Grated zest of 1 lime

¾ teaspoon kosher salt

Oil of choice, for brushing the dough

directions

1. Preheat the oven to 325 degrees. Line 2 baking sheets with parchment paper.

2. In the bowl of a stand mixer, using the whisk attachment, mix the ingredients for the chips.

3. Remove the bowl from the stand mixer and, using your hands, mix the dough further until it holds together. (This extra step is necessary with doughs made from almond flour.)

4. Divide the dough in half. Roll out one half of the dough between 2 sheets of parchment paper as thinly as possible. Carefully remove the top layer of parchment.

5. Cut the dough into triangles and place them on a prepared baking sheet.

6. Repeat the process with the second half of the dough and the other baking sheet.

7. If using the lime salt, mix together the lime zest and salt in a small bowl. Brush the dough triangles with oil and sprinkle with the lime salt.

8. Bake the chips for 13 minutes, until firm to the touch. Let them cool on the baking sheets. Store the cooled chips in a sealed bag or container at room temperature.

PREP TIME: 10 to 15 minutes
COOK TIME: 50 minutes
YIELD: 32 to 40 bagel chips

DAIRY *free*, **EGG** *free*, **NUT** *free*, **GRAIN** *free*, **COCONUT** *free*

bagel chips

Remember bagel chips from the store? Holy cow, did I love those things. Now I make my own all the time! They are a blast to throw together because you can sprinkle on just about any spice blend you want. I typically use garlic powder and sea salt, but if you want sweet chips, try sprinkling on some cinnamon and coconut palm sugar.

ingredients

1 batch Yeast-Free Mini Bagels (page 84)

Oil of choice, melted salted butter, or melted ghee, for brushing the chips

Coarse sea salt, for sprinkling the chips

Garlic powder and/or other spice(s) of choice, for sprinkling the chips

directions

1. Preheat the oven to 250 degrees. Line a baking sheet with parchment paper.

2. Cut the bagels into ⅛- to ¼-inch-thick rounds. (The thinner you slice them, the crispier they will get!)

3. Place them on the prepared baking sheet and brush the rounds liberally with oil on both sides.

4. Sprinkle on the salt and garlic powder.

5. Bake for 50 minutes, until crisp and lightly golden brown. Let the chips cool on the baking sheet. Store the cooled chips in a sealed bag or container at room temperature.

notes

I like using Yeast-Free Mini Bagels to make these chips, but feel free to use any of the other bagel recipes in this book instead. Even the Cinnamon Raisin Bagels (page 86) would taste great toasted with some butter!

PREP TIME: 20 minutes
COOK TIME: 20 to 25 minutes
YIELD: 1 tray

DAIRY *free*, EGG *free*, NUT *free*, GRAIN *free*, COCONUT *free*

fish-shaped crackers

Kids (and adults, too) shouldn't have to miss out on beloved fish-shaped crackers due to food allergies! I created this recipe to be as simple as possible—no eggs needed. If you need to avoid dairy as well, I suggest using Daiya nondairy "cheese" shreds, which are made from tapioca. I found my fish-shaped cookie cutter on Amazon.com, but if you can't track one down, just about any small cookie cutter will do.

ingredients

137 grams blanched almond flour (about ¾ cup plus 3 tablespoons)

71 grams tapioca starch (about ½ cup plus 1½ teaspoons)

1 teaspoon double-acting, aluminum-free baking powder

½ teaspoon kosher salt

¼ teaspoon garlic powder

⅛ teaspoon cayenne pepper

2 cups shredded sharp cheddar cheese (dairy or nondairy)

3 tablespoons hot water

notes

This dough tends to get crumbly and will break easily if it sits too long, so it's important to use it right away.

I used Makin's USA Clay Cutters to make my fish crackers!

directions

1. Preheat the oven to 315 degrees. Line a baking sheet with parchment paper.

2. Place the almond flour, tapioca starch, baking powder, salt, garlic powder, and cayenne in a food processor and pulse to blend. Add the cheese and hot water and process until combined into a dough that sticks together.

3. Roll out the dough between 2 sheets of parchment paper into a rectangle about 12 by 17 inches.

4. Using a fish-shaped or other small cookie cutter, cut fish shapes out of the dough.

5. Carefully place the fish cutouts on the prepared baking sheet. Gather up the leftover dough, roll it out, and cut out more fish shapes. (Do this no more than twice; otherwise, the dough will begin to get too greasy and will not stick together.)

6. Bake for 20 to 25 minutes. The exact time will vary based on how thin you rolled out the dough. You will know that they're done when they are firm and crisp. (Break off a piece and take a bite—they should be crunchy all the way through.)

7. Let the crackers cool on the baking sheet. Store the cooled crackers in a sealed bag or container at room temperature, or freeze for another day.

PREP TIME: 15 to 20 minutes
COOK TIME: 15 to 25 minutes
YIELD: 2 trays

DAIRY *free*, **EGG** *free*, NUT *free*,
GRAIN *free*, **COCONUT** *free*

cheese crackers

I've gotten a ton of requests for a mock Cheez-Its recipe over the years, so I knew I would have to include it in this book. I like to roll these out to about ¼ inch thick so that they resemble the real thing. They have an incredible cheesy taste and can be made dairy-free using Daiya shreds.

ingredients

137 grams blanched almond flour (about ¾ cup plus 3 tablespoons)

71 grams tapioca starch (about ½ cup plus 1½ teaspoons)

1 teaspoon double-acting, aluminum-free baking powder

½ teaspoon kosher salt

1½ cups shredded sharp cheddar cheese (dairy or nondairy)

3 tablespoons hot water

directions

1. Preheat the oven to 315 degrees. Have on hand 2 baking sheets.

2. Using a food processor, pulse the almond flour, tapioca starch, baking powder, and salt until blended. Add the cheese and hot water and process until the ingredients come together as a dough. (Almond flour slowly releases its fat and moisture as you mix it, so it may take longer than you would expect for the dough to come together.)

3. Divide the dough in half. Roll out one half of the dough between 2 sheets of parchment paper into a rectangle about 12 by 17 inches.

4. Using a pizza cutter or knife, cut the dough into ½-inch squares and pierce each square with a fork. (Do not separate the squares.)

5. Slide the piece of parchment paper with the dough squares onto a baking sheet.

6. Repeat this process with the second half of the dough.

7. Bake for 15 to 25 minutes. The exact time will depend on how thin you rolled out the dough. You will know that the crackers are done when they are firm and crisp. (Break off a piece and take a bite—they should be crunchy all the way through.)

8. Break along the seam lines that you cut and let the crackers cool on the baking sheet. Store the cooled crackers in a sealed bag or container at room temperature, or freeze for another day.

PREP TIME: 15 to 20 minutes
COOK TIME: 25 to 27 minutes
YIELD: 1 tray

DAIRY *free*, **EGG** *free*, **NUT** *free*,
GRAIN *free*, **COCONUT** *free*

oyster crackers

These Oyster Crackers are a cinch to make and are great to use in salads or soups. I didn't have the proper tool to cut out the traditional shape, so I improvised and used an apple corer. It worked like a charm!

ingredients

91 grams blanched almond flour (about a scant ⅔ cup)

142 grams tapioca starch (about 1 cup plus 1 tablespoon)

1 tablespoon xanthan gum or guar gum

1 teaspoon double-acting, aluminum-free baking powder

¾ teaspoon kosher salt

1 large egg

3 tablespoons water

82 grams Spectrum vegetable shortening (about ½ cup plus ½ tablespoon)

Fine sea salt, for sprinkling the crackers (optional)

directions

1. Preheat the oven to 315 degrees. Line a baking sheet with parchment paper.

2. In the bowl of stand mixer, using the whisk attachment, mix the almond flour, tapioca starch, xanthan gum, baking powder, and salt until blended. Add the egg, water, and shortening and continue mixing on medium-high speed until a dough forms.

3. Roll out the dough between 2 sheets of parchment paper to ¼ inch thick. Carefully remove the top sheet of parchment.

4. Use an apple corer to cut out small circles of dough. Place the dough circles on the prepared baking sheet.

5. If you like your crackers salty, sprinkle the circles with salt.

6. Bake for 25 to 27 minutes, until the bottoms are lightly golden and the edges are ever so slightly brown.

7. Let the crackers cool on the baking sheet. Store the cooled crackers in a sealed bag or container at room temperature, or freeze for another day.

PREP TIME: 15 to 20 minutes
COOK TIME: 20 to 25 minutes
YIELD: 1 tray

DAIRY *free*, **EGG** *free*, **NUT** *free*,
GRAIN *free*, **COCONUT** *free*

no-wheat crackers

I often ask my husband to blind-taste-test things and guess what I made. A silly game for sure, but it really helps me know if I got the results I wanted. After biting into one of these crackers, he knew right away that it was my version of Wheat Thins! The mixture of shortening and oil allows them to be a bit flaky and crispy at the same time.

ingredients

137 grams blanched almond flour (about ¾ cup plus 3 tablespoons)

91 grams tapioca starch (about ½ cup plus 3 tablespoons)

1 teaspoon double-acting, aluminum-free baking powder

1 tablespoon xanthan gum or guar gum

¾ teaspoon kosher salt

1 large egg

2 tablespoons oil of choice

2 tablespoons water

1 tablespoon Spectrum vegetable shortening

directions

1. Preheat the oven to 315 degrees. Line a baking sheet with parchment paper.

2. In the bowl of a stand mixer, using the whisk attachment, mix the almond flour, tapioca starch, baking powder, xanthan gum, and salt until blended. Add the egg, oil, water, and shortening and continue mixing on medium-high speed until a dough forms.

3. Roll out the dough between 2 sheets of parchment paper until it is paper-thin. Carefully take off the top sheet of parchment.

4. Cut the dough into 1-inch squares using a pizza cutter. Separate the squares and place them on the prepared baking sheet.

5. Bake for 20 to 25 minutes, until the bottoms are lightly golden and the edges are ever so slightly brown.

6. Store the cooled crackers in a sealed bag or container at room temperature, or freeze for another day.

notes

Feel free to experiment and add dried seasonings to the dough to make various flavors.

PREP TIME: 15 to 20 minutes
COOK TIME: 12 to 13 minutes
YIELD: 1 tray

DAIRY *free*, EGG *free*, NUT *free*, GRAIN *free*, COCONUT *free*

black pepper bacon biscuit-crackers

When I began making these crackers, I intended them to be just that: crackers. However, when the first batch came out of the oven, they tasted like a cross between biscuits and crackers. They tasted so delicious that I knew I couldn't change the recipe. Here I've included a version with eggs and a version without. The egg-free variation is a bit on the crumbly side, but still delicious!

ingredients

142 grams tapioca starch (about 1 cup plus 1 tablespoon)

91 grams blanched almond flour (about a scant ⅔ cup), plus more for rolling the dough

1 teaspoon black pepper

1 teaspoon garlic powder

½ teaspoon double-acting, aluminum-free baking powder

½ teaspoon kosher salt

⅛ teaspoon xanthan gum or guar gum

1 large egg

80 grams bacon fat (about ⅓ cup plus 2 tablespoons)

directions

1. Preheat the oven to 350 degrees. Line a baking sheet with parchment paper.

2. In the bowl of a stand mixer, using the whisk attachment, mix the tapioca starch, almond flour, pepper, garlic powder, baking powder, salt, and xanthan gum until blended. Add the egg and bacon fat and mix on medium-high speed until a dough forms.

3. Place the dough on a sheet of parchment paper and sprinkle with tapioca starch. Roll out the dough to ¼ inch thick.

4. Using the cookie cutter of your choice, cut the dough into shapes and place them ¼ inch apart on the prepared baking sheet.

5. Bake for 12 to 13 minutes, until the bottoms are lightly golden and the edges are ever so slightly brown.

6. Let the biscuit-crackers cool on the baking sheet, as they may be crumbly until cool. Store the cooled biscuit-crackers in a sealed bag or container at room temperature, or freeze for another day.

variation:

Egg-Free Black Pepper Bacon Biscuit-Crackers

Follow the recipe as written, but omit the egg and add 3 tablespoons water. Bake for 13 to 14 minutes.

PREP TIME: 15 to 20 minutes
COOK TIME: 25 minutes
YIELD: 1 tray

DAIRY *free*, **EGG** *free*, **NUT** *free*,
GRAIN *free*, **COCONUT** *free*

rosemary crackers

Rosemary is one of those beautiful, woodsy herbs that I love to use in my cooking because it fills the kitchen with its wonderful aroma. To get lovely fluted edges on your crackers, use a fluted wheel pastry cutter to cut the dough.

ingredients

119 grams blanched almond flour (about ¾ cup plus 1 tablespoon)

106 grams tapioca starch (about ¾ cup plus 2 teaspoons)

1 teaspoon double-acting, aluminum-free baking powder

½ teaspoon kosher salt

2 teaspoons dried rosemary leaves

3 tablespoons oil of choice

3 tablespoons very hot water

notes

If you would like light, airy crackers, replace the oil with ¼ cup shortening.

directions

1. Preheat the oven to 315 degrees.

2. In a bowl, whisk the almond flour, tapioca starch, baking powder, and salt until blended. Add the rosemary, oil, and hot water and mix with a wooden spoon until a dough forms. (Anytime you use almond flour, you may need to mix the dough a little longer for it to become wet. Almond flour slowly releases its fat and moisture as you mix it, so it may take longer than you would expect for the dough to come together. If, after a few minutes of mixing, you can't get the dough to come together, you can add an additional tablespoon or so of water, but if you use the gram weights, that shouldn't be necessary.)

3. Divide the dough in half. Roll out one half of the dough between 2 sheets of parchment paper into a rectangle about 12 by 17 inches.

4. Using a pizza cutter or knife, cut squares in the dough and pierce each square with a fork. (Do not separate the squares.) Slide the piece of parchment with the dough squares onto a baking sheet.

5. Bake for 25 minutes. You will know that the crackers are done when they are firm and crisp. (Break off a piece and take a bite—they should be crunchy all the way through.)

6. Break into crackers along the seam lines that you created and let the crackers cool on the baking sheet. Store the cooled crackers in a sealed bag or container at room temperature, or freeze for another day.

PREP TIME: 15 to 20 minutes
COOK TIME: 30 minutes
YIELD: 3 cups

DAIRY free, **EGG** free, **NUT** free, **GRAIN** free, **COCONUT** free

croutons

I have tried using all of my sandwich breads as the base for these Croutons, first letting them get stale and then beginning the fun. I like to make them pretty basic and throw them into salads or use them in stuffing, but you should feel free to have fun and experiment with different spice combinations! This recipe works with just about any of the bread recipes in this book. Even the Arepas (page 64), bagels (pages 82–87), and Extra-Crispy Paleo Waffles (page 144) can be made into Croutons.

ingredients

1 loaf stale sandwich bread of choice (see Notes)

½ cup olive oil

1 teaspoon kosher salt

1 teaspoon black pepper

notes

If you don't have a loaf of stale bread on hand, make a loaf (find recipes in Chapter 1) a day before you plan to make the Croutons and let it sit out overnight to harden.

For flavored Croutons, try adding 1 teaspoon garlic powder and 1 teaspoon dried parsley.

To make breadcrumbs, simply throw some Croutons into a food processor and process until you have crumbs.

directions

1. Preheat the oven to 325 degrees.

2. Cut the bread into cubes and place in a single layer on a rimmed baking sheet.

3. Drizzle with the olive oil and toss to coat evenly. Sprinkle with the salt and pepper and toss again.

4. Bake for 30 minutes, until lightly golden and completely dried out.

5. Let the Croutons cool on the baking sheet. Store the cooled Croutons in a sealed bag or container at room temperature, or freeze for another day.

PREP TIME: 15 to 20 minutes
COOK TIME: 10 to 12 minutes
YIELD: 1 tray

DAIRY *free,* **EGG** *free,* **NUT** *free,*
GRAIN *free,* **COCONUT** *free*

circus animal crackers

Three trial batches and these circus critters were created. I wanted a cracker with nice crunch, so I played around with the amounts of almond flour and sugar until I got the perfect texture and taste.

ingredients

Crackers:

144 grams blanched almond flour (about 1 cup)

146 grams tapioca starch (about 1 cup plus 1 tablespoon), plus more for rolling the dough

1 teaspoon double-acting, aluminum-free baking powder

¼ teaspoon kosher salt

⅛ teaspoon xanthan gum or guar gum

77 grams powdered coconut palm sugar or maple sugar (about ½ cup) (see tutorial, page 26)

1 large egg

60 grams Spectrum vegetable shortening (about ¼ cup plus 1 tablespoon)

1 tablespoon vanilla extract

White chocolate frosting (optional):

1 cup store-bought white chocolate chips, melted, or homemade Dairy-Free White Chocolate (page 336)

1 to 3 tablespoons Spectrum vegetable shortening

Natural pink or red food coloring, or ¼ cup powdered freeze-dried strawberries (see Notes)

Gluten-free sprinkles

directions

1. Preheat the oven to 350 degrees. Line a baking sheet with parchment paper.

2. In the bowl of a stand mixer, using the whisk attachment, mix the almond flour, tapioca starch, baking powder, salt, xanthan gum, and powdered sugar until blended.

3. Add the egg, shortening, and vanilla and mix until a dense yet soft and pliable dough forms.

4. Place the dough on a sheet of parchment paper and sprinkle with tapioca starch. Roll out the dough to ¼ inch thick.

5. Using the animal-shaped cookie cutter(s) of your choice, cut the dough into shapes. Place the dough shapes on the prepared baking sheet.

6. Bake for 10 to 12 minutes, until the bottoms are lightly golden and the edges are ever so slightly brown. Remove from the oven and transfer to a cooling rack.

7. While the crackers are cooling, make the frosting, if using: Place the white chocolate in a bowl. If using melted, store-bought white chocolate chips, add 3 tablespoons shortening and whip with a hand-held electric mixer until fluffy. If using homemade Dairy-Free White Chocolate, add 1 tablespoon shortening and whip until fluffy.

8. Transfer half of the frosting to another bowl and color it with red food coloring or powdered freeze-dried strawberries.

9. Once the crackers have cooled, dip half of them in the pink frosting and half of them in the white frosting. Top all of them with sprinkles! Store at room temperature in a sealed bag or container, or freeze for later use.

notes

To make powdered freeze-dried strawberries, place the freeze-dried strawberries in a coffee grinder or spice grinder and process until powdery. Mixing this powder into the frosting adds great natural color and flavor!

PREP TIME: 15 to 20 minutes
COOK TIME: 9 to 10 minutes
YIELD: 1 tray

DAIRY *free,* **EGG** *free,* **NUT** *free,*
GRAIN *free,* **COCONUT** *free*

chocolate animal grahams

These little crackers are so yummy and fun to make with kids. You can order a mini teddy bear cookie cutter to mimic the ones from the store, or just use some cute little animal-shaped cutters like I did!

ingredients

1 large egg

77 grams powdered coconut palm sugar or maple sugar (about ½ cup) (see tutorial, page 26)

60 grams Spectrum vegetable shortening (about ¼ cup plus 1 tablespoon)

2 tablespoons raw honey

1 tablespoon vanilla extract

144 grams blanched almond flour (about 1 cup)

146 grams tapioca starch (about 1 cup plus 1 tablespoon), plus more for rolling the dough

50 grams cocoa powder (about ½ cup)

1 teaspoon double-acting, aluminum-free baking powder

¼ teaspoon kosher salt

⅛ teaspoon xanthan gum or guar gum

directions

1. Preheat the oven to 350 degrees. Line a baking sheet with parchment paper.

2. In the bowl of a stand mixer, using the whisk attachment, mix the egg, powdered sugar, shortening, honey, and vanilla on medium speed until well combined.

3. In a separate bowl, whisk the dry ingredients until blended. With the mixer running on low speed, gradually add the dry ingredients to the wet ingredients. Once all the dry ingredients have been added, increase the speed to medium-high and continue mixing until the dough holds together (see Notes).

4. Lay a sheet of parchment paper on your work surface and sprinkle it with tapioca starch. Place the dough on the dusted parchment and roll it out to ¼ inch thick.

5. Using your cookie cutter of choice, cut the dough into shapes. Place the dough shapes on the prepared baking sheet.

6. Bake for 9 to 10 minutes, until the bottoms are lightly golden and the edges are ever so slightly brown.

7. Let cool on the baking sheet. Store the cooled crackers in a sealed bag or container at room temperature, or freeze for later use.

notes

Anytime you use almond flour, you may need to mix the dough a little longer for it to become fully combined. Almond flour slowly releases its fat and moisture as you mix it, so it may take longer than you would expect for the dough to come together.

PREP TIME: 15 to 20 minutes
COOK TIME: 26 to 34 minutes
YIELD: 2 trays

DAIRY *free*, **EGG** *free*, NUT *free*,
GRAIN *free*, COCONUT *free*

graham crackers

This recipe combines almond flour and chestnut flour to make an egg-free cracker that tastes spot-on to the ones from the store. These crackers hold up beautifully in s'mores and are awesome as the base for piecrust. Or do what I do and eat them all within an hour of making them!

ingredients

173 grams blanched almond flour (about ¾ cup plus 3 tablespoons)

136 grams chestnut flour (about ¾ cup plus 1½ tablespoons)

117 grams coconut palm sugar (about ¾ cup)

2½ teaspoons double-acting, aluminum-free baking powder

2 teaspoons ground cinnamon

¼ teaspoon kosher salt

½ teaspoon ginger powder

74 grams applesauce (about ¼ cup plus 1 tablespoon)

directions

1. Preheat the oven to 315 degrees. Have on hand 2 baking sheets.

2. In a bowl, whisk the dry ingredients until well blended. Add the applesauce and, using your hands, mix until you have a thick dough that holds together. Knead for a few minutes until it is smooth. (This step can also be done in a food processor. If using a food processor, dump the dough onto a clean surface before kneading.)

3. Lay a sheet of parchment paper on your work surface. Divide the dough in half and place one half on the parchment. Roll out the dough to a large rectangle no thicker than ⅛ inch.

4. Using a knife or pizza cutter, cut the dough into squares. Gently separate the pieces so that all of the edges are exposed. Score a line down the middle of each square (but do not cut through!). Using a fork, prick a few holes into each square. Carefully slide the sheet of parchment with the squares onto a baking sheet.

5. Bake for 13 to 17 minutes, until crispy and lightly browned. Keep an eye on them toward the end of the baking time to make sure that the edges don't burn. Remove from the oven and allow the crackers to cool and harden before removing them from the baking sheet.

6. Repeat Steps 3 to 5 with the second half of the dough.

7. Store the cooled crackers in a sealed bag or container at room temperature, or freeze for later use.

CHAPTER 9
Pizza, Calzones, and More

PREP TIME: 50 to 55 minutes, including proofing time
COOK TIME: 22 to 26 minutes
YIELD: 2 large or 4 small calzones

DAIRY *free*, EGG *free*, NUT *free*, GRAIN *free*, COCONUT *free*

classic calzones

Here's a recipe for those who love working with yeast breads. Fill this calzone with any combination of cooked or cured meats, veggies, sauce, and cheese that you like!

ingredients

1 cup plus 3½ tablespoons lukewarm water

1 tablespoon instant yeast

1 tablespoon coconut palm sugar

108 grams coconut flour (about ½ cup plus 2 tablespoons)

129 grams potato starch or sweet potato starch (about ⅔ cup plus 1 tablespoon)

2 tablespoons potato flour

1 tablespoon xanthan gum or guar gum

2 teaspoons double-acting, aluminum-free baking powder

¼ teaspoon kosher salt

60 grams Spectrum vegetable shortening (about ¼ cup plus 1 tablespoon)

2 large eggs

Olive oil or other oil of choice, for the work surface and for brushing the calzones

Filling(s) of choice

directions

1. Preheat the oven to 375 degrees to warm it up as a "hot box" for the calzones to proof. Line a baking sheet with parchment paper.

2. In a small bowl or cup, combine the lukewarm water, yeast, and sugar. Mix and set aside.

3. In the bowl of a stand mixer, using the whisk attachment, whisk the coconut flour, potato starch, potato flour, xanthan gum, baking powder, and salt until blended.

4. Add the shortening, eggs, and yeast mixture and mix on low speed until combined. Increase the speed to high and continue to mix for a few minutes until you have a slightly tacky dough that holds together.

5. Place a sheet of parchment paper on your work surface. Oil the paper and your hands, and then divide the dough into 2 equal portions to make large calzones or 4 equal portions to make single-serving calzones.

6. Place a portion of dough on the oiled parchment paper and press it into a circle about ¼ to ½ inch thick. Add ¼ cup filling for a large calzone (or less for smaller calzones) to one side of the circle, leaving about a ½-inch border.

7. Using the parchment as a guide, fold the dough over the filling and seal the edge with your fingers or a fork.

8. Prepare the remaining calzones and brush the tops with olive oil. Place the calzones on the prepared baking sheet and cover with a kitchen towel.

9. Turn off the oven and place the covered calzones in the warm oven to proof for a total of 30 minutes. Leave the oven door open a crack for the first 15 minutes, and close the door for the last 15 minutes.

10. After 30 minutes of proofing, remove the calzones from the warm oven. Preheat the oven to 375 degrees.

11. Remove the towel from the calzones, brush them with more oil, and place them in the fully preheated oven. Bake for 22 to 26 minutes, until perfectly golden brown.

12. Enjoy! These calzones taste best hot or warm.

bbq chicken yeast-free calzones

I love making calzones; you can fill them any way you like. I like to keep my filings simple; I often use leftover meat with whatever sauce I have in the pantry. They always seem to end up delicious!

ingredients

BBQ chicken filling:

½ pound cooked chicken, shredded

Barbecue sauce of choice

Calzone dough:

108 grams coconut flour (about ⅔ cup)

129 grams potato starch or sweet potato starch (about ⅔ cup)

2 tablespoons potato flour

1 tablespoon plus 1 teaspoon xanthan gum or guar gum

1 tablespoon double-acting, aluminum-free baking powder

¼ teaspoon kosher salt

265 grams water (about 1¼ cups)

60 grams Spectrum vegetable shortening (about ¼ cup plus 1 tablespoon)

3 large eggs

1 tablespoon apple cider vinegar

2 cups shredded mozzarella cheese (dairy or nondairy; optional)

directions

1. In a bowl, mix together the shredded chicken and barbecue sauce; set aside.

2. Preheat the oven to 350 degrees.

3. In the bowl of a stand mixer, using the whisk attachment, mix the coconut flour, potato starch, potato flour, xanthan gum, baking powder, and salt until blended.

4. Add the water, shortening, eggs, and vinegar and mix on high speed until combined.

5. Lay a sheet of parchment paper on your work surface. Oil the paper and your hands, and then divide the dough into 2 equal portions to make large calzones or 4 equal portions to make single-serving calzones. Pat out each piece of dough into a ½-inch-thick circle.

6. Divide the sauced, shredded chicken between the dough circles, placing the filling to one side of the circle and leaving about a ½-inch border. Sprinkle with cheese, if desired.

7. Using the parchment paper as a guide, fold the dough over the filling and seal the edge with your fingers or a fork. Do not move the dough after it is shaped, or it may break. Carefully slide the parchment paper with the calzones on it onto a baking sheet.

8. Bake for 40 minutes, until the calzones are firm to the touch and lightly golden brown. Store any leftovers in the fridge in a sealed bag or container for up to 3 days.

PREP TIME: 30 minutes
COOK TIME: 35 to 37 minutes
YIELD: 2 large pizzas

DAIRY *free*, EGG *free*, NUT *free*,
GRAIN *free*, COCONUT *free*

thin-crust white pizza
with spinach

White pizza is my weakness! The beauty of this recipe is that it has no cheese and can be made with or without dairy. Both ways are equally delicious!

ingredients

Pizza dough:

432 grams blanched almond flour (about 3 cups) (see Notes)

77 grams potato, sweet potato, tapioca, or arrowroot starch (about ¼ cup plus 3 tablespoons) (see Notes)

2 teaspoons double-acting, aluminum-free baking powder

¼ teaspoon kosher salt

56 grams flaxseed meal, preferably golden (about ⅔ cup)

220 grams warm water (about 1 cup)

1 tablespoon mild-flavored oil, melted salted butter, or melted ghee

White sauce:

1 tablespoon salted butter or ghee

12 cloves garlic, minced

⅓ cup minced shallots

½ teaspoon black pepper

2½ teaspoons tapioca starch

1 cup heavy cream or coconut cream

2 tablespoons blanched almond flour

¼ to ½ teaspoon kosher salt (or to taste)

½ cup fresh spinach leaves

notes

Instead of almond flour, feel free to use another mild-flavored homemade nut or seed flour. If you choose to experiment, be aware that sunflower seed flour reacts with baking powder and turns green if you use more than ¼ teaspoon baking powder in a recipe.

If using tapioca or arrowroot starch and measuring with a cup, use ½ cup plus 1 tablespoon.

directions

1. Preheat the oven to 375 degrees. Line 2 baking sheets with parchment paper.

2. In the bowl of a stand mixer, using the whisk attachment, mix the almond flour, starch, baking powder, and salt until blended.

3. In a separate bowl, combine the flaxseed meal, warm water, and oil. Whisk until thickened.

4. Add the thickened flaxseed meal mixture to the dry ingredients and mix until well combined and the dough holds together enough to roll out. (This step can also be done by hand; just make sure to mix it really well!)

5. Divide the dough in half. Place one half on a prepared baking sheet and roll it out into a really thin rectangle, about 12 by 16 inches and no more than 1/16 inch thick. Oil your hands and the parchment as needed to keep the dough from sticking. (You can also roll it out between 2 sheets of parchment paper.)

6. Repeat with the other half of the dough on the other prepared baking sheet.

7. Parbake each crust for 10 to 12 minutes, until the edges are golden and the crust is cooked through. (If you want to bake them at the same time, you can, but you might need to increase the baking time by a few minutes, and I suggest swapping the trays halfway through.)

8. Meanwhile, prepare the white sauce: In a saucepan, heat the butter over medium-low heat.

9. Add the garlic, shallots, and pepper and cook for 2 to 3 minutes.

10. In a bowl, whisk the tapioca starch and cream. Add to the pan and cook for another 3 minutes, until thickened.

11. Add the almond flour, stirring to make sure that there are no clumps.

12. Add ¼ teaspoon salt, stir, and taste! Season with additional salt, if needed. Remove from the heat.

13. Remove the pizza crusts from the oven and increase the oven temperature to 400 degrees. Top the crusts with the white sauce and spinach. Return the pizzas to the oven and bake for an additional 14 to 16 minutes, until golden brown.

PREP TIME: 20 to 25 minutes
COOK TIME: 18 to 26 minutes
YIELD: One 8-inch pizza

DAIRY *free,* **EGG** *free,* **NUT** *free,*
GRAIN *free,* COCONUT *free*

butter chicken naan pizza

This Indian-inspired pizza is the epitome of decadence. The crust, based on my Naan recipe (page 60), is topped with gingery butter chicken. The rich sauce for the chicken is built from cream, tomato sauce, and a spice blend called garam masala. The longer you allow it to cook, the more the flavors will develop.

ingredients

Butter chicken sauce:

1 tablespoon oil of choice

1¼ teaspoons grated fresh ginger

1¼ teaspoons garlic powder

1 medium onion, chopped

⅛ to ¼ teaspoon cayenne pepper (depending on how spicy you want it)

1¼ teaspoons garam masala

1¼ cups tomato sauce

1 pound boneless, skinless chicken breasts or thighs, chopped into bite-sized pieces

¼ cup heavy cream or coconut cream (from a can of coconut milk; see tutorial, page 26)

1 batch Naan dough (page 60)

1 tablespoon oil of choice, plus more for the skillet (if using)

1 to 2 cups shredded mozzarella cheese (dairy or nondairy)

3 tablespoons sliced scallions

notes

Depending on the type of tomato sauce you use, you may need to add a tablespoon or so of sugar to the sauce to cut the sourness.

directions

1. Make the sauce: In a pot, warm the oil over low heat. Add the ginger, garlic powder, and onion and cook for 3 minutes, until the onion has softened.

2. Add the cayenne and garam masala and cook for 30 seconds, stirring constantly.

3. Add the tomato sauce, chicken, and cream and simmer over low heat for about 10 minutes, until the chicken is cooked through and the sauce is reduced and thickened.

4. While the sauce cooks, prepare the pizza crust: Preheat the oven to 350 degrees. Have on hand a large rimmed baking sheet or an 8-inch cast-iron skillet.

5. Form the Naan dough into one large ball (do not divide it into 4 pieces as per the Naan recipe).

6. If using a rimmed baking sheet, roll out the dough on a sheet of parchment paper until it is about 10½ inches in diameter and ¼ inch thick. Slide the parchment with the dough onto the baking sheet. If using a cast-iron skillet, coat the bottom and sides well with oil. Place the ball of dough in the skillet and, using your hands, press the dough into the pan, pushing some of the dough up the sides.

7. Brush the top of the dough with the tablespoon of oil.

8. Bake for 15 to 22 minutes, depending on how well-done you want your pizza crust.

9. Remove the crust from the oven. Spread the sauce over the crust, and then top with the mozzarella cheese.

10. Broil on low until the cheese melts, 3 to 4 minutes, keeping an eye on it. Sprinkle with the scallions before serving.

PREP TIME: 45 minutes, including proofing time
COOK TIME: 30 minutes
YIELD: One 8-inch pizza

DAIRY *free*, EGG *free*, NUT *free*,
GRAIN *free*, COCONUT *free*

chicago deep-dish pizza

Chicago Deep-Dish Pizza is my husband's number-one most requested recipe. This recipe is for him. And me, too! I made it egg-free so I could enjoy it with him. The outside of the crust is crispy, and the bottom layer under the cheese is doughy—the perfect combination. Once you make it, you'll see why we love it so much.

ingredients

Yeast mixture:

100 grams lukewarm water (about a scant ½ cup)

1 tablespoon instant yeast

2 teaspoons coconut palm sugar

1 teaspoon gelatin

Pizza dough:

97 grams blanched almond flour (about ⅔ cup)

55 grams potato starch or sweet potato starch (about ⅓ cup)

47 grams tapioca starch (about ⅓ cup plus 2 teaspoons)

2 teaspoons xanthan gum or guar gum

1 teaspoon kosher salt

1 teaspoon double-acting, aluminum-free baking powder

62 grams oil of choice (about ¼ cup plus 1 tablespoon), plus more for the pan

1 tablespoon apple cider vinegar

Toppings:

6 links hot Italian sausage

1½ cups shredded mozzarella cheese (dairy or nondairy)

1 (14½-ounce) can diced tomatoes, slightly drained

½ cup grated Parmesan cheese (optional)

directions

1. Preheat the oven to 400 degrees to warm it up as a "hot box" for the pizza dough to proof. Oil an 8-inch round pan, an 8-inch cast-iron skillet, or, for a pretty presentation, a springform pan.

2. In a small bowl, mix together the lukewarm water, yeast, sugar, and gelatin; set aside.

3. In the bowl of a stand mixer, using the whisk attachment, mix the almond flour, starches, xanthan gum, salt, and baking powder until blended.

4. Add the oil, vinegar, and yeast mixture and mix until it comes together into a sticky dough that holds together.

5. Place the dough in the prepared pan. Press the dough across the bottom of the pan and 1 inch up the sides. Cover the pan with a towel.

6. Turn off the oven and place the covered pan in the warm oven to proof for a total of 30 minutes. Leave the oven door open a crack for the first 15 minutes, and then close the door for the last 15 minutes.

7. While the dough is proofing, cook the sausage: Remove the casings. Break the sausage meat into small pieces and brown in a skillet over medium heat. Remove with a slotted spoon and set on paper towels to drain.

8. After 30 minutes of proofing, remove the pan from the oven. Preheat the oven to 400 degrees.

9. When the oven is fully preheated, remove the towel from the pan and place the pan in the oven. Parbake the crust for 5 minutes, and then remove from the oven. (But leave the oven on!)

10. It's time to layer on the toppings! Put the mozzarella cheese on the bottom, followed by a layer of sausage, then pour on the diced tomatoes, and top with the Parmesan cheese, if using.

11. Bake for 30 minutes, until the cheese has melted and the crust is golden brown.

PREP TIME: 10 minutes
COOK TIME: 15 minutes
YIELD: 16 to 20 bites

DAIRY *free*, **EGG** *free*, **NUT** *free*, **GRAIN** *free*, **COCONUT** *free*

pizza bagel bites

This used to be my all-time favorite after-school snack. I couldn't wait to remake it with my Yeast-Free Mini Bagels!

ingredients

1 batch Yeast-Free Mini Bagels (page 84)

Pizza sauce of choice

Shredded mozzarella cheese (dairy or nondairy)

directions

1. Preheat the oven to 400 degrees.

2. Cut the mini bagels in half and place them on a baking sheet.

3. Spread with pizza sauce and sprinkle with cheese. If using nondairy cheese shreds, tent the baking sheet with foil.

4. Bake for 15 minutes, or until the cheese has melted and the bagels are starting to get a little golden.

PREP TIME: 10 to 15 minutes
COOK TIME: 40 to 42 minutes
YIELD: 24 pieces

DAIRY *free*, **EGG** *free*, **NUT** *free*,
GRAIN *free*, **COCONUT** *free*

bruschetta

Bruschetta is the perfect appetizer for entertaining. The Baguette (page 48) can be made a few days prior, and the topping can be whipped up the day of the party, making for an easy prep day.

ingredients

1 head garlic

Oil of choice, for the garlic and bread slices

1 Baguette (page 48)

4 plum tomatoes, chopped

¼ packed cup fresh basil, chopped

Kosher salt and black pepper to taste

Balsamic vinegar, for drizzling the bruschetta

directions

1. Preheat the oven to 400 degrees. Line a rimmed baking sheet with parchment paper.

2. Peel away the outer layers of the garlic and cut ½ inch off the top. Drizzle with oil, wrap in foil, and roast for 35 minutes. Remove the garlic from the oven and reduce the oven temperature to 375 degrees.

3. Meanwhile, cut the Baguette into ½-inch slices. Brush both sides of the slices with oil and place on the prepared baking sheet.

4. In a bowl, mix together the tomatoes and basil and season with salt and pepper.

5. When the roasted garlic is cool enough to handle, press the soft garlic out of the cloves and smash them with a fork to make a paste.

6. Spread the Baguette slices with the roasted garlic paste and place in the oven. Toast for 5 to 7 minutes, until golden brown.

7. Top the slices with the tomato-basil mixture and drizzle with balsamic vinegar. Serve immediately.

PREP TIME: 15 to 20 minutes
COOK TIME: 25 minutes
YIELD: 4 breadsticks

DAIRY *free*, **EGG** *free*, **NUT** *free*,
GRAIN *free*, **COCONUT** *free*

breadsticks

Who doesn't love garlicky breadsticks? Dip these guys in marinara sauce and serve them with zucchini noodles. Paleo at its best!

ingredients

4 large egg whites

132 grams tapioca starch (about 1 cup), plus more for the work surface

108 grams blanched almond flour (about ¾ cup)

2 teaspoons double-acting, aluminum-free baking powder

1 teaspoon xanthan gum or guar gum

1¼ teaspoons garlic powder

½ teaspoon onion powder

¼ teaspoon kosher salt

48 grams Spectrum vegetable shortening (about ¼ cup)

1 tablespoon water

1 tablespoon apple cider vinegar

Olive oil, for brushing the breadsticks

directions

1. Preheat the oven to 350 degrees. Line a baking sheet with parchment paper.

2. In the bowl of a stand mixer, using the whisk attachment, whip the egg whites until frothy.

3. In a separate bowl, whisk the tapioca starch, almond flour, baking powder, xanthan gum, garlic powder, onion powder, and salt until well blended.

4. Add the dry ingredients to the egg whites and mix on medium-high speed until a dough forms. Add the shortening, water, and vinegar and mix until combined.

5. Dust your work surface and your hands with tapioca starch. Shape the dough into 4 equal portions and, using your palms, roll each portion into a cylinder about 6 inches long and 1 inch in diameter. Place the breadsticks on the prepared baking sheet and brush them with olive oil.

6. Bake for 25 minutes or until golden brown.

CHAPTER 10
Tacos, Quesadillas, and More

PREP TIME: 15 to 20 minutes
COOK TIME: 9 to 12 minutes
YIELD: 6 taco shells

DAIRY *free*, EGG *free*, NUT *free*,
GRAIN *free*, COCONUT *free*

plantain taco shells

Plantains are so versatile. I make them into just about everything! You'll start to see that more clearly as you continue deeper into this book. In this recipe, they result in super-crispy taco shells. Just be sure to press or roll the dough out thin!

ingredients

2 green plantains, peeled (about 1 pound)

210 grams potato starch or sweet potato starch (about 1¼ cups)

44 grams bacon fat or Spectrum vegetable shortening (about ¼ cup) (do not use any other oil)

1 teaspoon baking soda

1 teaspoon garlic powder

¾ teaspoon kosher salt

Oil of choice, for the parchment paper

directions

1. Preheat the oven to 400 degrees.

2. Place the plantains in a food processor and process until totally smooth.

3. Add the rest of the ingredients, except for the oil, and process until a dough forms.

4. Oil 2 small squares of parchment paper. Roll 1 tablespoon of the dough into a ball and place it between the sheets of oiled parchment. Using either a tortilla press or a rolling pin, press or roll the dough into a thin circle.

5. Carefully remove the top sheet of parchment paper and place the rolled-out tortilla (still stuck to the bottom sheet of parchment) on a baking sheet, parchment side down. Do not try to remove the dough from the bottom sheet of parchment at this point, or it will break.

6. Repeat this process until you have 6 tortillas on 6 squares of parchment placed on the baking sheet.

7. Bake the tortillas for 4 to 5 minutes, until they are firm to touch and can be removed from the parchment paper without breaking.

8. Remove the parchment paper and fold the tortillas to create taco shells.

9. Hang the shells upside-down on the rungs of an oven rack to maintain the shape, and bake for an additional 5 to 7 minutes, until crisp.

10. Fill the shells with the taco fillings of your choice! Store leftover shells at room temperature in a sealable plastic or similar container. Handle these fragile taco shells very gently; do not store them in a bag, where they are likely to be crushed.

PREP TIME: 15 to 20 minutes
COOK TIME: 10 to 13 minutes
YIELD: 8 tortillas

DAIRY *free*, **EGG** *free*, **NUT** *free*,
GRAIN *free*, **COCONUT** *free*

soft plantain tortillas

This recipe was one of my recipe testers' favorites because these plantain tortillas are so much like real tortillas! You can bend them without fear of breaking them, and they taste great eaten with fajitas.

ingredients

2 green plantains, peeled (about 1 pound)

2 tablespoons oil of choice

1 teaspoon garlic powder

½ teaspoon kosher salt

2 tablespoons water

directions

1. Preheat the oven to 400 degrees. Line 2 baking sheets with parchment paper.

2. Cut the plantains into chunks and place in a food processor. Add the oil, garlic powder, and salt and process until smooth.

3. With the machine running, drizzle in the water and process until smooth.

4. Spoon a portion of dough onto a prepared baking sheet and, using the back of a spoon, smooth it out as thinly possible into a circle about 6 inches in diameter.

5. Repeat with the remaining dough, placing 4 circles of dough on each baking sheet.

6. Bake for 8 minutes, flip the tortillas, and then bake for an additional 2 to 3 minutes.

7. *Optional:* If you want your tortillas to be a bit crispy on the outside, after removing them from the oven, lightly oil a skillet, place over medium heat, and cook the tortillas for 1 to 2 minutes per side.

PREP TIME: 10 to 15 minutes
COOK TIME: 12 minutes
YIELD: 12 tortillas

DAIRY *free,* **EGG** *free,* **NUT** *free,*
GRAIN *free,* **COCONUT** *free*

cheesy
soft plantain tortillas

This is a cheesy variation of my Soft Plantain Tortillas (page 240) because...why not? Cheese makes everything better!

ingredients

1 tablespoon salted butter, ghee, or mild-flavored oil, plus more for the pan as needed

2 green plantains, peeled (about 1 pound)

89 grams water (about ¼ cup plus 2 tablespoons)

1 teaspoon garlic powder

60 grams Spectrum vegetable shortening (about ¼ cup plus 1 tablespoon)

¾ teaspoon kosher salt

141 grams potato starch or sweet potato starch (about ¾ cup plus 1 tablespoon)

211 grams tapioca starch (about 1½ cups plus 1 tablespoon), plus more for the work surface

2 to 2½ cups shredded cheese of choice (dairy or nondairy)

notes

Use these tortillas right away. As they sit, they harden, because the starch continues to soak up moisture.

directions

1. Place the butter in a cast-iron skillet over low heat.

2. Place the plantains and water in a food processor and process until smooth.

3. Add the garlic powder, shortening, salt, starches, and cheese to the food processor and process until smooth.

4. Sprinkle a sheet of parchment paper with tapioca starch. Take a heaping tablespoon of the dough, roll it into a ball, and place it in the center of the parchment. Sprinkle with tapioca starch and place a second sheet of parchment on top.

5. Using a tortilla press or rolling pin, flatten the dough out as thinly as possible between the sheets of parchment paper. Carefully peel off the top sheet.

6. Increase the heat under the skillet to medium-low. Using the parchment paper, slide the tortilla onto the palm of your hand. Flip your hand over to drop the tortilla into the skillet, parchment side up. Cook for 2 to 3 minutes per side, peeling away the parchment before flipping. Place on a cooling rack.

7. Repeat with the rest of the dough, adding more butter to the pan as needed.

PREP TIME: 20 minutes
COOK TIME: 35 to 38 minutes
YIELD: 2 servings

DAIRY *free*, EGG *free*, NUT *free*,
GRAIN *free*, COCONUT *free*

taco bowls
with taco salad

This may be my favorite recipe in the entire book! These crunchy taco bowls may be even better than the wheat-based ones. Adding another dimension of deliciousness to your taco salads, they are loaded with spices. To make them, I use a special taco bowl–shaped pan; however, if you don't want to buy one, feel free to make mini taco bowls in a muffin tin instead (see Notes).

ingredients

Taco bowls:

26 grams flaxseed meal, preferably golden (about ¼ cup plus 1 tablespoon)

110 grams hot water (about ½ cup)

56 grams oil of choice (about ¼ cup)

176 grams tapioca starch (about 1⅓ cups)

36 grams blanched almond flour (about ¼ cup)

1 teaspoon chili powder

½ teaspoon ground cumin

½ teaspoon garlic powder

¼ teaspoon cayenne pepper

¾ teaspoon kosher salt

⅛ teaspoon double-acting, aluminum-free baking powder

Meat filling:

1 pound ground beef

½ cup minced onion

1 teaspoon kosher salt

1 teaspoon chili powder

½ teaspoon ground cumin

½ teaspoon garlic powder

¼ teaspoon cayenne pepper

Toppings (optional):

Diced tomatoes

Shredded lettuce

Cilantro-Avocado Mousse (page 350), Guacamole (page 170), or diced avocado

directions

1. Preheat the oven to 350 degrees. Have on a hand 2 taco bowl pans or a muffin tin.

2. Make the dough for the taco bowls: In a small bowl, mix together the flaxseed meal, hot water, and oil; set aside.

3. In a larger bowl, whisk the tapioca starch, almond flour, spices, salt, and baking powder.

4. Add the flaxseed mixture to the dry ingredients and mix to combine. Then knead the dough in the bowl until it's stretchy and well combined.

5. Divide the dough in half. Place one half on a sheet of parchment paper and roll it out as thinly as possible into a circle about 12 inches in diameter.

6. Carefully flip the dough into the taco bowl pan using the parchment paper as your guide. Gently press the dough into the crevices of the pan.

7. Repeat the process with other half of the dough and taco bowl pan. (This dough will dry out if it sits out. If that happens, work in a little bit of water.)

8. Bake the taco bowls for 35 to 38 minutes, until golden brown and as crisp as crackers.

9. Meanwhile, make the meat filling: Place the ingredients for the filling in a large skillet and cook over medium heat until the meat is no longer pink and the onion has softened.

10. Place the meat filling and any additional toppings in your taco bowls and enjoy!

notes

If you use a muffin tin instead of a taco bowl pan to make mini taco bowls, the baking time may be different. Keep an eye on them and remove them from the oven when they are nice and crispy.

chicken taquitos

I absolutely love street food...I mean, who doesn't, right? But with street food, you have no control over the quality of the ingredients. My solution? Make your own street food! These Chicken Taquitos are so tasty, you will forget that you're standing in your own kitchen, not outside a food truck. I like to eat them with Cilantro-Avocado Mousse (page 350) or salsa.

ingredients

Chicken filling:

2 tablespoons coconut oil or other mild-flavored oil

1 pound boneless, skinless chicken thighs

¾ teaspoon chili powder

½ teaspoon cayenne pepper

½ teaspoon onion powder

½ teaspoon kosher salt

Taquito shells:

26 grams flaxseed meal, preferably golden (about ¼ cup plus 1 tablespoon)

55 grams hot water (about ¼ cup)

176 grams tapioca starch (about 1⅓ cups)

36 grams blanched almond flour (about ¼ cup)

½ teaspoon ground cumin

½ teaspoon garlic powder

¼ teaspoon cayenne pepper

¼ teaspoon chili powder

1 tablespoon plus 1½ teaspoons grapeseed oil or melted coconut oil

½ cup shredded cheese of choice (dairy or nondairy; optional)

directions

1. Preheat the oven to 350 degrees.

2. Make the filling: In a skillet over medium-high heat, melt the coconut oil. While the skillet is heating up, slice the chicken thighs into thin strips.

3. Once the skillet is hot and the coconut oil has melted, drop in the sliced chicken. Add the chili powder, cayenne, onion powder, and salt and toss to coat. Stir occasionally until the chicken is cooked through, about 8 to 10 minutes. Set aside.

4. Make the taquito shells: Mix the flaxseed meal and hot water in a small bowl. Set aside.

5. In a large bowl, mix together the tapioca starch, almond flour, cumin, garlic powder, cayenne, and chili powder.

6. Add the oil and the flaxseed mixture to the dry ingredients. Mix until you can form it into a firm ball. You may need to add additional hot water 1 teaspoon at a time to bring the dough together.

7. On a piece of parchment paper, roll out the dough as thin as you can get it without it breaking. It should be about as thick as construction paper.

8. Cut the dough into 5-inch circles. (You can use a small bowl as a guide.) Gather up the leftover dough, reroll it, and continue cutting it into circles until you have used up all of the dough.

9. In the center of each shell, place 1 tablespoon of the chicken filling and about 3 teaspoons of the cheese, if using. Roll it up and place on a rimmed baking sheet, seam side down.

10. Bake the taquitos for 40 minutes, until the shells are crispy and the cheese (if using) has melted.

PREP TIME: 25 minutes
COOK TIME: 12 to 15 minutes
YIELD: 6 quesadillas

DAIRY *free*, **EGG** *free*, **NUT** *free*,
GRAIN *free*, COCONUT *free*

bbq chicken quesadillas

These quesadillas are winners—barbecue sauce plus cheese, and Bacon Jam (page 348), too! You'll be shocked by the flavors. Sarah and Sarah, my darling kitchen assistants while writing this book, and I especially love this recipe.

ingredients

1 pound boneless, skinless chicken thighs

½ cup barbecue sauce of choice

Oil of choice, for the pan

1 batch Cheesy Soft Plantain Tortillas (page 242)

Shredded cheese of choice (dairy or nondairy)

1 batch Bacon Jam (page 348; optional)

directions

1. Bring a pot of water to a boil. Add the chicken thighs and cook until no longer pink, about 8 minutes.

2. Remove the chicken from the water and set aside until cool enough to handle. Using 2 forks, shred the chicken and place in a bowl along with the barbecue sauce. Toss the meat in the sauce until evenly coated.

3. Place a skillet over medium heat with a skim of oil.

4. Assemble the quesadillas! On a tortilla, arrange a layer of the shredded BBQ chicken followed by a layer of cheese.

5. Place in the pan and heat until the cheese melts, flipping one side over the other once the cheese has melted. Serve hot with Bacon Jam on the side, if you wish.

PREP TIME: 15 to 20 minutes
COOK TIME: 12 to 16 minutes
YIELD: 6 to 8 tortillas

DAIRY *free*, **EGG** *free*, **NUT** *free*,
GRAIN *free*, **COCONUT** *free*

soft almond flour tortillas

Yet another soft tortilla recipe—this one made with almond flour. These soft tortillas are the real deal: they're soft and chewy, and they bend without breaking! Use them as a base for my Tapas-Style Fish Tacos (page 252).

ingredients

99 grams tapioca starch (about ¾ cup), plus more for the work surface

66 grams blanched almond flour (about a scant ½ cup)

1 teaspoon xanthan gum or guar gum

½ teaspoon kosher salt

⅛ teaspoon double-acting, aluminum-free baking powder

2 tablespoons Spectrum vegetable shortening

2 large egg whites

notes

These tortillas can also be formed using the method in the Cheesy Soft Plantain Tortillas recipe (page 242), where the dough is separated into small balls and rolled out with a rolling pin or pressed with a tortilla press.

These tortillas tend to harden as they sit. To bring them back to life, simply heat them up again!

directions

1. In a bowl, whisk the tapioca starch, almond flour, xanthan gum, salt, and baking powder until blended.

2. Add the shortening and egg whites and mix with your hands to create a smooth, slightly sticky dough.

3. Sprinkle some tapioca starch on a sheet of parchment paper. Place the dough on the parchment. Dust a little more starch on top of the dough, and then roll out the dough paper-thin. The tortillas will double in thickness when you cook them.

4. Cut the dough into 5-inch circles using a small bowl as a guide. Carefully remove each circle, using the parchment paper to help you.

5. Place a dry skillet over medium heat. Cook the tortillas one at a time for 20 to 30 seconds on each side. Remove to a cooling rack. If you want to make them into taco shapes, bend them while warm and allow them to cool in that shape.

6. After cooking all of the cut tortillas, gather up the leftover dough, roll it out again, and continue cutting out tortillas until you have used up all of the dough. Cook and shape the remaining tortillas.

7. Store the cooled tortillas in a sealed bag or container at room temperature.

PREP TIME: 1 hour, including time to chill the onions
COOK TIME: 23 to 24 minutes
YIELD: 14 to 16 mini tacos

DAIRY *free,* **EGG** *free,* **NUT** *free,*
GRAIN *free,* **COCONUT** *free*

tapas-style fish tacos

Fish Friday can now be a part of your grain-free life with the help of these incredible-tasting tacos filled with crispy pieces of fish. Though baked, they have plenty of crunch—just as if they'd been fried.

ingredients

Pickled red onions:

1¼ cups apple cider vinegar

½ cup raw honey

1 red onion, sliced

Tortillas:

1 batch Soft Almond Flour Tortillas dough (page 250)

Wet mixture for the fish:

2 tablespoons tapioca, arrowroot, potato, or sweet potato starch

1⅓ cups milk (dairy or nondairy)

1 cup (2 sticks) plus 2 tablespoons salted butter, ghee, or mild-flavored oil

Breading mixture for the fish:

½ cup tapioca, arrowroot, potato, or sweet potato starch

½ cup blanched almond flour

1 teaspoon black pepper

½ teaspoon kosher salt

¼ teaspoon paprika

¼ teaspoon cayenne pepper

½ teaspoon garlic powder

10 ounces haddock fillets

Oil of choice, for drizzling the fish sticks

Toppings:

1 batch Cilantro-Avocado Mousse (page 350) or Guacamole (page 170)

Torn lettuce leaves

Lime wedges

directions

1. Make the pickled red onions: Heat the vinegar and honey in a small saucepan over medium-low heat, stirring. Once the honey has dissolved, pour the mixture into a bowl. When cool, add the onion. Place in the fridge, covered, for at least 1 hour.

2. Cut the tortilla dough into 3½-inch rounds. Cook, following Step 5 in the Soft Almond Flour Tortillas recipe. After cooking, fold them into taco shapes while warm. Place on a cooling rack and allow to cool.

3. Prepare the fish: Preheat the oven to 425 degrees. Line a rimmed baking sheet with foil.

4. Make the wet mixture for the fish: In a bowl, combine the starch and milk and mix until there are no clumps.

5. Melt the butter in a saucepan over low heat. Add the starch-milk mixture, increase the heat to medium, and whisk continuously until it thickens.

6. Pour into a pie pan or shallow dish that is long enough to fit the fish fillets.

7. While this mixture cools slightly, combine the breading ingredients in another bowl.

8. Drop a fish fillet into the wet mixture and then heavily dredge it in the breading mixture. Remove from the breading mixture, place in the wet mixture, and then again into the breading mixture. Repeat, coating both fillets twice.

9. Place the coated fish fillets on the prepared baking sheet and drizzle with oil. Bake for 20 minutes, until the fish is cooked through and the breading is crispy.

10. Broil on high for 3 to 4 minutes, until golden brown.

11. Remove the fish from the oven and cut into strips.

12. Assemble the tacos! Place the fish strips, pickled red onions, Cilantro-Avocado Mousse, and lettuce in the tortillas. Squeeze fresh lime juice over the top and enjoy!

CHAPTER 11
Comfort Foods

PREP TIME: 20 to 25 minutes
COOK TIME: 30 minutes
YIELD: 12 to 15 buns

DAIRY *free*, **EGG** *free*, **NUT** *free*,
GRAIN *free*, **COCONUT** *free*

chinese-style bbq pork buns

This has to be one of my favorite dim sum comfort food treats. These buns are light and filled with shredded BBQ pork. Using plantains as the base for the dough adds a fun flavor twist and allows them to be egg-free, too!

ingredients

Bun dough:

2 green plantains, peeled

89 grams water (about ¼ cup plus 2 tablespoons)

146 grams tapioca starch (about 1 cup plus 1 tablespoon)

141 grams potato starch or sweet potato starch (about ¾ cup plus 1 tablespoon)

60 grams Spectrum vegetable shortening (about ¼ cup plus 1 tablespoon)

2 teaspoons double-acting, aluminum-free baking powder

1 teaspoon garlic powder

¾ teaspoon kosher salt

Filling:

2 cups shredded cooked pork

⅔ to 1 cup barbecue sauce of choice

directions

1. Line a steamer basket with parchment paper. Place the basket in a pot with a few inches of water and place over medium heat.

2. Place the plantains and water in a food processor and process until smooth.

3. Add the remaining ingredients for the dough and process until smooth.

4. In a bowl, combine the shredded pork and barbecue sauce and toss until the meat is evenly coated. (You want the meat to be sauced well, as the plantains will soak up a lot of liquid.)

5. Press ¼ cup of dough between your palms until it is about ¼ inch thick. Place about 1 tablespoon of the filling in the center. Gather up the sides and press them together, like a purse, to seal in the filling. Roll gently in your hand to form into a ball. Repeat with the remaining dough and filling.

6. Place the buns in the steamer basket and steam for 30 minutes.

notes

If you aren't using a steamer basket, make sure to oil the surface of the steamer before placing the buns inside.

PREP TIME: 15 to 20 minutes
COOK TIME: 40 to 46 minutes
YIELD: 24 buns

DAIRY *free*, **EGG** *free*, **NUT** *free*,
GRAIN *free*, **COCONUT** *free*

brazilian cheese buns

I first tried these buns when visiting a Brazilian steakhouse years ago. Talk about addicting! Using the versatile plantain as my base (once again!), I made them grain- and egg-free. They are the perfect comforting indulgence!

ingredients

1 tablespoon salted butter, ghee, or mild-flavored oil

2 green plantains, peeled (see Notes)

89 grams water (about ¼ cup plus 2 tablespoons)

146 grams tapioca starch (about 1 cup plus 1 tablespoon)

141 grams potato starch or sweet potato flour (about ¾ cup)

60 grams Spectrum vegetable shortening (about ¼ cup plus 1 tablespoon)

1 tablespoon double-acting, aluminum-free baking powder

1 teaspoon garlic powder

¾ teaspoon kosher salt

2 to 2½ cups shredded sharp cheddar cheese (dairy or nondairy)

directions

1. Melt the butter in a large cast-iron skillet over medium-low heat.
2. Place the plantains and water in a food processor and process until smooth.
3. Add the remaining ingredients and process until smooth.
4. Shape 1 heaping tablespoon of the dough into a ball. Repeat with the remaining dough.
5. Place the first batch of 12 balls in the skillet and cook, covered, for 20 to 23 minutes, turning once or twice during cooking. Do not pack too tightly in the pan, as they will spread during cooking. Keep a careful eye on them, because the cheese tends to burn quickly.
6. Remove the buns from the skillet and set aside in a low oven to keep warm.
7. Repeat the process with the second batch of dough balls. Store any leftovers in a sealed container at room temperature or in the fridge for up to 3 days.

notes

You want green plantains for this recipe. If they aren't as green, the buns will spread as they bake, resembling pancakes more than buns, and the flavor will change slightly. They still taste delicious, but I prefer them when they are made with green plantains!

If you do not have a cast-iron skillet, you can bake these buns on a rimmed baking sheet in a 400-degree oven for 15 to 20 minutes. Be sure to brush them with melted butter or oil before they go into the oven!

PREP TIME: 20 to 25 minutes
COOK TIME: 1 hour 10 minutes
YIELD: 8 to 10 cups

DAIRY *free*, EGG *free*, NUT *free*,
GRAIN *free*, COCONUT *free*

clam chowder

This lovely recipe was created by my seafood-loving former kitchen assistant, Sarah Rothberg. Her redo of this classic chowder has a creamy consistency without using a ton of cream. Her secret? Puréed cauliflower (see Notes below)—though leaving the cauliflower chunky is delicious, too! Be sure to try this soup with Oyster Crackers (page 202).

ingredients

8 slices bacon

¼ cup chopped shallots

½ cup chopped onion

1 cup chopped carrots

1 cup chopped celery

½ head cauliflower

1 (13½-ounce) can full-fat coconut milk

2 cups chicken broth

3 tablespoons salted butter, ghee, or mild-flavored oil

¼ cup blanched almond flour

1 tablespoon dried parsley

¼ teaspoon cayenne pepper

½ teaspoon kosher salt

¼ teaspoon black pepper

3 bay leaves

2 (6½-ounce) cans chopped clams

directions

1. In a large pot over medium-low heat, cook the bacon until crispy.

2. Using a slotted spoon, remove the cooked bacon from the pot and set on paper towels to drain, reserving 1 tablespoon of the fat.

3. Add the shallots, onion, carrots, and celery to the same pot, increase the heat to medium, and cook for 4 to 5 minutes.

4. While the vegetables are cooking, chop up the cauliflower and cooled bacon.

5. Place the cauliflower, bacon, coconut milk, chicken broth, and butter in the pot with the vegetables.

6. Whisk in the almond flour. Then add the parsley, cayenne, salt, pepper, and bay leaves and simmer for 1 hour, until the soup has thickened and all of the vegetables are cooked.

7. Add the clams and cook for 2 to 3 minutes to heat through.

8. Remove the bay leaves, pour into bowls, and enjoy!

notes

If you want a thicker, creamier soup, cook the cauliflower separately (in a pot of water or a steamer) until tender. Chop it up and throw half of it into the soup. Purée the rest of the cauliflower and then add it back to the soup.

PREP TIME: 20 to 25 minutes
COOK TIME: 1 hour
YIELD: 8 cups

DAIRY *free*, EGG *free*, NUT *free*,
GRAIN *free*, COCONUT *free*

roasted tomato soup
with grilled cheese croutons

Taking the time to roast the tomatoes and garlic before adding them to the pot creates a beautiful depth of flavor in the finished soup. The Grilled Cheese Croutons are there to plop into the soup and eat with a spoon, adding fun sophistication!

ingredients

Soup:

9 vine-ripe tomatoes (about 3 pounds), cut in half

2 heads garlic (roughly 23 cloves), cloves separated and peeled

1 large onion, cut into quarters

3 to 4 tablespoons olive oil

1 teaspoon kosher salt, plus more for sprinkling

Black pepper

4 cups chicken broth or vegetable broth

3 tablespoons dried basil

2 teaspoons garlic powder

Pinch of dried oregano leaves (optional)

2 bay leaves

3 tablespoons salted butter, ghee, or mild-flavored oil

¾ cup heavy cream or coconut cream (from a can of coconut milk; see tutorial, page 26)

2 tablespoons coconut palm sugar

Grilled Cheese Croutons:

1 batch sandwich bread of choice (from Chapter 1) or Extra-Crispy Paleo Waffles (page 144)

Cheddar cheese or other cheese slices (dairy or nondairy)

directions

1. Preheat the oven to 400 degrees.

2. Spread the tomato halves, peeled garlic cloves, and onion quarters on a rimmed baking sheet. Drizzle them with the olive oil and sprinkle with salt and pepper. Roast for 45 minutes to 1 hour.

3. Place the roasted tomatoes, garlic, and onion in a stockpot. Add the broth, basil, garlic powder, oregano, bay leaves, 1 teaspoon salt, and butter and bring to a boil.

4. Reduce the heat to maintain a simmer and cook for 15 minutes or until the liquid reduces.

5. Remove the bay leaves. Using either a blender or an immersion blender/hand mixer, blend the soup until smooth. If you're using a blender, blend in small batches.

6. Return the soup to the pot and place over medium-low heat. Add the cream and sugar and simmer for a few minutes. Taste for seasoning and add salt and pepper if needed.

7. Make the Grilled Cheese Croutons: Preheat a skillet to medium-high heat. Place a slice or two of cheese between two slices of bread or two waffles. Lightly butter the outsides of the bread or waffles to prevent sticking and help brown the outside.

8. Cook for a few minutes on each side, until golden brown. During the last minute or two of cooking, cover the skillet with a lid to melt the cheese even more.

9. Cut into crouton-sized pieces and place in each bowl of soup. Enjoy!

notes

You can use a panini press to make the Grilled Cheese Croutons if you wish.

PREP TIME: 25 to 30 minutes
COOK TIME: 30 minutes
YIELD: 8 servings

DAIRY *free*, **EGG** *free*, **NUT** *free*,
GRAIN *free*, **COCONUT** *free*

sage sausage stuffing

Stuffing isn't just for Thanksgiving. You can eat this comfort food at any time of the year. My family loves it prepared with spicy Italian sausage for a little kick. The Croutons (page 210) can be made from any of the breads in this book.

ingredients

1 pound sausage links (about 5), casings removed

1 tablespoon salted butter, ghee, or mild-flavored oil

3 stalks celery, chopped (about 1 heaping cup)

1 medium onion, chopped (about 1 heaping cup)

2 cloves garlic, minced

1½ teaspoons dried ground sage

1¼ teaspoons black pepper

1 teaspoon fresh or ½ teaspoon dried thyme leaves

½ teaspoon kosher salt

¼ cup white wine

6 cups Croutons (page 210)

3 cups chicken broth

directions

1. Preheat the oven to 350 degrees. Grease a 2½-quart casserole dish.

2. Brown the sausage in a skillet over medium heat, using a spatula to break it up into bite-sized pieces.

3. Remove the cooked sausage from the pan and place on a paper towel to drain. Drain the excess fat from the skillet.

4. In the same skillet, melt the butter. Reduce the heat to medium-low and sauté the celery, onion, and garlic until softened. Be careful not to burn the garlic!

5. Sprinkle in the sage, pepper, thyme, and salt.

6. Once the vegetables have softened, deglaze the pan with the white wine and cook for about 2 more minutes. Make sure that the heat is not too high!

7. In a large bowl, combine the Croutons, sausage, and vegetable mixture. Pour in the chicken broth and mix well to coat the Croutons evenly.

8. Pour the mixture into the prepared casserole dish and cover with foil.

9. Bake for 20 minutes. Remove the foil and bake for another 10 minutes or until the top is golden brown.

PREP TIME: 15 to 20 minutes
COOK TIME: 16 to 20 minutes
YIELD: 8 to 10 corn dogs

DAIRY *free*, **EGG** *free*, **NUT** *free*,
GRAIN *free*, **COCONUT** *free*

corn dogs

Corn dogs typically get their slightly golden color from corn. Since my recipe leaves out the corn, I added a little turmeric for color. My Corn Dogs ended up looking and tasting spot-on! I love using Applegate brand hot dogs to keep these treats fairly healthy. You will need wooden skewers; 8-inch skewers are ideal.

ingredients

Coconut oil or grapeseed oil, for deep-frying

Batter:

1 cup blanched almond flour

½ cup tapioca starch

½ cup potato or sweet potato starch

2 teaspoons double-acting, aluminum-free baking powder

1 teaspoon garlic powder

¼ teaspoon ground turmeric

¼ teaspoon kosher salt

2 tablespoons granulated maple sugar or coconut palm sugar

3 large eggs

¼ cup mild-flavored oil, melted salted butter, or melted ghee

1 teaspoon lemon juice or apple cider vinegar

1 (12-ounce) package hot dogs of choice

directions

1. In heavy-bottomed pot that's wide enough to deep-fry the corn dogs sideways, such as a Dutch oven, heat about 2 inches of oil over medium heat to 365 degrees.

2. While the oil is heating, prepare the batter: In a mixing bowl, whisk the almond flour, starches, baking powder, garlic powder, turmeric, and salt. Add the sugar, eggs, oil, and lemon juice and mix until smooth.

3. Pour the batter into a tall glass.

4. Wipe off all the excess liquid from a hot dog with a paper towel. Insert a skewer lengthwise in the center of the hot dog, leaving a couple of inches sticking out at the top for a handle. Holding the hot dog by the skewer, stick it in the batter and let the extra batter drip off. (But keep as much on as possible! Making sure that the hot dog is very dry before dipping it in the batter will help the batter stick.)

5. Place the corn dog in the hot oil (submerging the dog and skewer) and fry until golden brown on all sides, about 2 minutes.

6. Place on a paper towel to cool briefly, and repeat with the remaining hot dogs and batter. Serve warm with your favorite condiments.

PREP TIME: 30 to 35 minutes
COOK TIME: 35 to 38 minutes
YIELD: 8 to 10 pieces

DAIRY *free*, EGG *free*, NUT *free*,
GRAIN *free*, COCONUT *free*

crab rangoon

This is an American classic made a brand-new way, with an easy-to-use grain- and egg-free dough that is baked rather than fried. Healthier, but no less delicious! One of my closest friends, Hayley Mason Staley from PrimalPalate.com, helped me figure out this dough. For real-deal multipurpose wontons, be sure to pick up a copy of her forthcoming book, Make it Paleo II.

ingredients

Crab filling:

2½ ounces crab meat

2 ounces cream cheese or fresh goat cheese (chèvre)

¼ teaspoon garlic powder

Kosher salt and black pepper to taste

Wonton wrappers:

26 grams flaxseed meal, preferably golden (about ¼ cup plus 1 tablespoon)

110 grams hot water (about ½ cup)

60 grams oil of choice (about ¼ cup plus ½ tablespoon)

176 grams tapioca starch (about 1⅓ cups), plus more for the work surface

36 grams blanched almond flour (about ¼ cup)

1 teaspoon double-acting, aluminum-free baking powder

¾ teaspoon kosher salt

Melted butter or oil of choice, for brushing the wontons

directions

1. Preheat the oven to 350 degrees. Line a baking sheet with parchment paper.

2. Make the crab filling: In a bowl, mix together the filling ingredients. Set aside.

3. Make the wonton wrappers: In a small bowl, mix together the flaxseed meal, hot water, and oil. Set aside.

4. In a larger bowl, whisk the tapioca starch, almond flour, baking powder, and salt until blended. Add the flaxseed meal mixture and mix until combined. Knead the dough in the bowl until it's stretchy and well mixed. If you find that your dough is not coming together, add an additional tablespoon of water.

5. Dust a sheet of parchment paper with tapioca starch. Roll out the dough as thinly as possible on the dusted parchment (or between 2 sheets of parchment). It should be paper-thin!

6. Using a 2½- to 3-inch round cookie cutter, biscuit cutter, or glass, cut out circles of dough.

7. Place 1 to 2 teaspoons of crab filling in the center of each wonton. Lift the edges of each circle up and around the filling and pinch together to seal. The wontons will resemble small coin purses.

8. Place the sealed wontons on the prepared baking sheet and brush them with melted butter. Bake for 35 to 38 minutes, until the wonton wrappers are crispy.

9. Serve hot!

notes

As this dough sits, it tends to dry out and start breaking easily. If this occurs, you can add a little more water to bring it back to life.

PREP TIME: 10 to 15 minutes
COOK TIME: 8 to 12 minutes
YIELD: 8 to 10 pancakes

DAIRY *free*, EGG *free*, NUT *free*, GRAIN *free*, COCONUT *free*

chinese scallion pancakes

These Chinese-style pancakes are truly unique! They deliver an intense, delicious flavor in a small package. I like to eat them warm and plain, but they are also delicious dipped in coconut aminos!

ingredients

200 grams superfine white rice flour (about 1¼ cups)

132 grams tapioca starch (about 1 cup)

1 teaspoon kosher salt

1 teaspoon garlic powder

¾ teaspoon xanthan gum or guar gum

½ cup (1 stick) salted butter, semi-chilled, or ghee, room temperature

110 grams water (about ½ cup)

3 to 4 scallions, chopped

1 tablespoon oil of choice, plus more for the pan

directions

1. In a bowl, whisk the rice flour, tapioca starch, salt, garlic powder, and xanthan gum until blended. Cut in the butter until small pea-sized clumps form.

2. Add the water and scallions and mix well with your hands to combine.

3. Heat the oil in a large skillet over medium-high heat.

4. Taking about ⅓ cup of the pancake batter, form a patty about ¼ inch thick. Form 2 or 3 more patties, depending on the size of your pan, and place them in the hot pan, being sure not to crowd the pan.

5. Cook for about 2 minutes. Flip and cook for an additional 2 to 3 minutes, until lightly golden brown, and then remove to a warm oven to keep warm while you cook the rest of the pancakes.

6. Repeat with the remaining pancake batter, adding more oil to the pan if needed.

PREP TIME: 20 to 25 minutes
COOK TIME: 2 hours
YIELD: 8 cups

DAIRY *free*, EGG *free*, NUT *free*, GRAIN *free*, COCONUT *free*

chili

This hearty chili doesn't need beans to make it amazing! Be sure to serve it with a side of Honey "Cornbread" Muffins (page 66).

ingredients

2 pounds ground beef

1½ cups chopped onion

1 green bell pepper, chopped

1 yellow bell pepper, chopped

3 garlic cloves, chopped (about 2 teaspoons)

1 jalapeño pepper, seeded and diced (optional)

1 (28-ounce) can crushed tomatoes

1 cup brewed coffee

2 tablespoons ground cumin

1 tablespoon chili powder

1 tablespoon dried oregano leaves

1 teaspoon garlic powder

1 teaspoon onion powder

1 teaspoon ground cinnamon

1 teaspoon ground nutmeg

½ teaspoon cayenne pepper

1½ teaspoons kosher salt, or to taste

1 teaspoon black pepper

directions

1. In a large skillet, brown the ground beef.
2. Place all of the ingredients in a large soup pot.
3. Bring to a simmer, cover, and cook for 2 hours.
4. Enjoy!

PREP TIME: 5 minutes
COOK TIME: 15 to 20 minutes
YIELD: 8 to 10 pieces

DAIRY *free*, **EGG** *free*, **NUT** *free*,
GRAIN *free*, **COCONUT** *free*

texas toast

Ever sunk your teeth into a thick slice of buttery Texas Toast? If you have, then you know it's real-deal comfort food. If not, take my word for it and make this garlic bread ASAP!

ingredients

1 Round Loaf (page 52)

¼ cup (½ stick) salted butter or ghee

2 cloves garlic, minced, or ½ teaspoon garlic powder

Kosher salt and black pepper

directions

1. Cut the Round Loaf into ½-inch-thick slices.
2. Preheat the oven to 350 degrees. Line a baking sheet with parchment paper.
3. In a saucepan over medium heat, melt the butter with the garlic and a pinch each of salt and pepper.
4. Brush the bread slices with the garlic butter.
5. Place the slices on the prepared baking sheet. Bake until golden and perfectly toasted, about 15 to 20 minutes.

CHAPTER 12

Soft Pretzels — Sweet and Savory

PREP TIME: 50 minutes, including proofing time
COOK TIME: 24 to 26 minutes
YIELD: 8 pretzels

DAIRY *free*, **EGG** *free*, **NUT** *free*, **GRAIN** *free*, COCONUT *free*

classic soft pretzels

I don't know about your household, but pretzels don't last long in mine—especially pretzels like these. Dunk them in mustard and enjoy!

ingredients

Yeast mixture:

416 grams lukewarm water (about 1¾ cups)

1 tablespoon coconut palm sugar

1½ teaspoons instant yeast

Pretzel dough:

129 grams coconut flour (about ¾ cup)

162 grams potato starch or sweet potato starch (about 1 cup)

132 grams tapioca starch (about 1 cup)

2 tablespoons potato flour

2½ teaspoons double-acting, aluminum-free baking powder

1½ teaspoons xanthan gum or guar gum

½ teaspoon kosher salt

60 grams Spectrum vegetable shortening (about ¼ cup plus 1 tablespoon)

1 tablespoon raw honey

Oil of choice, for brushing the pretzels

Coarse sea salt, for topping the pretzels

directions

1. Preheat the oven to 375 degrees to create a "hot box" for the pretzels to proof. Line a baking sheet with parchment paper.

2. In a small bowl, combine the lukewarm water, sugar, and yeast; set aside.

3. In a mixing bowl, whisk the coconut flour, starches, potato flour, baking powder, xanthan gum, and salt until blended. Add the shortening, honey, and yeast mixture and mix until a smooth dough forms.

4. Coat your hands in oil and divide the dough into 8 equal-sized balls. Working on a dry surface, gently roll each ball into a rope at least 12 inches long. Crisscross each rope into the classic pretzel shape.

5. Place the pretzels on the prepared baking sheet, brush them with oil, and cover them with a towel.

6. Turn off the oven and place the pretzels in the warm oven. Open the oven door a crack and allow the pretzels to proof for 20 to 25 minutes.

7. When the pretzels have finished proofing, remove them from the oven. Preheat the oven to 375 degrees.

8. Brush the pretzels with oil and top with coarse sea salt.

9. When the oven is fully preheated, bake the pretzels for 24 to 26 minutes, until firm to the touch and golden brown.

10. Store at room temperature in a sealed bag or container, or freeze for another day.

PREP TIME: 20 to 25 minutes
COOK TIME: 50 to 55 minutes
YIELD: 4 sandwiches

DAIRY *free*, **EGG** *free*, **NUT** *free*, **GRAIN** *free*, COCONUT *free*

bavarian pretzel sandwiches
with kielbasa, mustard, and caramelized onions

What goes better with a pretzel than some smoked sausage, mustard, and onions? I used kielbasa here because I love its rich, fatty flavor. The caramelized onions add another layer of flavor, and the mustard blends it all together!

ingredients

1 pound kielbasa

1 tablespoon salted butter, ghee, or mild-flavored oil

2 medium yellow onions, sliced

4 slices or ⅓ cup shredded mozzarella cheese (dairy or nondairy)

Prepared yellow mustard

1 batch Classic Soft Pretzels (page 278)

directions

1. Cook the kielbasa in a skillet over medium heat until cooked through. Set the sausage aside and drain the fat from the pan.

2. In the same pan, melt the butter over medium-low heat. Add the onions and cook until caramelized, 30 to 35 minutes.

3. When the onions are almost done, slice the kielbasa.

4. Assemble the sandwiches: Smear mustard on a pretzel and top with sliced kielbasa, caramelized onions, and cheese. Place another pretzel on top. Repeat with the rest of the pretzels and sandwich fixings.

5. Place the sandwiches in a dry pan over medium heat, covered with a lid, to melt the cheese.

PREP TIME: 20 to 25 minutes
COOK TIME: 4 to 6 minutes
YIELD: 4 sandwiches

DAIRY *free*, **EGG** *free*, **NUT** *free*,
GRAIN *free*, COCONUT *free*

grilled cheese pretzel sandwiches with bacon

I'm always looking to create an updated, adult spin on a classic. Here we have grilled cheese made with fluffy pretzels, plus bacon! I prefer American or cheddar cheese, but any cheese will do.

ingredients

8 slices bacon

1 batch Classic Soft Pretzels (page 278)

4 slices American or cheddar cheese (dairy or nondairy)

1 tablespoon salted butter, mild-flavored oil, or other fat of choice, for the pan

directions

1. In a skillet over medium heat, fry the bacon until crispy.

2. Assemble the sandwiches, using 2 pretzels, 2 slices of bacon, and a slice of cheese per sandwich.

3. Heat the butter in a large skillet over medium heat. Cook the sandwiches for 2 to 3 minutes per side, until the cheese has melted.

PREP TIME: 50 minutes, including proofing time
COOK TIME: 29 to 33 minutes
YIELD: 6 to 8 pretzels

. . . .

DAIRY *free,* **EGG** *free,* **NUT** *free,*
GRAIN *free,* COCONUT *free*

mexican hot chocolate
pretzels with caramel sauce

. . . .

Pretzels for dessert? You betcha! You can't go wrong with anything made with Mexican chocolate—especially with Caramel Sauce drizzled on top.

ingredients

Yeast mixture:

377 grams lukewarm water or brewed coffee (about 1⅔ cups)

1 tablespoon raw honey

1½ teaspoons instant yeast

Pretzel dough:

129 grams coconut flour (about ¾ cup)

162 grams potato starch or sweet potato starch (about 1 cup)

132 grams tapioca starch (about 1 cup), plus more for the work surface

2 tablespoons potato flour

1¾ teaspoons xanthan gum or guar gum

1 teaspoon double-acting, aluminum-free baking powder

½ teaspoon kosher salt, plus more for sprinkling the pretzels (optional)

50 grams cocoa powder (about ½ cup)

2½ teaspoons chili powder

2 teaspoons ground cinnamon

½ to ¾ teaspoon cayenne pepper (depending how spicy you like things)

½ teaspoon ground nutmeg

60 grams Spectrum vegetable shortening (about ¼ cup plus 1 tablespoon)

160 grams coconut palm sugar (about 1 cup)

84 grams raw honey (about ¼ cup)

Melted butter, for brushing the pretzels

Caramel Sauce:

¼ cup (½ stick) salted butter, ghee, or mild-flavored oil

½ cup coconut palm sugar

1 tablespoon heavy cream or coconut cream (from a can of coconut milk; see tutorial, page 26)

Pinch of kosher salt

directions

1. Preheat the oven to 375 degrees to create a "hot box" for the pretzels to proof. Line a baking sheet with parchment paper.

2. In a small bowl, combine the lukewarm water, honey, and yeast; set aside.

3. In a mixing bowl, whisk the coconut flour, starches, potato flour, xanthan gum, baking powder, salt, cocoa powder, chili powder, cinnamon, cayenne, and nutmeg until blended.

4. Add the shortening, sugar, honey, and yeast mixture and, using a hand-held electric mixer, beat on high speed for 30 seconds to 1 minute, until the ingredients have come together into a smooth dough.

5. Divide the dough into 6 to 8 equal-sized balls. Sprinkle a clean work surface with tapioca starch and gently roll each ball into a rope at least 12 inches long. Crisscross each rope into the classic pretzel shape.

6. Place the pretzels on the prepared baking sheet, brush them with melted butter, and cover with a towel.

7. Turn off the oven and place the pretzels in the warm oven. Open the oven door a crack and allow the pretzels to proof for 20 to 25 minutes.

8. When the pretzels have finished proofing, remove them from the oven. Preheat the oven to 375 degrees.

9. Brush the pretzels with melted butter and top with coarse sea salt.

10. When the oven is fully preheated, bake the pretzels for 29 to 33 minutes, until firm to the touch. Remove the pretzels from the oven and brush them with butter again.

11. While the pretzels are cooling, make the Caramel Sauce: In a saucepan over medium heat, combine the butter, sugar, cream, and salt. Heat, stirring constantly, until the caramel boils, and then remove from the heat.

12. Drizzle the Caramel Sauce over the pretzels and sprinkle with salt, if desired. Store at room temperature in a sealed bag or container, or freeze for another day.

PREP TIME: 10 to 15 minutes
COOK TIME: 3 to 5 minutes
YIELD: 4 s'mores

. . . .

DAIRY *free*, **EGG** *free*, **NUT** *free*,
GRAIN *free*, **COCONUT** *free*

chocolate pretzel s'mores

. . . .

This is my spin on an old favorite, but you don't have to wait for warm weather to eat these s'mores! Use my Mexican Hot Chocolate Pretzels (page 284) to sandwich the marshmallows.

ingredients

1 batch White Honey Marshmallows (page 306) or Chocolate Marshmallows (page 308)

1 batch Mexican Hot Chocolate Pretzels (page 284), without the Caramel Sauce

directions

1. Place 1 or 2 marshmallows on a chocolate pretzel.
2. Microwave for 30 seconds or until the marshmallow(s) begin to melt.
3. Remove from the microwave and smush the top pretzel on.
4. Repeat with the remaining pretzels and marshmallows.

PREP TIME: 40 minutes, including proofing time
COOK TIME: 22 to 26 minutes
YIELD: 1 tray

DAIRY *free,* **EGG** *free,* **NUT** *free,* **GRAIN** *free,* COCONUT *free*

cinnamon sugar pretzel bites

Bite-sized cinnamon sugar pretzels made Paleo! Thought it wasn't possible? Think again. You'll love these little pretzel bites tossed in coconut palm sugar.

ingredients

Yeast mixture:

377 grams lukewarm water (about 1⅔ cups)

1 tablespoon coconut palm sugar

1½ teaspoons instant yeast

Pretzel dough:

129 grams coconut flour (about ¾ cup)

162 grams potato starch or sweet potato starch (about 1 cup)

66 grams tapioca starch (about ½ cup)

2 tablespoons potato flour

1¾ teaspoons xanthan gum or guar gum

1 teaspoon double-acting, aluminum-free baking powder

½ teaspoon kosher salt

60 grams Spectrum vegetable shortening (about ¼ cup plus 1 tablespoon)

40 grams coconut palm sugar (about ¼ cup)

Coating:

¼ cup (½ stick) salted butter or ghee

½ cup coconut palm sugar

1 teaspoon ground cinnamon

directions

1. Preheat the oven to 375 degrees to create a "hot box" for the pretzels to proof. Line a baking sheet with parchment paper.

2. In a small bowl, combine the lukewarm water, sugar, and yeast; set aside.

3. In a mixing bowl, whisk the coconut flour, starches, potato flour, xanthan gum, baking powder, and salt until blended. Add the shortening and sugar and mix briefly.

4. Add the yeast mixture and, using a hand-held electric mixer, beat on high speed for about 1 minute, until a smooth dough comes together.

5. Working with about 2 tablespoons of dough at a time, shape the dough into balls.

6. Melt the butter in a microwave-safe bowl in the microwave.

7. In another bowl, mix together the sugar and cinnamon for the coating.

8. Working with one ball at a time, drop the dough balls into the butter and then roll them around in the cinnamon-sugar mixture.

9. Place the dough balls on the baking sheet and cover with a towel. Turn off the oven and place the baking sheet in the warm oven. Open the oven door a crack and allow the dough to proof for 20 to 25 minutes.

10. When the dough has finished proofing, preheat the oven to 375 degrees.

11. When the oven is fully preheated, bake the pretzel bites for 22 to 26 minutes, until firm to the touch and golden brown.

12. When the pretzel bites come out of the oven, roll them in a little extra cinnamon sugar. Store the cooled pretzel bites at room temperature in a sealed bag or container, or freeze for another day.

PREP TIME: 40 minutes, including proofing time
COOK TIME: 17 to 19 minutes
YIELD: 6 to 8 pretzel sticks

DAIRY *free*, **EGG** *free*, **NUT** *free*, **GRAIN** *free*, **COCONUT** *free*

jalapeño cheddar pretzel sticks

These pretzel sticks are absolutely delicious. I seed my jalapeño to tame the spiciness, but depending on how hot you like your food, you can opt to leave some seeds in. Be sure to put on gloves when cutting up the jalapeño; otherwise, your fingers may feel tingly for the rest of the day.

ingredients

Yeast mixture:

416 grams lukewarm water (about ¾ cup)

1 tablespoon sugar

1½ teaspoons instant yeast

Pretzel dough:

129 grams coconut flour (about ¾ cup)

162 grams potato starch or sweet potato starch (about 1 cup)

66 grams tapioca starch (about ½ cup)

2 tablespoons potato flour

1½ teaspoons xanthan gum or guar gum

1 teaspoon double-acting, aluminum-free baking powder

½ teaspoon kosher salt

60 grams Spectrum vegetable shortening (about ¼ cup plus 1 tablespoon)

1 jalapeño pepper, seeded and minced

1½ cups shredded cheddar cheese (dairy or nondairy)

Oil of choice, for brushing the pretzels

Coarse sea salt, for topping the pretzels

directions

1. Preheat the oven to 375 degrees to create a "hot box" for the pretzels to proof. Line a baking sheet with parchment paper.

2. In a small bowl, combine the lukewarm water, sugar, and yeast; set aside.

3. In a mixing bowl, whisk the coconut flour, starches, potato flour, xanthan gum, baking powder, and salt until blended. Add the shortening and mix briefly to work the shortening through the dry ingredients.

4. Add the yeast mixture and, using a hand-hand electric mixer, beat on high speed until a dough comes together.

5. Fold in the jalapeño and cheddar cheese.

6. Coat your hands in oil and divide the dough into 6 to 8 equal-sized balls. On a dry surface, gently roll each ball into a rope at least 12 inches long.

7. Place on the prepared baking sheet, 1½ inches apart. Brush with oil and cover with a towel. Turn off the oven and place the baking sheet in the warm oven. Open the door a crack and allow the pretzel sticks to proof for 20 to 25 minutes.

8. Remove the pretzel sticks from the oven. Preheat the oven to 375 degrees.

9. Brush the pretzel sticks with oil and top with coarse sea salt.

10. When the oven is fully preheated, bake the pretzel sticks for 17 to 19 minutes, until firm to the touch and golden brown.

11. Store the cooled pretzel sticks at room temperature in a sealed bag or container, or freeze for another day.

PREP TIME: 10 minutes
COOK TIME: 18 minutes
YIELD: 6 waffles

DAIRY *free*, **EGG** *free*, **NUT** *free*,
GRAIN *free*, **COCONUT** *free*

soft pretzel waffles

This recipe is serious fun! If you own a waffle iron, then you need to give it a go. I took my Classic Soft Pretzels recipe (page 278), sans yeast, and, rather than baking the dough, smushed it into my waffle iron. The results were truly amazing. These waffles are super-chewy and would be wonderful dipped in a sauce or used to make a sandwich.

ingredients

168 grams coconut flour (about 1 cup plus 2 tablespoons)

166 grams potato starch or sweet potato starch (about 1 cup)

132 grams tapioca starch (about 1 cup)

2 tablespoons potato flour

2½ teaspoons double-acting, aluminum-free baking powder

2 teaspoons kosher salt

1½ teaspoons xanthan gum

400 grams warm water (about 1¾ cups plus 1 tablespoon)

60 grams Spectrum vegetable shortening (about ¼ cup plus 1 tablespoon)

1 tablespoon raw honey

Oil of choice, for the waffle iron

directions

1. Preheat a waffle iron.

2. In a mixing bowl, whisk the dry ingredients until well blended. Add the warm water, shortening, and honey and, using a hand-held electric mixer, beat on high speed until a dough forms.

3. Liberally oil the preheated waffle iron. Form ½ cup of the dough into a ball, and then flatten it out until it's about the size of your hand. Place in the center of the iron and close.

4. Cook for about 3 minutes, until it reaches the desired level of crispiness.

5. Repeat with the remaining batter.

6. Serve warm or reheat before serving; the waffles will harden as they sit out. Store them in a sealed container at room temperature, or freeze for later.

PREP TIME: 10 minutes
COOK TIME: 21 minutes
YIELD: 7 waffles

DAIRY *free*, **EGG** *free*, **NUT** *free*,
GRAIN *free*, **COCONUT** *free*

honey mustard pretzel waffles

What's better than dipping a hot pretzel into gooey honey mustard? Well, not much, except having a honey mustard–flavored pretzel—which is exactly what you get with this fun waffle recipe! Great on its own as an on-the-go snack or used as the bread for your favorite sandwich, this pretty yellow waffle is going to be your new go-to.

ingredients

168 grams coconut flour (about 1 cup plus 2 tablespoons)

166 grams potato starch or sweet potato starch (about 1 cup)

132 grams tapioca starch (about 1 cup)

2 tablespoons potato flour

1 tablespoon dry mustard

2½ teaspoons double-acting, aluminum-free baking powder

1½ teaspoons xanthan gum

1 teaspoon kosher salt

½ teaspoon ground turmeric

385 grams warm water (about 1¾ cups)

60 grams Spectrum vegetable shortening (about ¼ cup plus 1 tablespoon)

84 grams raw honey (about ¼ cup)

1 tablespoon prepared yellow mustard

directions

1. Preheat a waffle iron.

2. In a mixing bowl, whisk the dry ingredients until well blended. Add the warm water, shortening, honey, and mustard and, using a hand-held electric mixer, beat on high speed until a dough forms.

3. Liberally oil the preheated waffle iron. Form ½ cup of the dough into a ball, and then flatten it out until it's about the size of your hand. Place in the center of the iron and close.

4. Cook for about 3 minutes, until it reaches the desired level of crispiness.

5. Repeat with the remaining batter.

6. Serve warm or reheat before serving; the waffles will harden as they cool. Store them in a sealed container at room temperature, or freeze for later.

CHAPTER 13

Desserts

PREP TIME: 10 to 15 minutes, plus 1 hour to chill the frosting
COOK TIME: 23 minutes
YIELD: 10 cupcakes

DAIRY *free*, **EGG** *free*, **NUT** *free*, GRAIN *free*, **COCONUT** *free*

red velvet cupcakes
with cream cheese frosting

Here we have an American favorite made without eggs! I used natural food coloring to give them a lovely red color without any scary unnatural dye. To help provide that characteristic color, I used Hershey's Special Dark cocoa powder. A dark Dutch-process cocoa powder would do the trick, too. If you are looking to avoid dairy, use the "Cream Cheese" Frosting paired with the Carrot Cake recipe on page 332 instead.

ingredients

Cupcake batter:

186 grams superfine white rice flour (about 1 cup plus 2½ tablespoons)

42 grams potato starch or sweet potato starch (about ¼ cup)

42 grams tapioca starch (about ⅓ cup)

160 grams coconut palm sugar (about 1 cup)

2 tablespoons dark cocoa powder

½ teaspoon double-acting, aluminum-free baking powder

¼ teaspoon xanthan gum

½ teaspoon kosher salt

100 grams Spectrum vegetable shortening (about ½ cup plus 2 tablespoons)

2 tablespoons salted butter or ghee, room temperature

1 tablespoon vanilla extract

2 tablespoons milk (dairy or nondairy)

83 grams natural red food coloring (about ¼ cup plus 2 tablespoons)

Cream Cheese Frosting:

1 (8-ounce) package cream cheese, softened

¼ cup (½ stick) butter, softened

¼ cup plus 1 tablespoon raw honey

½ teaspoon vanilla extract

Pinch of salt

directions

1. Preheat the oven to 350 degrees. Line 10 cups of a muffin tin with cupcake liners.

2. In a bowl, mix together the rice flour, starches, sugar, cocoa powder, baking powder, xanthan gum, and salt until blended.

3. Add the shortening and butter and, using a hand-held electric mixer, beat on high speed for 20 seconds. Add the vanilla, milk, and food coloring and mix on high speed until well combined.

4. Pour the batter into the lined muffin cups, filling each about three-quarters full.

5. Bake for 23 minutes or until a toothpick inserted comes out clean. After removing the cupcakes from the oven, allow them to cool in the pan.

6. While the cupcakes are baking, make the frosting: In a mixing bowl, combine all of the frosting ingredients. Using the hand-held mixer, beat until fluffy. Chill the frosting in the refrigerator for 1 hour before frosting the cupcakes.

7. Once the frosting has chilled and the cupcakes are cool, either pipe or spoon the frosting onto the cupcakes.

8. Store the frosted cupcakes at room temperature in a sealed container. If it is warm in your house, keep them in the fridge to prevent the frosting from melting.

notes

To make a chocolate and vanilla swirl frosting as pictured, you will need a double frosting pastry bag. Place half of the frosting in a separate bowl. Add 1½ tablespoons dark cocoa powder, ½ teaspoon vanilla extract, and 1 teaspoon honey. Beat again until fluffy. Place the vanilla frosting on one side of the double frosting pastry bag and the chocolate frosting on the other side. Chill the frosting in the fridge for about 1 hour. Then pipe onto the cooled cupcakes.

PREP TIME: 20 minutes
COOK TIME: 30 to 35 minutes
YIELD: Sixteen 2-inch bars

DAIRY *free*, EGG *free*, NUT *free*,
GRAIN *free*, COCONUT *free*

coffee and cookie brownie bars

Sometimes it's hard to choose between cookies and brownies for a treat. In this recipe, you can have both! The best part of these fun bars is that they are relatively low-carb and free of both dairy and eggs.

ingredients

Brownie batter:

216 grams blanched almond flour (about 1½ cups)

30 grams cocoa powder (about ⅓ cup)

2 teaspoons double-acting, aluminum-free baking powder

¼ teaspoon kosher salt

100 grams granulated maple sugar or coconut palm sugar (about ½ cup plus 2 tablespoons)

3 tablespoons milk (dairy or nondairy)

1 tablespoon vanilla extract

3 tablespoons Spectrum vegetable shortening

2 tablespoons finely ground coffee (preferably a dark roast for bolder flavor)

Cookie dough:

288 grams blanched almond flour (about 2 cups)

2 teaspoons double-acting, aluminum-free baking powder

⅛ teaspoon kosher salt

100 grams granulated maple sugar or coconut palm sugar (about ½ cup plus 2 tablespoons)

3 tablespoons milk (dairy or nondairy)

3 tablespoons Spectrum vegetable shortening

1 tablespoon vanilla extract

¾ cup chocolate chips

directions

1. Preheat the oven to 350 degrees. Line an 8-inch square baking pan with parchment paper.

2. Make the brownie batter: In a mixing bowl, whisk together the almond flour, cocoa powder, baking powder, and salt until blended. Add the sugar, milk, vanilla, shortening, and ground coffee and mix until the ingredients are fully incorporated and you have a thick dough. (You may need to mix for some time or use your hands; almond flour tends to remain dry and not incorporate into wet ingredients until it's mixed really well.)

3. Make the cookie dough: In a separate mixing bowl, whisk the almond flour, baking powder, and salt until blended. Add the sugar, milk, shortening, and vanilla and mix until the dry and wet ingredients are fully incorporated. (Again, you may need to mix for some time or use your hands.) Fold in the chocolate chips.

4. To get a nice checkered effect, roll the brownie batter into heaping tablespoon-sized balls. Wash your hands, and then do the same for the cookie dough. Drop the balls of dough into the pan so that they alternate in color.

5. Once all the dough is in the pan, lightly press down on the top with a sheet of parchment paper so that the brownie and cookie balls come together.

6. Bake for 30 to 35 minutes, until lightly browned. Store at room temperature in a sealed bag or container, or freeze for later.

PREP TIME: 15 minutes, plus about 1 hour to set
COOK TIME: n/a
YIELD: 16 sunbutter cups

DAIRY *free*, **EGG** *free*, **NUT** *free*, **GRAIN** *free*, **COCONUT** *free*

sunbutter cups

My all-time favorite candy growing up was (and still is) peanut butter cups. I could eat them by the dozen! This adapted version tastes even better than the real thing, and no one would ever know that they are made with sunflower seed butter and not peanut butter.

ingredients

2½ cups chocolate chips, melted

½ cup sunflower seed butter

¼ cup powdered coconut palm sugar or maple sugar (see tutorial, page 26)

1½ teaspoons vanilla extract

Pinch of kosher salt

Melted coconut oil, if needed

directions

1. Line a mini muffin pan with mini foil cupcake liners. Spoon the melted chocolate into the lined cups, filling each about one-quarter full. Place in the freezer to set, about 5 to 10 minutes.

2. In a bowl, combine the sunflower seed butter, powdered sugar, vanilla, and salt and stir until well blended.

3. Take a heaping teaspoonful of the sunbutter mixture and roll it into a ball. Flatten slightly and place on top of the set chocolate in a foil liner. Repeat with the remaining sunbutter mixture.

4. Spoon the remaining melted chocolate on top of the sunbutter in the cups, being sure to cover it completely. You may need to add a teaspoon of melted coconut oil to your melted chocolate to thin it out a bit.

5. Tap the pan on the countertop to even out and smooth the chocolate. Place in the fridge or freezer until set. Store these Sunbutter Cups at room temperature in a sealed container, or in the fridge or freezer for later if your kitchen is hot!

PREP TIME: 30 minutes
COOK TIME: 45 minutes
YIELD: Sixteen 2-inch brownies

DAIRY *free*, EGG *free*, NUT *free*,
GRAIN *free*, COCONUT *free*

pms brownies

Extreme indulgence. EXTREME. Make this recipe on the worst day of your life, and I promise it will be a game-changer. I call these PMS brownies for obvious reasons. Sometimes you just need something crazy delicious. This recipe is that.

ingredients

Brownies:

1 (10-ounce) package Enjoy Life brand chocolate chips, melted but not hot

140 grams salted butter or ghee, softened (½ cup/1 stick plus 2 tablespoons)

2 teaspoons vanilla extract

3 tablespoons finely ground coffee (preferably a dark roast for bolder flavor)

188 grams coconut palm sugar (about 1 cup plus 2 tablespoons)

28 grams blanched almond flour (about a scant ¼ cup)

30 grams tapioca starch (about ¼ cup)

2 large eggs

1 large egg yolk

1 cup chocolate chips (optional)

Ganache:

¾ cup chocolate chips

½ cup coconut cream (from a can of coconut milk; see tutorial, page 26) or heavy cream

Additional toppings:

8 to 10 Sunbutter Cups (page 302), chopped into large pieces

More chocolate chips

Caramel:

¾ cup (1½ sticks) salted butter or ghee

1¼ cups coconut palm sugar

1 tablespoon coconut cream (from a can of coconut milk; see tutorial, page 26) or heavy cream

Pinch of kosher salt

directions

1. Preheat the oven to 350 degrees. Line an 8-inch square pan with parchment paper.

2. Make the brownies: In a large bowl, mix together the melted chocolate chips and softened butter. Once incorporated, mix in the vanilla and ground coffee.

3. In a separate bowl, combine the sugar, almond flour, and tapioca starch. Gradually add the dry mixture to the chocolate mixture, stirring to combine. Add the eggs and yolk and beat until fully combined.

4. If you are adding the optional 1 cup chocolate chips to the batter, make sure that it is no longer warm before folding them in.

5. Pour the batter into the prepared pan and tap on the countertop to settle the batter. Bake for 35 minutes or until the brownies have set and do not jiggle in the pan.

6. Remove the brownies from the oven and allow them to cool in the pan.

7. While the brownies are cooling, make the ganache: Place the chocolate chips in the microwave and melt for roughly 1 minute. Remove and add the coconut cream, stirring until it comes together.

8. Spoon the ganache over the cooled brownies. Then drop the chopped Sunbutter Cups and chocolate chips on top. While that is cooling, make the caramel.

9. Make the caramel: In a heavy-bottomed saucepan, bring the caramel ingredients to a gentle boil over medium heat, stirring constantly. Continue to boil gently, while stirring, until it thickens. Remove from the heat and drizzle the caramel on top of the brownies.

10. Let the caramel sit and harden. Then cut the brownies into squares and serve. Store leftovers in a sealed bag or container at room temperature, or freeze for later.

PREP TIME: 30 minutes
COOK TIME: 9 to 14 minutes
YIELD: Sixteen 2-inch marshmallows

DAIRY *free*, EGG *free*, NUT *free*, GRAIN *free*, COCONUT *free*

white honey marshmallows

Before you make these, let me tell you: You will need a candy thermometer! If you wanted, you could even make this recipe into peeps by adding a little natural food coloring while whipping the marshmallows and using a fun cookie cutter to cut them into shapes.

ingredients

½ cup cold water

2 packets gelatin (2 tablespoons)

1 cup raw honey

½ cup water

1 teaspoon vanilla extract

¼ teaspoon kosher salt

Tapioca starch, for dusting

directions

1. In the bowl of a stand mixer, using the whisk attachment, mix together the cold water and gelatin.

2. In a deep pot with a candy thermometer attached to the side, combine the honey, water, vanilla, and salt. Heat the mixture over medium-high heat until it reaches 240 degrees, the hardball stage (roughly 9 to 14 minutes).

3. Carefully pour this mixture into the gelatin mixture (it will be very hot).

4. Starting with the mixer on low speed and gradually increasing to high speed, whip for 8 to 10 minutes, until the mixture becomes white and thick.

5. Meanwhile, line an 8-inch square baking pan with parchment paper and dust it with tapioca starch.

6. As soon as the mixture is thick and white in color, quickly pour the marshmallow fluff into the prepared pan, as it will get thicker by the second.

7. Dust with more tapioca starch (this will help you smooth out the surface).

8. Let cool for several hours in the fridge, which will allow the marshmallows to set.

9. Cut the marshmallows into squares. If you find that the knife is sticking, coat it in tapioca starch before each cut. Store the marshmallows in a sealed bag or container at room temperature, or freeze for later use.

DAIRY *free*, **EGG** *free*, **NUT** *free*,
GRAIN *free*, **COCONUT** *free*

chocolate marshmallows

What would life be without variety? I used my White Honey Marshmallows base (page 306) to create these Chocolate Marshmallows!

ingredients

½ cup cold water

3 packets gelatin (3 tablespoons)

1 cup raw honey

½ cup water

1 teaspoon vanilla extract

¼ teaspoon kosher salt

½ cup cocoa powder, plus more for the pan

directions

1. In the bowl of a stand mixer, using the whisk attachment, mix together the cold water and gelatin.

2. In a deep pot with a candy thermometer attached to the side, combine the honey, water, vanilla, and salt. Heat the mixture over medium-high heat until it reaches 240 degrees, the hardball stage (roughly 9 to 14 minutes).

3. Carefully pour this mixture into the gelatin mixture (it will be very hot).

4. Starting with the mixer on low speed and gradually increasing to high speed, whip for 8 to 10 minutes, until the mixture becomes white and thick. In the last 4 minutes, add the cocoa powder.

5. Meanwhile, line an 8-inch baking pan with parchment paper and lightly dust it with cocoa powder.

6. As soon as the mixture has fully thickened and the chocolate is incorporated, quickly pour the marshmallow fluff into the pan.

7. Lightly dust with more cocoa powder (this will help you smooth out the surface).

8. Let cool for several hours in the fridge, which will allow the marshmallows to set.

9. Cut the marshmallows into squares. If you find that the knife is sticking, coat it in cocoa powder before each cut. Store the marshmallows in a sealed bag or container at room temperature, or freeze for later use.

PREP TIME: 15 minutes
COOK TIME: 12 minutes
YIELD: 12 cones

DAIRY *free*, EGG *free*, NUT *free*,
GRAIN *free*, COCONUT *free*

waffle cones

I love ice cream. What do I love even more? Being able to scoop it into a grain-free waffle cone, of course! You will need a waffle cone form to make this recipe, plus a waffle cone maker if you want the signature waffle pattern on your cones.

ingredients

2 large eggs

80 grams granulated sugar of choice (about ½ cup)

56 grams melted (but not hot) salted butter, melted ghee, or mild-flavored oil (about ¼ cup)

3 tablespoons milk (dairy or nondairy)

1 teaspoon vanilla extract

118 grams potato starch (about ⅔ cup)

72 grams blanched almond flour (about ½ cup)

¼ teaspoon double-acting, aluminum-free baking powder

⅛ teaspoon xanthan gum or guar gum

⅛ teaspoon kosher salt

Flourishes (optional):

½ cup chocolate chips, melted

Gluten-free sprinkles

directions

1. Preheat a waffle cone maker to medium-high.

2. In the bowl of a stand mixer, using the whisk attachment, whip the eggs until slightly frothy.

3. Add the sugar, melted butter, milk, and vanilla and mix until incorporated.

4. In a separate bowl, whisk the potato starch, almond flour, baking powder, xanthan gum, and salt until blended. Add the dry ingredients to the wet ingredients and mix until well combined, scraping down the sides of the bowl.

5. Pour 2 tablespoons of the batter into the preheated waffle cone maker and cook for 50 to 60 seconds. Remove when it starts to get ever so slightly golden on the edges. The more golden it is, the harder it will be to handle.

6. Wrap the cooked waffle around the waffle cone form. Press and seal the side seam and bottom.

7. Leave on the cone form for a minute so that it holds its shape, and then transfer to a tall glass to cool further.

8. Repeat the process with the remaining batter.

9. For fun, you can dip the end of each cone in melted chocolate and then in sprinkles. These are great for kids' birthday parties! Store the waffle cones in the freezer if you aren't using them the day you make them.

variation :

Baked Waffle Cones

If you don't have a waffle cone maker, you may bake the waffle cones, although you will still need a waffle cone form to shape them.

To make baked waffle cones, preheat the oven to 325 degrees. Prepare the batter for the waffles, following Steps 2 to 4 above, but omit the xanthan gum. Line a baking sheet with parchment paper and, using a bowl, trace 2 circles roughly 6 inches in diameter.

Pour about 3 tablespoons of the batter into the center of each circle and, using the back of a spoon, evenly spread the batter to fill out the circle.

Bake for 7 to 8 minutes, until the waffles are golden but still malleable. Remove from the oven and roll the cooked waffle onto the waffle cone form. Press down on the bottom to seal and let cool and harden. Repeat the process with the remaining batter.

PREP TIME: 15 minutes
COOK TIME: 12 minutes
YIELD: 12 cones

DAIRY *free,* **EGG** *free,* **NUT** *free,*
GRAIN *free,* **COCONUT** *free*

chocolate waffle cones

For all you chocolate lovers out there, here's a waffle cone just for you!

ingredients

2 large eggs

80 grams granulated sugar of choice (about ½ cup)

56 grams melted (but not hot) salted butter, melted ghee, or mild-flavored oil (about ¼ cup)

3 tablespoons milk (dairy or nondairy)

1 teaspoon vanilla extract

162 grams potato starch (about ⅔ cup plus ¼ cup)

72 grams blanched almond flour (about ½ cup)

¼ teaspoon double-acting, aluminum-free baking powder

⅛ teaspoon kosher salt

2 tablespoons cocoa powder

Flourishes (optional):

½ cup chocolate chips, melted

Gluten-free sprinkles

directions

1. Preheat a waffle cone maker to medium-high.

2. In the bowl of a stand mixer, using the whisk attachment, whip the eggs until slightly frothy.

3. Add the sugar, melted butter, milk, and vanilla and mix until incorporated.

4. In a separate bowl, whisk the potato starch, almond flour, baking powder, salt, and cocoa powder until blended. Add the dry ingredients to the wet ingredients and mix until well combined, scraping down the sides of the bowl.

5. Pour 2 tablespoons of the batter into the preheated waffle cone maker and cook for 50 to 60 seconds. Remove when it starts to get ever so slightly golden on the edges. The more golden it is, the harder it will be to handle.

6. Wrap the cooked waffle around the waffle cone form. Press and seal the side seam and bottom.

7. Leave on the cone form for a minute so that it holds its shape, and then transfer to a tall glass to cool further.

8. Repeat the process with the remaining batter.

9. For fun, you can dip the end of each cone in melted chocolate and then in sprinkles. These are great for kids' birthday parties! Store the waffle cones in the freezer if you aren't using them the day you make them.

variation:

Chocolate Waffle Bowls

To make Chocolate Waffle Bowls, follow Steps 1 to 5 above. Then, instead of shaping the hot cooked waffle into a cone, gently press it over an upside-down ramekin or small bowl. These bowls are great for serving ice cream, like my Chocolate and Red Wine Ice Cream (page 316).

PREP TIME: 30 to 40 minutes
COOK TIME: 1 hour 20 minutes
YIELD: 8 to 10 servings

DAIRY *free,* **EGG** *free,* **NUT** *free,*
GRAIN *free,* **COCONUT** *free*

angell food cake

We call this "Angell" Food Cake, as that's my last name, and it's a bit famous around here! It's one of my most requested recipes when I attend family gatherings. While this cake has a few extra steps, it's worth the process! No one will guess that it's free of refined sugar.

ingredients

12 large eggs

120 grams superfine white rice flour (about ¾ cup)

90 grams tapioca starch (about ½ cup plus 3 tablespoons)

50 grams potato starch or sweet potato starch (about ¼ cup plus 2 teaspoons)

160 grams granulated maple sugar or coconut palm sugar (about 1 cup) (see Notes)

1 teaspoon xanthan gum or guar gum

¼ teaspoon kosher salt

1¼ teaspoons cream of tartar

120 grams powdered maple sugar or coconut palm sugar (about 1 cup) (see tutorial, page 26)

1 teaspoon vanilla extract

notes

If you use coconut palm sugar rather than granulated maple sugar, the cake will be darker and rise slightly less.

Sifting the flour and starches together makes a big difference. You want them perfectly blended.

Your cake must be baked in a grease-free pan. Do not use a pan with a nonstick surface. The cake needs to stick to the pan!

If you have never made an angel food cake before, watch a video tutorial first on YouTube. All angel food cakes are made in basically the same way!

directions

1. Remove the eggs from the fridge and allow them to sit on the counter until they have come to room temperature. (Do not use a boxed egg white variation; only real eggs will do the job.) Depending on the temperature of your kitchen, this could take anywhere from 30 minutes to 1 hour.

2. In a bowl, sift together the rice flour, starches, sugar, and xanthan gum (see Notes). Set aside.

3. Separate the egg whites from the yolks. Place the egg whites in the stainless-steel bowl of a stand mixer. Save the yolks for another use.

4. Preheat the oven to 325 degrees. Set an oven rack in the bottom position.

5. Double-check to see if the egg whites are at room temperature. If they are, add the salt to the egg whites and begin whipping on high speed. Once the egg whites are foamy, add the cream of tartar.

6. Continue to whip on high speed until soft peaks begin to form. Add the powdered sugar, a little at a time.

7. Beat until stiff peaks form. Add the vanilla and beat for another second, and then turn off the mixer.

8. Using a spatula, gently fold in the flour mixture, little by little. The key here is gentle movement so that you don't destroy the peaks, but it's crucial that the flour is thoroughly mixed in. Your peaks are going to lose a little bit of their volume as you do this—and that's okay!

9. Place the fully incorporated mixture into an ungreased angel food cake pan (see Notes). Using a spatula, smooth out the top.

10. Place the cake on the bottom rack of the oven and bake for exactly 1 hour and 20 minutes. Tent with foil for the last 20 minutes, opening and shutting the oven door quickly but gently. Do not open the oven door at other time during baking. (If you open the oven door more than once, the cake is likely to fall.)

11. Gently remove the cake from the oven and allow it to cool in the pan.

12. When the cake is fully cooled, and not before, remove it from the pan: Run a serrated knife around the edge to loosen it, and then flip it onto a serving platter. If needed, use a knife to loosen the top of the cake from the pan.

PREP TIME: 30 minutes, plus 1 hour 10 minutes to chill and churn
COOK TIME: 20 minutes
YIELD: 3 cups ice cream, ½ cup sauce

DAIRY *free*, EGG *free*, NUT *free*, GRAIN *free*, COCONUT *free*

chocolate and red wine ice cream

For those who consume dairy, this is some seriously grown-up ice cream with rich flavors that will have you making the recipe again and again. The combination of dark chocolate and red wine is life-changing. It is served with a cherry wine sauce that is quick to throw together. For an extra-fancy (and delicious!) treat, I like to serve this ice cream in Chocolate Waffle Bowls (page 312) topped with Coconut Whipped Topping (page 318).

ingredients

Chocolate and red wine flavoring:

½ cup cocoa powder

½ cup red wine

½ cup coconut palm sugar

1½ ounces bittersweet chocolate (55% to 70% cacao), finely chopped

Ice cream base:

2 cups whole milk

1 cup heavy cream

½ cup coconut palm sugar

2 tablespoons coconut nectar

1 tablespoon plus 1 teaspoon tapioca starch

⅛ teaspoon kosher salt

3 tablespoons cream cheese, softened

Cherry wine sauce:

1 cup sweet cherries, pitted and chopped, plus more for garnish (garnish optional)

¼ cup coconut palm sugar

¼ cup red wine of choice

¼ cup water

½ teaspoon tapioca, potato, or sweet potato starch

Pinch of kosher salt

For serving (optional):

1 batch Chocolate Waffle Bowls (page 312)

1 batch Coconut Whipped Topping (page 318)

directions

1. Make the chocolate and red wine flavoring: In a small saucepan over medium heat, bring the cocoa powder, red wine, and sugar to a simmer, stirring to dissolve the cocoa powder and sugar.

2. Once the sugar has dissolved, allow to simmer for 30 more seconds. Remove from the heat and set aside for 5 minutes to cool slightly, and then stir in the bittersweet chocolate.

3. Make the ice cream base: In a medium saucepan, whisk the milk, cream, sugar, coconut nectar, tapioca starch, and salt until blended. Bring the mixture to a boil over medium-high heat.

4. Boil for 5 minutes, and then remove the pan from the heat. Add the chocolate and red wine flavoring and the cream cheese and mix well to combine and remove any lumps. Set aside and let cool slightly, about 5 minutes. If the mixture has any lumps in it, use a blender or an immersion blender to purée it until smooth.

5. Prepare an ice water bath in a large bowl. Pour the slightly cooled ice cream base into a zip-top bag, seal, and place in the ice water bath for 30 minutes to chill.

6. Pour the chilled ice cream base into an ice cream machine and churn, following the manufacturer's directions, for 35 to 40 minutes. (Because of the alcohol content in the wine, the ice cream may not freeze 100 percent.)

7. Place the ice cream in an airtight container and freeze for 8 hours or more before serving.

8. When you're ready to serve the ice cream, make the cherry wine sauce: Put the cherries in a small saucepan and cover with the sugar and red wine. Place the pan over medium-low heat to slowly warm the cherries and melt the sugar.

9. In a small bowl, whisk together the water and starch, making sure that there are no clumps. Add to the saucepan with the cherries. Cook, covered, for about 5 minutes to allow the sugar to fully dissolve and the cherries to soften.

10. Remove the lid and increase the heat to medium-high to bring the mixture to a simmer, stirring often.

11. Simmer, lowering the heat if needed, for about 8 to 10 minutes, until it thickens. Add the salt and stir to combine. Let cool to room temperature before using.

12. To serve, scoop the ice cream into Chocolate Waffle Bowls, if using, or other serving bowls. Spoon the cherry wine sauce over the ice cream, and top with Coconut Whipped Topping and a cherry, if desired.

PREP TIME: 20 minutes
COOK TIME: n/a
YIELD: 2 cups

DAIRY *free*, **EGG** *free*, **NUT** *free*, **GRAIN** *free*, **COCONUT** *free*

coconut whipped topping

This whipped topping is the real deal! It can be made ahead and stored in the fridge in a sealed container for up to a week. Thanks to the use of gelatin, it is stable and will hold up like regular whipped cream without deflating or melting into a puddle. Be sure to stick your cans of coconut milk in the fridge the night before you plan to make this recipe!

ingredients

2 tablespoons hot water

1 teaspoon vanilla extract

½ teaspoon gelatin

¼ cup raw honey

2 (13½-ounce) cold cans full-fat coconut milk (chilled in the fridge overnight)

directions

1. In a microwave-safe bowl, whisk the hot water, vanilla, and gelatin very thoroughly, making sure that there are no clumps.

2. Microwave the gelatin mixture for 20 seconds.

3. Place the gelatin mixture and honey in the bowl of a stand mixer outfitted with a whisk attachment, or in a metal bowl if using a hand-held electric mixer. Whip on high speed for 6 to 7 minutes, until the mixture thickens.

4. Open the cans of coconut milk and scoop off the heavy cream that has risen to the top. Be careful to remove just the fatty cream, leaving the watery liquid in the can. (Stick the leftover coconut water in the fridge for use in another recipe or to drink.)

5. Add the coconut cream to the bowl and whip until frothy and thickened; this will take a minute or two.

PREP TIME: 20 minutes
COOK TIME: 16 to 17 minutes
YIELD: 12 cookies

DAIRY *free*, **EGG** *free*, **NUT** *free*, **GRAIN** *free*, **COCONUT** *free*

chocolate chip cookies— two ways!

Chocolate chip cookies can be made in so many ways! I couldn't resist including two versions: The almond flour cookies are soft and chewy, and the coconut flour recipe makes cookies similar in texture to crispy sugar cookies. Make both versions, and then weigh in online using the hashtag #Everylastcrumb. Let me know which recipe wins!

ingredients

Almond flour version:

288 grams blanched almond flour (about 2 cups)

1 teaspoon double-acting, aluminum-free baking powder

¼ teaspoon kosher salt

80 grams granulated maple sugar or coconut palm sugar (about ½ cup)

3 tablespoons salted butter, Spectrum vegetable shortening, or coconut oil, room temperature

2 tablespoons milk (dairy or nondairy)

1 tablespoon vanilla extract

½ to 1 cup chocolate chips

directions (almond flour version)

1. Preheat the oven to 350 degrees. Line 2 standard-sized or 1 large baking sheet with parchment paper.

2. In the bowl of a stand mixer, using the whisk attachment (or by hand in a mixing bowl), mix the almond flour, baking powder, and salt until blended. Add the rest of the ingredients, except the chocolate chips, and mix until combined. Stir in the chocolate chips by hand.

3. Divide the dough into 12 equal portions. Using your hands, form each portion into a patty about ¾ inch thick and 3 inches in diameter. (*Note:* This dough may be a little crumbly—don't fret if it is!) Place the cookies on the prepared baking sheet(s), 1½ inches apart.

4. Bake for 16 to 17 minutes, until the bottoms and edges start to turn lightly golden brown.

5. Allow the cookies to cool on the pan(s). Store the cooled cookies at room temperature in a sealed bag or container, or freeze for another day.

variation:

Soft Baked Chocolate Chip Cookies (Coconut Flour–Based)

The coconut flour recipe on the opposite page creates delightfully crispy chocolate chip cookies. But with the simple addition of flaxseed meal and hot water, you can give the same cookies a soft baked texture. Mix together 1 tablespoon flaxseed meal (preferably golden) and 1 tablespoon hot water and add it to the cookie dough with the rest of the ingredients.

PREP TIME: 20 minutes
COOK TIME: 16 to 18 minutes
YIELD: 6 to 8 cookies

DAIRY *free*, EGG *free*, NUT *free*,
GRAIN *free*, COCONUT *free*

ingredients

Coconut flour version:

40 grams tapioca starch (about ¼ cup plus 1 tablespoon)

42 grams coconut flour (about ¼ cup)

1 teaspoon double-acting, aluminum-free baking powder

¼ teaspoon kosher salt

72 grams salted butter or Spectrum vegetable shortening, room temperature (about ¼ cup plus 2 tablespoons) (see Notes)

69 grams milk (dairy or nondairy) (about ¼ cup plus 1 tablespoon)

40 grams granulated maple sugar or coconut palm sugar (about ¼ cup)

1 teaspoon vanilla extract

½ cup chocolate chips

directions (coconut flour version)

1. Preheat the oven to 350 degrees. Line a baking sheet with parchment paper.

2. In the bowl of a stand mixer, using the whisk attachment (or by hand in a mixing bowl), mix the tapioca starch, coconut flour, baking powder, and salt until blended. Add the rest of the ingredients, except the chocolate chips, and mix until combined. Stir in the chocolate chips by hand.

3. Take 2 heaping tablespoons of dough and form into a ½-inch-thick patty. Place on the prepared baking sheet. Repeat with the rest of the dough, spacing the cookies 1½ inches apart.

4. Bake for 16 to 18 minutes, until golden brown on the bottoms and edges.

5. Allow the cookies to cool on the baking sheet. Store the cooled cookies at room temperature in a sealed bag or container, or freeze for another day.

notes

Butter tastes better in this recipe, but in a pinch, shortening will work.

PREP TIME: 20 minutes
COOK TIME: 11 to 14 minutes
YIELD: 14 to 16 cookies

DAIRY *free*, EGG *free*, **NUT** *free*,
GRAIN *free*, COCONUT *free*

cinnamon roll cookies

I don't know a single person who doesn't love cinnamon rolls! For fun, I turned the holiday classic into a cookie that has the texture of a sugar cookie with pretty layers of cinnamon and sugar. Not only do these cookies taste incredible, but they are fun to make, too. Bring them to your next cookie exchange!

ingredients

Cookie dough:

126 grams coconut flour (about ¾ cup)

99 grams tapioca starch (about ¾ cup)

205 grams granulated maple sugar or coconut palm sugar (about 1¼ cups)

2 teaspoons double-acting, aluminum-free baking powder

¼ teaspoons kosher salt

216 grams Spectrum vegetable shortening (about 1 cup plus 2 tablespoons)

2 tablespoons plus 1 teaspoon unsweetened applesauce

2 teaspoons vanilla extract

1 large egg

Cinnamon filling:

¾ cup coconut palm sugar

2 tablespoons melted salted butter or mild-flavored oil

2 teaspoons ground cinnamon

Glaze:

1 cup granulated maple sugar or coconut palm sugar

1 tablespoon plus 2 teaspoons milk (dairy or nondairy) or water

1 teaspoon vanilla extract

directions

1. Preheat the oven to 325 degrees. Line a baking sheet with parchment paper.

2. Make the cookie dough: Mix together the coconut flour, tapioca starch, sugar, baking powder, and salt.

3. Add the shortening and thoroughly mix into the flour mixture.

4. Add the applesauce, vanilla, and egg to the flour and shortening mixture and mix well with your hands until a dough forms. Roll the dough into a large ball, place it in a bowl, and set aside.

5. Make the cinnamon filling: In a small bowl, combine the sugar, melted butter, and cinnamon. Stir until well combined.

6. Roll out the dough between 2 sheets of parchment paper into a square that is about ¼ inch thick. Occasionally remove the top sheet of parchment and, using your hands or the rolling pin, straighten the sides of the dough to form a square. Return the top sheet of parchment and continue gently rolling the dough.

7. Remove the top sheet of parchment and spread the cinnamon filling from edge to edge across the entire surface of the dough. Replace the top sheet of parchment and very gently roll the rolling pin over the surface to work the cinnamon filling into the dough.

8. Remove the top sheet of parchment and, grabbing one end of the dough with the bottom layer of parchment, begin to tightly roll the dough into a log, peeling back the parchment as you go. Take your time with this step—you want to roll the dough tightly, as this will be what keeps everything intact when you make your slices!

9. Once the cookie log is formed, use unflavored dental floss to slice it into ½- to ¾-inch-thick cookies.

10. Place the cookies about ½ inch apart on the prepared baking sheet. Bake for 11 to 14 minutes, until lightly golden. Remove from the oven and allow to cool completely on the baking sheet. If you take them off too soon, they will crumble!

11. While the cookies are cooling, make the glaze: Place the sugar in a coffee grinder or spice grinder and grind until it is a powder. Place the powdered sugar in a small bowl and mix it with the milk and vanilla. Drizzle the glaze over the cooled cookies.

extra-moist
triple chocolate cake

Back before I quit gluten, I made mile-high cakes that were over-the-top moist. I would replace the milk in my cake recipes with store-bought pudding. Nowadays, I'm not exactly buying pudding, and I'm working with a brand-new set of flours. I replaced the pudding with a puréed avocado to get the same effect and swapped out the all-purpose flour with coconut flour. Instead of using white sugar to make the frosting, I used a second avocado. This cake is very dark, rich, and all-around wonderful.

ingredients

Cake batter:

72 grams coconut flour (about ⅔ cup plus 2 tablespoons)

88 grams potato starch or sweet potato starch (about ½ cup)

25 grams cocoa powder (about ¼ cup)

1 tablespoon double-acting, aluminum-free baking powder

⅛ teaspoon kosher salt

1 avocado, pitted, peeled, and puréed

4 large eggs

165 grams coconut palm sugar or granulated maple sugar (about 1 cup)

120 grams milk (dairy or nondairy) (about ½ cup plus 2 teaspoons)

44 grams melted salted butter, melted ghee, or mild-flavored oil (about a scant ¼ cup)

1 teaspoon lemon juice or apple cider vinegar

1 cup chocolate chips

Chocolate espresso frosting:

1 avocado, pitted, peeled, and puréed

¾ cup Spectrum vegetable shortening

⅔ cup powdered coconut palm sugar or maple sugar (see tutorial, page 26)

½ cup cocoa powder

Pinch of kosher salt

2 to 3 teaspoons finely ground coffee

directions

1. Preheat the oven to 350 degrees. Spray an 8-inch round cake pan with nonstick spray.

2. Make the batter: In a food processor or blender, briefly mix together the coconut flour, potato starch, cocoa powder, baking powder, and salt. Add the rest of the batter ingredients, except the chocolate chips, and process until light and fluffy. Stir in the chocolate chips.

3. Pour the batter into the prepared cake pan. Bake for 40 minutes or until a toothpick inserted comes out clean.

4. Remove the cake from the oven and allow it to cool in the pan.

5. While the cake is cooling, prepare the frosting: In a food processor or blender, combine the avocado, shortening, powdered sugar, cocoa powder, salt, and 2 teaspoons ground coffee. Blend until light and fluffy. Taste for coffee flavor and add up to 1 teaspoon more ground coffee, if desired, but note that the flavor will intensify as the frosting sits.

6. Chill the frosting in the fridge before icing the cake.

notes

This recipe makes one cake layer. If you would like to make more than one layer, bake another batch while the first cake is cooling. You will also need to double the frosting amount.

PREP TIME: 15 minutes
COOK TIME: 38 to 40 minutes
YIELD: 8 to 10 servings

DAIRY *free*, **EGG** *free*, **NUT** *free*,
GRAIN *free*, **COCONUT** *free*

banana-chocolate bundt cake with candied bacon

This cake brings together three flavors that were made for each other: banana, chocolate, and bacon. They are combined in an egg-free cake that tastes like a cross between banana bread and cake. Elvis would be proud!

ingredients

Cake batter:

316 grams chestnut flour (about 2 cups)

168 grams potato starch or sweet potato starch (about 1 cup)

1 tablespoon double-acting, aluminum-free baking powder

2 teaspoons ground cinnamon

1 teaspoon xanthan gum or guar gum

½ teaspoon kosher salt

240 grams coconut palm sugar (about 1½ cups)

260 grams puréed banana (about 1 cup, or 2 medium bananas)

96 grams mild-flavored oil, melted salted butter, or melted ghee (about ½ cup)

1 tablespoon plus 1 teaspoon apple cider vinegar

1 tablespoon vanilla extract

Toppings:

1 cup chocolate chips

1 tablespoon coconut oil or Spectrum vegetable shortening

5 slices Candied Bacon (page 328), roughly chopped

directions

1. Preheat the oven to 350 degrees. Lightly oil a nonstick Bundt pan.

2. Make the batter: In the bowl of a stand mixer, using the whisk attachment (or by hand in a large bowl), mix the chestnut flour, potato starch, baking powder, cinnamon, xanthan gum, and salt until blended. Add the rest of the batter ingredients and mix until smooth.

3. Pour the batter into the prepared Bundt pan. Bake for 38 to 40 minutes, until a toothpick inserted comes out clean. Remove from the oven and allow to cool in the pan.

4. Place the chocolate chips in a microwave-safe bowl and microwave for 1 minute or until melted. Add the coconut oil to thin the chocolate (it will melt once it's added to the warm chocolate).

5. Flip the cake out of the Bundt pan onto a serving plate. Drizzle the melted chocolate over the top, and then add the chopped Candied Bacon. Store at room temperature, covered, for a few days, or freeze for later use.

PREP TIME: 10 to 15 minutes
COOK TIME: 28 to 30 minutes
YIELD: 5 slices

DAIRY *free,* **EGG** *free,* **NUT** *free,*
GRAIN *free,* **COCONUT** *free*

candied bacon

Candied Bacon is one of my favorite indulgences. Eat it by itself, or use it to top Banana-Chocolate Bundt Cake (page 326)!

ingredients

1 tablespoon maple syrup

¼ cup plus 2 tablespoons coconut palm sugar

½ teaspoon kosher salt

5 slices thick-cut bacon

notes

When the sugar hits the pan, it can cause some burning and smoking. If this starts to happen, pull the bacon out of the oven, swap out the foil for a new sheet, and then continue baking.

directions

1. Preheat the oven to 350 degrees. Line a rimmed baking sheet with foil and place a wire rack on top; set aside.

2. In a bowl, mix together the maple syrup, sugar, and salt.

3. Rub this mixture all over the slices of bacon, front and back.

4. Place the bacon on the wire rack on the baking sheet. Bake for 28 to 30 minutes, until crispy.

5. Let cool on the wire rack for 5 minutes, and then remove. Store in the fridge in a sealed container for up to 3 days.

PREP TIME: 25 to 30 minutes
COOK TIME: 35 to 45 minutes
YIELD: 12 slices

DAIRY *free,* **EGG** *free,* **NUT** *free,*
GRAIN *free,* **COCONUT** *free*

candied oranges

These delicate candied orange slices taste like sugared orange gummies. Boiling the orange slices helps take away the bitterness from the peel, allowing you to eat the whole slice in one bite!

ingredients

2 medium organic oranges

1½ cups raw honey

1 cup water

Granulated maple sugar

directions

1. Slice the oranges about ⅛ inch thick, trimming off each end. Carefully remove the seeds.

2. Bring a pot of water to a boil. Blanch the orange slices in the boiling water for about 2 minutes. Remove from the water and set aside.

3. Bring the honey and 1 cup water to a boil in a medium saucepan. When boiling, carefully drop in the blanched orange slices, reduce the heat to low, and simmer for 35 to 45 minutes, until the oranges are soft and translucent. Remove the oranges from the honey water.

4. Roll each orange slice in sugar and allow to cool in a single layer on a cooling rack.

PREP TIME: 20 minutes
COOK TIME: 18 to 23 minutes
YIELD: One 9-inch single-layer cake
or one 5-inch triple-layer cake

DAIRY *free*, EGG *free*, NUT *free*
GRAIN *free*, COCONUT *free*

carrot cake
with "cream cheese" frosting

This cake is special because it is free of so many allergens: no eggs or dairy, and it tastes great. So many things to be thrilled about!

ingredients

Cake batter:

160 grams coconut palm sugar (about 1 cup)

110 grams milk (dairy or nondairy) (about ½ cup)

75 grams applesauce (about ¼ cup plus 1 tablespoon)

56 grams mild-flavored oil, melted salted butter, or melted ghee (about ¼ cup)

1 teaspoon vanilla extract

208 grams chestnut flour (about 1¼ cups plus 1 tablespoon)

1 tablespoon ground cinnamon

2 teaspoons double-acting, aluminum-free baking powder

⅛ teaspoon xanthan gum or guar gum

Pinch of kosher salt

1 teaspoon apple cider vinegar

1 cup grated carrots (about 2 medium)

½ cup chopped raw nuts of choice and/or raisins (optional)

Frosting:

½ cup coconut butter

½ cup plus 1 tablespoon Spectrum vegetable shortening

¼ cup plus 3 tablespoons raw honey

1½ tablespoons lemon juice

¼ teaspoon xanthan gum or guar gum

Pinch of kosher salt

directions

1. Preheat the oven to 325 degrees. Grease one 9-inch round cake pan or three 5-inch springform pans.

2. Make the batter: In a large bowl, mix together the sugar, milk, applesauce, oil, and vanilla.

3. In a separate bowl, whisk the chestnut flour, cinnamon, baking powder, xanthan gum, and salt until blended. Add the dry ingredients to the wet mixture and mix until well combined.

4. Add the vinegar and mix well.

5. Gently fold in the carrots and nuts/raisins, if using, until evenly distributed.

6. Pour the batter into the prepared pan(s). Bake for 18 to 23 minutes, until a toothpick inserted comes out clean.

7. Let the cake(s) cool for a bit, and then flip the cake(s) out of the pan(s) and allow to cool completely before frosting.

8. Make the frosting: Melt the coconut butter in the microwave for 30 seconds to 1 minute.

9. Combine the melted coconut butter, shortening, honey, lemon juice, xanthan gum, and salt in a food processor and pulse until smooth and creamy.

10. Refrigerate until just hardened, 2 to 3 hours. If you leave the frosting in the fridge for more than a few hours, it may become too hard to spread. If this happens, place the frosting back in the food processor to get it soft and fluffy again for spreading.

11. Frost the cake using an offset spatula and serve! Store at room temperature in a cake holder.

notes

This recipe makes one 9-inch cake and enough frosting for that cake. If you wish to make a multi-tiered cake that is full-sized (unlike the mini tiered cake pictured), you will need to double or triple this recipe. If you choose to bake multiple cakes in the oven at once, you will need to increase the baking time, or bake one cake at a time following the above instructions.

PREP TIME: 25 to 30 minutes
COOK TIME: 15 to 20 minutes
YIELD: One 6-inch-round cake

DAIRY free, EGG free, **NUT** free, **GRAIN** free, COCONUT free

tiramisu crepe cake

Light and fluffy mascarpone between layer upon layer of coffee-flavored crepes? Yes, please! This cake builds so beautifully that you almost won't want to eat it...almost. Before serving, chill it in the freezer to get perfect slices.

ingredients

Coffee-flavored crepes:

5 large eggs

1 tablespoon mild-flavored oil, melted salted butter, or melted ghee, plus more for the pan

57 grams tapioca starch (about ⅓ cup plus 2 tablespoons)

73 grams coconut flour (about ¼ cup plus 3 tablespoons)

193 grams espresso or strong brewed coffee, room temperature (about ¾ cup plus 2 tablespoons)

3 tablespoons milk (dairy or nondairy)

3 tablespoons maple syrup

1 tablespoon vanilla extract

⅛ teaspoon kosher salt

Coffee syrup:

½ cup espresso or strong brewed coffee

½ cup maple syrup

Mascarpone filling:

2 (8-ounce) packages mascarpone cheese

3 tablespoons maple syrup

1 teaspoon vanilla extract

Pinch of kosher salt

For serving:

Cocoa powder, for dusting the crepes

1 batch Coconut Whipped Topping (page 318)

directions

1. Make the crepes: In the bowl of a stand mixer, using the whisk attachment, mix all of the ingredients for the crepes on medium speed until well combined.

2. Heat a teaspoon of oil in a skillet over medium-high heat. Once hot, ladle ¼ cup of the batter into the pan and immediately begin to rotate the pan in a circular motion to even distribute and thin out the crepe. Cook for about 1 minute.

3. Flip the crepe and cook for 1 additional minute or until golden brown. Set aside on a plate. Repeat Steps 2 and 3 with the remaining batter.

4. Make the coffee syrup: In a small saucepan, mix together the espresso and maple syrup and bring to a boil. Allow to boil until it begins to thicken and develops a syruplike consistency, about 8 to 10 minutes. Remove the pan from the heat.

5. Make the mascarpone filling: In a bowl, mix together the mascarpone, maple syrup, vanilla, and salt until well combined.

6. Spoon the mascarpone filling into a disposable pastry bag or large zip-top bag. If using a zip-top bag, snip ¼ inch off of one corner.

7. Assemble the cake: Place a crepe on a serving plate. Using a pastry brush, coat the crepe with the coffee syrup.

8. Pipe a thick ring of the mascarpone filling around the outer edge of the crepe, and fill in the circle with a thinner layer.

9. Sift a small amount of cocoa powder onto the mascarpone and cover with the next crepe.

10. Repeat Steps 7 to 9 until you have used all of the crepes, coffee syrup, and mascarpone filling. Top with the last crepe.

11. Carefully place the fully constructed crepe cake in the freezer for 30 minutes to set.

12. Remove the cake from the freezer and top with Coconut Whipped Topping and some more sifted cocoa powder.

PREP TIME: 1 hour 15 minutes, including time to soak the cashews
COOK TIME: n/a
YIELD: One 6-by-6-inch block

DAIRY free, **EGG** free, **NUT** free, **GRAIN** free, **COCONUT** free

dairy-free white chocolate

For the dairy-free folks, I wanted to re-create white chocolate in a brand-new way. You'll love this recipe—it uses cashews to make the chocolate creamy. The vanilla bean is optional, but highly recommended. It adds a great flavor!

ingredients

½ cup cacao butter

¼ cup plus 2 tablespoons raw cashews

1 vanilla bean (optional)

¼ cup granulated maple sugar

directions

1. Melt the cacao butter. Pour it into a measuring cup to make sure that you have exactly ½ cup.

2. Stir the cashews into the melted cacao butter. Set aside for 1 hour for the cashews to soften.

3. If using a vanilla bean, use a pointy knife to cut the vanilla bean in half and scrape out the seeds. Add the seeds to the melted cacao butter mixture.

4. Pour the mixture into a small food processor. Add the sugar and process until very smooth.

5. To create solid chocolate for grating on top of cupcakes or peeling into pretty ribbons, line a small rimmed baking sheet with parchment paper. Pour the mixture onto the baking sheet and place in the freezer for 30 minutes or until solid. Store in the freezer.

CHAPTER 14

Condiments

PREP TIME: 10 minutes
COOK TIME: n/a
YIELD: ⅓ cup

DAIRY *free*, EGG *free*, NUT *free*,
GRAIN *free*, COCONUT *free*

classic mayo

There's nothing better than homemade mayo—no, really! The flavor and creaminess are bar none. Getting mayo right can be tricky, but I've found that my food processor works like magic every single time. This recipe can easily be doubled.

ingredients

1 large egg yolk

1 tablespoon lemon juice

1 tablespoon water

1 teaspoon Dijon mustard

1 cup oil of choice

Kosher salt

directions

1. In a food processor, combine the egg yolk, lemon juice, water, and mustard.

2. With the machine running, slowly drizzle in the oil. The mixture should begin to thicken almost instantly when the oil is mixed in.

3. Add salt to taste and pulse to combine. Store in a sealed jar in the fridge for up to 1 week.

PREP TIME: 10 minutes
COOK TIME: n/a
YIELD: ⅓ cup

DAIRY *free*, EGG *free*, NUT *free*,
GRAIN *free*, COCONUT *free*

egg-free mayo

This book is filled to the brim with fancy bread recipes that I still can't believe I was able to make grain-free. But this recipe is the one I'm most proud of. I'm allergic to eggs, so for years, if I wanted mayo, I had to resort to a jar made from soy that I never felt thrilled to eat. Those days are long gone, as this mayo is fantastic and takes literally three minutes from start to finish. It'll stay fresh in the fridge for at least a week. You can use coconut cream or heavy cream—both versions are equally delish. And this recipe can easily be doubled.

ingredients

¼ cup plus 3 tablespoons heavy cream or coconut cream (from a can of coconut milk; see tutorial, page 26)

¼ cup plus 3 tablespoons olive, grapeseed, or avocado oil

¼ teaspoon xanthan gum or guar gum

¼ teaspoon dry mustard

¼ teaspoon kosher salt

1 teaspoon lemon juice

directions

1. Place all of the ingredients in tall glass container, such as a mason jar, that is wide enough to accommodate an immersion blender. Using an immersion blender, blend until creamy.

2. Store in a sealed jar in the fridge for up to 1 week.

notes

Feel free to add additional spices. One of my recipe testers added a pinch of turmeric!

sriracha mayo

Here's a little spin on traditional mayo. I love the slightly sweet and spicy taste of Sriracha sauce!

ingredients

1 egg yolk

1 tablespoon lemon juice

1 tablespoon water

1 teaspoon Dijon mustard

1 cup oil of choice

1 to 2 tablespoons Sriracha sauce (depending on how spicy you like it)

Kosher salt

directions

1. In a food processor, combine the egg yolk, lemon juice, water, and mustard.

2. With the machine running, slowly drizzle in the oil. The mixture should begin to thicken almost instantly when the oil is mixed in.

3. Add the Sriracha and salt to taste and pulse to combine. Store in a sealed jar in the fridge for up to 1 week.

notes

To make this mayo egg-free, use the Egg-Free Mayo recipe as your base, then add Sriracha to taste.

PREP TIME: 10 minutes
COOK TIME: n/a
YIELD: ⅔ cup

DAIRY *free,* **EGG** *free,* **NUT** *free,*
GRAIN *free,* **COCONUT** *free*

tartar sauce

You can't have a fish sandwich without tartar sauce! Use this sauce on my "Fried" Fish Sandwiches on page 180.

ingredients

1 double batch Classic Mayo (page 340) or Egg-Free Mayo (page 340), or ⅔ cup store-bought mayonnaise

1 tablespoon white wine vinegar

1 tablespoon capers

1 teaspoon prepared yellow mustard

Kosher salt and black pepper to taste

2 tablespoons diced pickles

directions

1. Combine all of the ingredients, except for the pickles, in a food processor and process until smooth.

2. Stir in the pickles by hand. Store in a sealed jar in the fridge for up to 1 week.

homemade ketchup

Ketchup is so fun to make at home! This version is slightly sweet. Naturally, I use it on hamburgers and hot dogs.

ingredients

6 ounces tomato paste

¼ cup plus 2 tablespoons coconut palm sugar

⅓ cup white wine vinegar

½ cup water

¾ teaspoon kosher salt

¼ teaspoon onion powder

⅛ teaspoon garlic powder

directions

1. Combine all of the ingredients in a pot and bring to a boil over medium heat.
2. Once boiling, reduce the heat to maintain a simmer for 20 minutes or until thickened.
3. Remove from the heat and let cool. Transfer to a glass jar and store in the fridge for up to 1 week.

PREP TIME: 10 minutes, plus 24 hours to refrigerate
COOK TIME: n/a
YIELD: ½ cup

DAIRY *free*, **EGG** *free*, **NUT** *free*,
GRAIN *free*, **COCONUT** *free*

honey dijon mustard

I battled this recipe for days. It turns out that if you don't soak the mustard seeds, or if you heat the mustard, it becomes disgustingly bitter. I did everything wrong before I got it right! I'm thrilled with the final recipe. Be sure to give it a few days in the fridge to develop its best flavor and mellow out.

ingredients

½ cup mustard seeds

⅓ cup white wine

⅓ cup raw honey

3 tablespoons water

2 tablespoons apple cider vinegar

½ teaspoon kosher salt

¼ teaspoon ground turmeric

directions

1. In a sealable container, mix together all of the ingredients.
2. Cover and refrigerate for at least 24 hours.
3. Remove from the refrigerator, place in a food processor or blender, and process until smooth.
4. Refrigerate, covered, for at least 2 days before using.

notes

The flavor develops as it sits; if you taste it before the two days have elapsed, it will have a bitter aftertaste. If you want more bite, replace some of the water with more vinegar and let it sit in the fridge for an additional day before using.

DAIRY *free*, EGG *free*, NUT *free*, GRAIN *free*, COCONUT *free*

homemade relish

I love relish. Don't be afraid of the amount of salt in this recipe—it's used to draw out the extra liquid in the vegetables.

ingredients

4 cups seeded and finely chopped cucumber (about 2 to 3 English cucumbers, depending on size)

1 cup finely chopped onion (about 2 medium)

½ cup seeded and finely chopped red bell pepper (about 1 bell pepper)

1½ tablespoons kosher salt

½ cup apple cider vinegar

2 teaspoons gelatin

¾ cup coconut palm sugar

½ teaspoons celery seed

½ teaspoons dry mustard

¼ teaspoon ground turmeric

¼ teaspoon ground nutmeg

Black pepper to taste

directions

1. Place the vegetables in a large, nonreactive bowl. Add the salt and toss to evenly coat the vegetables.

2. Cover the bowl and set in the refrigerator for 24 hours. The salt and refrigeration will draw out the liquid in the vegetables.

3. Transfer the vegetables to a fine-mesh sieve or strainer to drain.

4. Rinse with cool water and then drain again, pressing the vegetables against the sieve or strainer with the back of a wooden spoon to get out as much water as possible.

5. In a large pot, whisk the vinegar and gelatin. Add the sugar and spices and mix well to make sure that there are no lumps.

6. Bring the mixture to a boil over medium heat. Once the syrup starts to boil, add the vegetables. Simmer for 20 minutes, stirring occasionally.

7. Let the relish cool completely, and then place in canning jars or sealed containers. Store in the refrigerator for up to 1 week.

PREP TIME: 20 to 25 minutes
COOK TIME: 3 hours 15 minutes
YIELD: ½ cup

DAIRY *free*, EGG *free*, NUT *free*,
GRAIN *free*, COCONUT *free*

bacon jam

I absolutely love the Bourbon Bacon Jam recipe that is posted on my blog, but it's not Paleo. So I decided to revamp it, and I may like this version even more than the original! Instead of bourbon whiskey, this recipe uses brewed coffee, which adds a complexity that pairs perfectly with the maple and bacon. I suggest making a double batch because you will want to put it on everything, including my BBQ Chicken Quesadillas (page 248).

ingredients

12 ounces bacon

1 medium onion, chopped

¼ cup coconut palm sugar

2 tablespoons maple syrup

¼ cup plus 2 tablespoons brewed coffee

½ teaspoon black pepper

¼ teaspoon kosher salt

Pinch of cayenne pepper

notes

After the jam is refrigerated, you may need to heat it slightly to make it easier to spread.

directions

1. In a medium saucepan over medium heat, cook the bacon until slightly crispy.

2. Remove the bacon and most of the drippings from the pan, leaving about 1 tablespoon of fat in the pan.

3. Add the chopped onion to the pan with the bacon drippings, reduce the heat to medium-low, and cook until caramelized, about 5 minutes.

4. Chop the cooled bacon and add it along with the remaining ingredients to the saucepan. Cook over low heat, covered, for 3 hours. (Less time is okay, but the flavor gets better the longer it cooks!) Stir every so often to make sure that the mixture is not burning.

5. Place the mixture in a food processor and pulse until it reaches the desired consistency.

6. Allow to cool, and then place in a jar. Store in the fridge for up to 1 week (if it lasts that long!).

cilantro-avocado mousse

I can't wait to spread this full-flavored, slightly spicy mousse on literally everything! If you love guacamole, you will go crazy for this upgraded variation.

ingredients

¼ cup Classic Mayo (page 340), Egg-Free Mayo (page 340), or store-bought mayonnaise

1½ teaspoons lemon juice

⅓ cup fresh cilantro leaves

Kosher salt and black pepper to taste

1 avocado, pitted and peeled

½ jalapeño pepper, seeded (optional)

directions

1. In a food processor, combine the mayo, lemon juice, cilantro, salt, pepper, avocado, and jalapeño, if using, and process until smooth.
2. Store in a sealed jar in the fridge for up to 3 days.

PREP TIME: 10 minutes
COOK TIME: n/a
YIELD: ½ cup

DAIRY *free*, **EGG** *free*, **NUT** *free*,
GRAIN *free*, **COCONUT** *free*

homemade remoulade

This mayo-based sauce is slightly spicy and perfect on top of my Po-Boys (page 176).

ingredients

¼ cup Classic Mayo (page 340), Egg-Free Mayo (page 340), or store-bought mayonnaise

2 teaspoons chopped cornichons

2 teaspoons capers

1 teaspoon Honey Dijon Mustard (page 344) or store-bought Dijon mustard

¼ teaspoon onion powder

¼ teaspoon cayenne pepper

directions

1. In a small bowl, mix together all of the ingredients until well blended. Store in a sealed jar in the fridge for up to 1 week.

PREP TIME: 10 minutes
COOK TIME: 10 minutes
YIELD: ½ cup

DAIRY *free*, **EGG** *free*, **NUT** *free*, **GRAIN** *free*, COCONUT *free*

ginger-teriyaki sauce

The name says it all! I created this sauce for burgers, but it would be a delicious addition to all kinds of dishes.

ingredients

½ cup coconut aminos

¼ cup plus 1 tablespoon coconut palm sugar

¼ cup water

2 tablespoons white wine

1 teaspoon minced fresh ginger

½ teaspoon garlic powder

¼ teaspoon black pepper

½ teaspoon tapioca starch

directions

1. In a saucepan over medium heat, mix together the coconut aminos, sugar, water, white wine, ginger, garlic powder, and pepper until the sugar has dissolved.

2. Place the tapioca starch in a small bowl. Remove about 2 tablespoons of the sauce and mix it with the tapioca starch, stirring until there are no clumps remaining. Add the mixture back to the saucepan. (This step is essential to keep the tapioca starch from clumping.)

3. Whisk over medium heat until thickened, and then let cool in the pan. Store in a sealed jar in the fridge for up to 1 week.

PREP TIME: 10 minutes
COOK TIME: 22 minutes
YIELD: 1½ cups

DAIRY *free*, **EGG** *free*, **NUT** *free*,
GRAIN *free*, **COCONUT** *free*

cranberry sauce

Put heaping spoonfuls of this delicious Paleo cranberry sauce on your day-after-Thanksgiving sandwiches.

ingredients

1 (16-ounce) bag frozen cranberries

1⅓ cups coconut palm sugar

¼ cup water

1 tablespoon lemon juice or orange juice

¼ to ½ teaspoon grated fresh ginger

directions

1. Combine all of the ingredients in a saucepan over low heat. Cook for 10 minutes, until the sugar has dissolved.

2. Increase the heat to medium and cook for an additional 12 minutes or until the cranberries begin to burst.

3. Using a potato masher or fork, mash up the cranberry sauce to the desired consistency.

Menu Ideas

Tailgating Food

Perfect treats for tailgating or watching the game at home.

274 texas toast

50 all-purpose flatbread

66 honey "cornbread" muffins

272 chili

166 meatball subs

196 bagel chips

194 lime tortilla chips

278 classic soft pretzels

290 jalapeño cheddar pretzel sticks

248 bbq chicken quesadillas

292 soft pretzel waffles

44 hot dog buns

40 hamburger buns

42 low-carb hamburger buns

220 classic calzones

222 bbq chicken yeast-free calzones

246 chicken taquitos

200 cheese crackers

204 no-wheat crackers

320 chocolate chip cookies—two ways!

Brunch

For your get-togethers with friends and family, these recipes will impress!

162 layered gingerbread crepes with orange-maple cream cheese filling

144 extra-crispy paleo waffles

152 classic french toast

154 egg-free banana french toast

72 croissants

76 chocolate croissants

78 danish

90 donuts

160 basic vanilla crepes

136 ham and cheese morning muffins

116 cherry chocolate chip scones

156 fluffy blueberry pancakes

114 "fried" chicken breakfast biscuit sandwiches

80 english muffins

146 coconut flour waffles

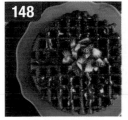
148 chocolate waffles with strawberries

150 strawberry waffles with coconut whipped topping

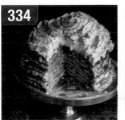
334 tiramisu crepe cake

128 blueberry muffins

134 strawberry cream cheese muffins

Winter Holiday Favorites

Traditional Thanksgiving and Christmas favorites!

118

gingerbread scones

158

pumpkin mug cakes

356

cranberry sauce

264

sage sausage stuffing

104

biscuits and sawmill gravy

46

parker house dinner rolls

96

classic biscuits

98

egg-free biscuits

106

biscuit pot pie

92

cinnamon rolls

322

cinnamon roll cookies

336

dairy-free white chocolate

298

red velvet cupcakes with cream cheese frosting

122

caramel apple muffins

124

coffee cake muffins

140

orange cranberry bread

108

monkey bread "cupcakes"

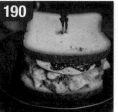
190

thanksgiving leftovers sandwiches

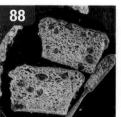
88

egg-free cinnamon raisin bread

318

coconut whipped topping

Easy Bread Recipes

Simple recipes that taste fancy! Perfect for the newbie Paleo baker.

84 yeast-free mini bagels

86 cinnamon raisin bagels

50 all-purpose flatbread

56 grain-free lavash

58 grain-free spinach lavash

36 low-carb honey "wheat" bread

64 arepas

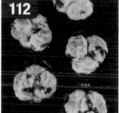
108 monkey bread "cupcakes"

112 strawberry shortcake monkey bread "cupcakes"

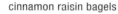

224 thin-crust white pizza with spinach

202 oyster crackers

208 rosemary crackers

240 soft plantain tortillas

242 cheesy soft plantain tortillas

250 soft almond flour tortillas

292 soft pretzel waffles

294 honey mustard pretzel waffles

270 chinese scallion pancakes

62 irish soda bread

288 cinnamon sugar pretzel bites

Index

Special Thanks

Sarah Rothberg—This book would not exist without you. Thank you for giving 110 percent each and every day. Not a day passes that you don't make me laugh. Your joy for life is infectious, and you make our days together in the kitchen a blast! Thank you for running recipe trials upwards of sixteen times without complaining once, and for your eagerness to learn. I'm incredibly lucky to have you!

Sarah Durie—My favorite little kitchen hurricane. Your hard work, creativity, and worth ethic came at the perfect time. You are a natural in the kitchen. Thanks for all your free time!

Amanda Hockham—Thanks for holding down the fort and giving me peace of mind to focus on writing this book. So thankful for you!

Rich Angell—To the man who picked me up through my hardest health struggles and loves me even when I'm overtired and crabby from spending too much time in the kitchen. To the man who will bend over backwards to help me in every way he can. I love you to the ends of the earth and back. I could not live so freely without you next to me.

Tré—My dear friend and go-to photographer! Thanks for being part of my projects the past few years! Your work never ceases to amaze, and I treasure your friendship.

The Gipson Family—Kenya, Brian, Nakiri, and Kaiya, my extended family. Thank you for supporting me in this journey and letting me stretch my wings to fly when the time came. I'll forever treasure the four years I spent with you!

My parents and brother—For your belief in me and for always celebrating my achievements!

Hayley Mason & Bill Staley—Thank you so much for dropping everything for me, just because you cared. I'll forever cherish you both and your big giving hearts! Every time I look at the beautiful cover of this book, I will be thankful for your kindness.

Diane Sanfilippo—You are a constant source of inspiration! Your kindness and support mean the world to me. THANK YOU for adding your magical touch to the pages of this book.

The Victory Belt team—For giving me this opportunity of a lifetime, and for the freedom to be as creative as my heart desires! A publishing team like this one is very hard to come by. I'm incredibly thankful.

My recipe testers—The time you spent to help me make sure that all the recipes are the best they can be made such a difference! I enjoyed your emails and learned so much from your suggestions. Thank you! Thank you!

Alisa Fairbanks, Amanda Gallagher, Amanda Hockham, Amy Menzies, Amy Thomas, Andrea Murdock, Anita Wilhite, Autumn Rolfe, Chelsea Connor, Christine Dufault, Dana Fait, Dani Jorgensen, Danielle Vargas, Diane Bramos, Elise Rees, Emily Jelassi, Emily Keeling, Hannah Pinkerton, Heather Kinnard, Heather Weiss, Jamie Busman, Jamie-Lynne Goodman, Jasmine King, Jen Bro, Jessica Angell, Jessica Sanders, Katherine Schoolcraft, Kelly Albertson, Kelly Amen, Kimberly Woodring, Kristen Noy, Kristi Drayovitch, Kymberly Oliver, Laura Spoerl, Laurel VanBlarcum, Leanna Harter, Leigh LaBrake, Lia Pearson, Lindsay Eberts, Linda Styles, Lindsey Erickson, Lucy McVicker, Marie Sorrento, Melanie Culbertson, Melanie Jewell, Melissa Theberge, Michele Paikin, Michelle Hartshorn, Michelle Lewis, Mimi Mendez, Nanci Selk, Rebecca Avery, Ronnda Staapleton, Shanna Freeman, Sherri Donohue, Simone Sandercombe, Susi LeMaire, Tammy McNair, Wendy Holnagel

Our three little Angell kids—Clyde, Chloe, and Cliff, thank you for being a constant source of happiness and love in my life. Very little compares to the affection and joy I experience every day with you three puppies. It's a gift to have you all in my life.